THE REVISED
ORWELL

THE REVISED
ORWELL

EDITED BY
JONATHAN ROSE

Michigan State University Press
East Lansing
1992

All Michigan State University Press books are produced on paper
which meets the requirements of American National Standard of
Information Sciences—Permanence of paper for printed materials
ANSI Z39.48-1984.

Michigan State University Press
East Lansing, Michigan 48823-5202

Printed in the United States of America

00 99 98 97 96 95 94 93 92 1 2 3 4 5 6 7 8 9

Library of Congress Cataloging-in-Publication Data

The Revised Orwell / edited by Jonathan Rose.
    p. cm.
    Includes bibliographical references.
    ISBN 0-87013-304-7 — ISBN 0-87013-311-X (pbk.)
    1. Orwell, George, 1903-1950. Nineteen eighty-four. I. Rose,
Jonathan.
PR6029.R8N667   1992
823'.912—dc20
                                    91-45257
                                        CIP

Cover photo courtesy of The George Orwell Archive, University
College, London.

Contents

Abbreviations
Used in the Text

AF	*Animal Farm*. New York: New American Library, 1974.
BD	*Burmese Days*. New York: New American Library, 1963.
CD	*A Clergyman's Daughter*. New York: Harcourt, Brace & World, 1968.
CEJL	*The Collected Essays, Journalism and Letters of George Orwell*. Ed. Sonia Orwell and Ian Angus. New York: Harcourt, Brace & World, 1968.
CUA	*Coming Up For Air*. New York: Harcourt, Brace & World, 1968.
DOPL	*Down and Out in Paris and London*. New York: Harcourt Brace Jovanovich, 1968.
HC	*Homage to Catalonia*. New York: Harcourt, Brace & World, 1952.
KAF	*Keep the Aspidistra Flying*. New York: Harcourt, Brace and World, 1968.
Ms	*Nineteen Eighty-Four: The Facsimile of the Extant Manuscript*. Ed. Peter Davison. London: Secker & Warburg; Weston, Mass.: M & S Press, 1984.
NEF	*Nineteen Eighty-Four*. New York: New American Library 1961.
RWP	*The Road to Wigan Pier*. New York: Harcourt Brace Jovanovich, 1968.
GO	Bernard Crick, *George Orwell*. Boston: Atlantic–Little, Brown, 1980.
OT	Peter Stansky and William Abrahams, *Orwell: The Transformation*. New York: Knopf, 1980.
UO	Peter Stansky and William Abrahams, *The Unknown Orwell*. New York: Knopf, 1972.

Introduction

The contributors to this book were brought together by a shared sense of disappointment with 1984. That year scholarly and unscholarly journals alike were flooded with Orwell retrospectives, and too many of them fell into one of two slots.

First, there were the commentators who debated whether *Nineteen Eighty-Four* had correctly foreseen 1984. They missed the rather obvious point that Orwell's intention was to avert rather than predict a nightmare. By that standard, *Nineteen Eighty-Four* has probably been the most effective defense of civil liberties written since the American Bill of Rights—an ideological superweapon in the battle for personal freedom and privacy. Even the Soviet press, one year before the inauguration of Gorbachev in 1985, felt compelled to pay some guarded homage to Orwell. "One could consider it one of the first unpremeditated appearances of pluralism," observed Victoria Chalikova, one of Orwell's Russian critics: "If we have not yet reached the future described by Orwell and Huxley, we are to some degree indebted to them."[1]

Meanwhile, back in the West, a great many critics fell to playing that intriguing faculty party game of guessing where Orwell would have stood on the Vietnam War, the 1984-85 British coal miners' strike, and all the other political controversies he never lived to see. Thus we had Irving Howe, Norman Podhoretz, and Christopher Hitchens hotly arguing whether Orwell would have eventually become the ideological comrade of Irving Howe, Norman Podhoretz, or Christopher Hitchens.

1

All that was perfectly harmless, but it is unfortunate that 1984 did not produce more in the way of original Orwell scholarship. With the publication of the Stansky/Abrahams and Crick biographies, the opening up of most of the Orwell Archive at University College, London, the ongoing discovery of Orwell's uncollected writings, and the publication of the facsimile manuscript of *Nineteen Eighty-Four*, the materials for reappraisal are available. For this volume, we made a point of soliciting contributions from a wide range of disciplines—intellectual history, literary criticism, communications, psychology, popular culture, sociology, linguistics, and even the classics—precisely in order to generate fresh perspectives on Orwell. Some of us set out to challenge broadly accepted appraisals of his work; others tried out new routes of investigation on *Nineteen Eighty-Four*, and still others explored the Orwell that remains unknown.

As this collection gelled, however, a deeper pattern emerged. In the course of untangling the many enigmas surrounding this guarded and private man, we discovered that the idea of *revision* itself was the key to breaking the code. Working from different directions, we converged on the conclusion that Orwell was a revisionist in every sense of the term: He revealed himself in his manuscript revisions; in his inveterate political revisionism; in the refashioning of his name and his persona; in his habit of turning on himself, of challenging and overturning his own convictions; in the way he borrowed and reworked pieces of other texts and incorporated them into his own writings. *Nineteen Eighty-Four* was itself the end product of thirty years' revision, stretching back to a schoolboy squib penned at Eton. Orwell would rewrite his childhood in "Such, Such Were the Joys," and in *Nineteen Eighty-Four* he would reverse some of the literary rules he had laid down a few years earlier in "Politics and the English Language." One could almost say that George Orwell and Winston Smith were in the same line of work.

At the present time, the most radical revision of Orwell and his work is taking place in the USSR. The initial response of the official Soviet press to *Nineteen Eighty-Four* was, needless to say, vilification. By 1984, however, *Izvestia* and *New Times* were prepared to admit that the novel had merit as a dystopian satire—of the United States. By 1988 *Literaturnaya Gazeta* could see Big Brother as an anticipation of Mao and Khomeini, but still shied away from comparisons with Stalin.[2] The first complete Russian translation of *Nineteen Eighty-Four* legally published in the Soviet Union appeared in 1989 in the magazine *Novy Mir*. Only then, in a critical afterword, did Victoria Chalikova openly confront Russian readers with the fact that their country was Airstrip Two.[3] The essay reprinted here, which appeared in the journal *Znamya* in

1989, is therefore remarkable as one of the first honest Soviet critiques of *Nineteen Eighty-Four*.

The next four essays in this collection aim to show that most critics, including Orwell himself, have greatly underestimated the literary artistry of *Nineteen Eighty-Four*. Those who have dismissed the construction of that novel as obvious and old-fashioned are only half correct, observes Alex Zwerdling. In fact, *Nineteen Eighty-Four* was written on two levels for two different audiences, one popular and one modernist. Drawing on the facsimile of the surviving manuscript, Sue Lonoff reconstructs the final revision of the novel to reveal its balance, patterning, and economy. Daniel Kies demonstrates that Orwell, breaking one of his own rules of language, artfully used every possible permutation of the passive voice to suggest the utter powerlessness of Winston Smith. A great many readers have dismissed *Nineteen Eighty-Four* as overwrought, unbelievable, or politically incorrect; but Laurence M. Porter's psychoanalytic reading reveals that what seem to be ideological and literary flaws may actually embody piercing psychological insights.

The next group of four articles explores the biographical and literary sources of Orwell's work, carrying forward the excellent work begun by William Steinhoff in *George Orwell and the Origins of 1984*. "Eric Blair's School Days" revises Bernard Crick's (and Orwell's) account of his boyhood. Though Orwell attempted to rewrite himself, adopting a new name and personality, everything he wrote bore the stamp of Eric Blair and the books he had read at school. He would always have a special knack for appropriating themes, images, ideas, and conventions from other texts—especially detective stories and science fiction—and reworking them into his own creations. Even in selecting the title of *Nineteen Eighty-Four*, he may have simply renumbered the title of some third-rate futuristic tale. While Russel Gray and I have rummaged through the dustbin of literary history, Arthur Eckstein has accounted Orwell's considerable debt to the Greek and Roman classics, showing how they impelled him to revise his whole philosophy of language.

The final essays locate Orwell in the context of British cultural history. His idiosyncratic politics have often baffled and irritated critics; William Laskowski makes sense of the apparent inconsistencies by placing Orwell in a Tory-Radical tradition that includes Jonathan Swift and William Cobbett. One piece of conventional wisdom that this book does *not* revise is that George Orwell died a socialist; but as Arthur Eckstein explains, he rethought and toned down his hostility to capitalism in his final years. John Rodden goes on to demonstrate that the anomalous example of Orwell—the odd man out in whatever crowd he happened to find himself—may compel us to revise several theories of the sociology of intellectuals. Finally, Rodden's reception history shows how the Movement writers of postwar Britain radically "rewrote" Orwell, continually recasting him in their own changing image.

That last article, "'The Rope that Connects Me Directly with You': John Wain and the Movement Writers' Orwell," was first published in the Spring 1988 issue of *Albion*. "Eric Blair's School Days" is an expanded version of an article that appeared in the Summer 1985 issue of the *Midwest Quarterly*, and "The Invisible Sources of *Nineteen Eighty-Four*" will be printed in the *Journal of Popular Culture*. "George Orwell's Second Thoughts on Capitalism" was published in the *Modern Age* in Winter 1985 and, in a very condensed form, in the proceedings of the 1984 Orwell conference at Hofstra University. We thank the editors of those publications for permission to reprint these articles. Several of the contributors made use of the Orwell Archive at the University College London Library, and we are most grateful to Mrs. Janet Percival and the entire staff there.

Jonathan Rose

Notes

1. Victoria Chalikova, "The Eternal Year," *Novy Mir*, April 1989, 128.
2. John Rodden, *The Politics of Literary Reputation: The Making and Claiming of "St. George" Orwell* (New York: Oxford University Press, 1989), 200-11.
3. Of course, that had been recognized all along by those Russians who, before glasnost, managed to obtain samizdat translations or smuggled English-language editions of *Nineteen Eighty-Four*. The novelist David Gurevich recalls that one scene in particular, "where Winston is bullied into reaching his toes, left me stunned. Morning exercise on the radio is a staple of Soviet life, and the announcer's voice, now sugary, now stern, had always made me feel I was being watched. How did Orwell know that?" David Gurevich, "Moscow Days: Liberated by Harold Robbins," *New York Times Book Review*, 11 March 1990, 26.

A Russian Preface to George Orwell

Victoria Chalikova

Any question, even the most abstract and unintelligible, can be examined in a literary form. But great books answer simple, direct questions. Is it permissible for a poor fellow full of noble intentions to kill a useless and evil, rich old woman? Can one judge a woman, energetic and full of passion, who deceives a husband she doesn't love? Anyone can pose such questions; no one can answer them; but for some people it is physically impossible to refrain from seeking an answer. An acute awareness of this impossibility gives birth to a great book.

George Orwell was tortured by a very simple question: What can and what cannot be done to a human being by force? The answers for him, an English intellectual, born of an impoverished aristocratic family,[1] graduate of an elite college, seemed to be ready-made in the enlightened, humanistic culture in which he grew up. We also have learned these answers from childhood on. Here they are: "A man can be deprived of his property, but not his honor"; "Faith and hope are immortal in man"; "One can take away man's physical freedom, but not his spiritual freedom"; "Love conquers death." And the capstone, the crown of all these, the famous: "It is better to die standing than to live on one's knees!"

But for the author of a great novel such answers are not necessary, for they are already there. A great novel is a laboratory in which unprecedented experiments are set up, new hypotheses checked in new conditions.

5

A spiritual, thinking, loving man—Winston Smith, who has been given sufficient autobiographical similarity to the author—is placed in the supertotalitarian world of "Ingsoc," in a society ruled by the Inner Party, an elite party that for the first time in history has refused to play at equality and justice and has transformed life into an open despotism and an absolute concentration camp. At the beginning of the novel, Winston is an intellectual who has adapted to this world—lying, humiliated, but filled with hatred toward power and with a secret dream of freedom. At the center of the story, after the meeting with Julia and the awakening of his repentant memory of his mother and sister, we see a new man, straightened out by love, inspired by truth, ready to fight evil. At the end, he is transformed by torture into a piece of pitifully quivering flesh, deprived of human thoughts and feelings, with drunken tears licking the hand of the master. The artistic experiment answers: If force is unlimited, it can do anything to man. Of course, it is better to die standing, it is beautiful to die standing, it is sweet to die standing. But they will not let you die standing. You will die on your knees, with blood and urine pouring over you, you will rot unknown, leaving not a trace, mourned by no one and remembered by no one, having betrayed and cursed everyone you loved.

But what follows from this? Why is this black truth opened up? So that you should not deceive yourself into hoping for the possibility of the coexistence of humanity and evil. Yes, it was possible in the past, when the power of evil over man was waning and limited. But as early as the end of the 1930s, Orwell wrote that nuclear weapons and the science of mind control will make evil all-powerful. They will not only destroy all that is best in reality, they will scrap utopia—the dream of brotherhood, equality, and freedom—and will transform existence into a bloody life of the moment, with no memory of the past nor dream of the future.

Is love stronger than death? Yes. But death in the form of hungry rats, springing from their cages at a human face—this is another death, and faced with such a death Winston cries out in an inhuman voice: "Not me! Julia!.... Tear her face off, strip her to the bones." And that is not the end. She indifferently confesses to him that she did the same thing, and that this shout was not a trick, a sop to the executioner— it was a shout of the soul, or more exactly, of what remained of it:

> "At the time you do not think to what you are condemning another person.[2] All you care about is yourself."
> "All you care about is yourself," he echoed.

"It is impossible to be a poet in the soul, just as it is impossible to be a shoemaker in the soul," sternly declared the poet Marina

Tsvetaeva. Ten years later (and what years they were!) Orwell answered even more terrifyingly: It is impossible to be a man in one's soul, it is only possible to be a man in reality. And if an all-embracing power replaces reality with an ideological fiction, there will simply be no place to be a man.

Here, perhaps, is the central revelation of the novel, mercilessly saying farewell to illusions of individual humanity, with the image so dear to our hearts of "secret freedom." "Pushkin! We sang of secret freedom after you," wrote Blok at the dawn of the first great revolution of the twentieth century. Orwell depicts a world after the last revolution, a world deprived even of the freedom to choose between common sense and absurdity.

George Orwell—a participant in the Spanish Civil War, a fighter for the militia of the independent Catalonian trade unions,[3] which was destroyed by local special organizations (directed by the Stalinist NKVD)—guessed the main secret of totalitarianism. In Spain, he wrote, there arose before him "a nightmare world in which the Leader...controls not only the future but *the past*.... If he says that two and two are five— well, two and two are five" (*CEJL*, 2:259). The formula $2 \times 2 = 4$ has long been a literary metaphor: for Dostoevsky, Proust, Chesterton, André Breton, Zamyatin. But Orwell's predecessors used it as a symbol of the "tyranny of reason." Dostoevsky's underground man rejects a world where two times two are four in the name of freedom, saying that "the idea of two times two being five can sometimes be a nice thing." In the anti-utopia of Evgeny Zamyatin, *We*, the faceless "numbers"—slaves of a totalitarian state—recite an ode to the formula $2 \times 2 = 4$.

Orwell did not accept this challenge to common sense. He saw in it not a love of freedom but the aggression of a superman, who is not capable of "behaving with ordinary decency." He wrote about this collision often: in an article on Baudelaire's "Flowers of Evil," in an article on *A Hero of Our Time*.[4] In *Nineteen Eighty-Four* the torment lasts long enough so that Winston really sees five fingers on the four-fingered hand of the executioner.

Thus, despite the preceding traditions, the formula for individual freedom in *Nineteen Eighty-Four* becomes $2 + 2 = 4$. Orwell was impelled to such an artistic solution by Eugene Lyons's book *Assignment in Utopia*, from which he extracted the following lines: "The slogan 'The Five-Year Plan in Four Years' was advanced, and...the formula $2 + 2 = 5$ instantly riveted my attention... —the daring and the paradox and the tragic absurdity of the Soviet scene, its mystical simplicity, its defiance of logic, all reduced to nose-thumbing arithmetic."[5] The author of *Nineteen Eighty-Four* included this book in his carefully collected "Russian library."

And how we used to read Orwell in Russia!: in third and fourth typewritten copies and in pale Xerox copies, we read "close to the text" in a literal sense—turning around and risking ourselves, in a tightly closed room, alone or two of us, just as in the novel Winston and Julia read the underground book. As in a mirror, the book and life observed each other! Yes, in spite of the prohibitions, Orwell forced his way through to at least part of the Russian reading audience, of whom he had so dreamed. *Animal Farm, Nineteen Eighty-Four,* and—to a lesser degree—*Homage to Catalonia* played their role in shaping the spirit of the writers, historians, and publicists who entered our culture after the Twentieth Party Congress of 1956.

However, Orwell undoubtedly took more from Russia than he gave it. One must bitterly confess that a special role in his comprehension of the essence of totalitarian terror (along with imperialism, racism, and fascism) was played by the tragedies and catastrophes of our history. The figures of Napoleon in *Animal Farm* and Big Brother in *Nineteen Eighty-Four* he consciously made similar to Stalin, fiercely polemicizing against all his Western apologists and advocates, who defended tyranny "in the interests of socialism."

In the preface to the second edition of *Animal Farm* he wrote: "The destruction of the Stalinist myth was essential if we wanted a revival of the Socialist movement" (*CEJL*, 3:405).[6] Recognizing socialism only as a utopia, as the faith of the "good and weak," he did not accept the socialism of organization and bureaucracy. Administrative socialism—that was unavoidably a "totalitarian version of socialism." For Orwell there were always two socialisms. One was that which he saw in revolutionary Barcelona. It was "a community where hope was more normal than apathy or cynicism, where the word 'comrade' stood for comradeship and not, as in most countries, for humbug." It was "a crude forecast of what the opening stages of Socialism might be like" (*HC*, 104-5). The other was that which Stalin set up, the "managerial revolution" anticipated in the West by the political scientist James Burnham, one of the most important thinkers for the author of *Nineteen Eighty-Four.* Socialism, if it means only "a planned and centralised society[,] is liable to develop into an oligarchy or a dictatorship"—so wrote Orwell in a review of Burnham's book *The Managerial Revolution* (*CEJL*, 4:163).

Concerning the ideological placement of Orwell, there are varying opinions in the West. His ideas are seen as moralism (Richard Rees); dissidence within the leftist movement (George Woodcock); the attempt of a conservative son of the nineteenth century to be a democratic socialist (Richard Voorhees); "revolutionary socialism," an anticipation of the New Left (Raymond Williams); but most of all, as "secular evangelism." The tragedy of this position lies in the fact that, being intellectual by nature, it does not strive to raise the consciousness and morality of people who do physical labor, of those about whom Winston writes in his secret diary: "If there is hope, it lies in the proles." But can and should an intellectual become a prole?

And Orwell continues to force us to think about that—about the fate of intellectuals in an era of scientific technology and mass propaganda. In his journalism, the phrase "totalitarian intellectual" (one of Orwell's neologisms) embraces the widest variety of sociopolitical types—devotees of fascism, pro-Stalin "fellow travellers," fanatically orthodox Catholics. "The countless English intellectuals who kiss the arse of Stalin are not different from the minority who give their allegiance to Hitler or Mussolini.... All of them are worshipping power and successful cruelty." He considered totalitarianism to be the characteristic mentality of the twentieth century, under which "people worship power in the form in which they are able to understand it.... An adolescent in a Glasgow slum worships Al Capone.... A *New Statesman* reader worships Stalin" (*CEJL*, 3:222-24). For him, the Stalin regime was not at all a power center for the mob or the pen-pushers, but "the dictatorship of a handful of intellectuals, ruling through terrorism."[7]

One of the deepest and most perceptive Orwell scholars, William Steinhoff, specifically defines *Nineteen Eighty-Four* as "a book about intellectuals, their beliefs, and their ways of thinking and feeling."[8] With a passion, Orwell investigates the "intellectual gang"[9] to which Orwell himself belongs to the very marrow of his bones. And he mercilessly notes the thirst for self-affirmation, the passion for order, the tendency toward reducing life to ideologies, toward orthodoxy. The problem is not in ideology—it is unavoidable for the active man—but in the degree of orthodoxy. "An ordinary Englishman, Conservative, Socialist, Catholic, Communist, or what not...almost always...utters heresies without noticing it. Orthodoxies, whether of the Right or the Left, flourish chiefly among the literary intelligentsia, the people who ought in theory to be the guardians of freedom of thought" (*CEJL*, 3:12). And no matter how strong or original the thinker, orthodoxy will kill in him "first the moral sense, and then the sense of reality" (*CEJL*, 4:18). Orwell showed us the corpse of the intellect in the demented O'Brien, but he did not show us the process of killing the intellect. That was done by his friend Arthur Koestler in *Darkness at Noon*, one of Orwell's favorite books.

In becoming political, the intellectual often is forced to reject spiritual subtleties, scrupulousness, and high aestheticism. Directly formulating his creative task, "to make political writing into an art" (*CEJL*, 1:6), Orwell used acutely topical material to create his widely

— acknowledged masterpiece *Animal Farm*. This was highly praised by
the democratic intelligentsia of the West as a revival of "a political sensibility of an ancient kind" (*GO*, xix), as the fulfillment of the testament
of Pericles: "Freedom is courage." Daring to follow his satiric tale with
a more risky genre, a political novel, Orwell had a rare success—the
creation of an artistic symbol of totalitarianism. His success is instructive for all those intellectuals who were long forced by bitter experience to flee from political passions. One must, however, understand
very precisely the strictness and firmness of the limits to political
involvement that Orwell set for himself. In the well-known article
"Writers and Leviathan" he said: "I do not think that [the writer] has the
right, merely on the score of his sensibilities, to shirk the ordinary dirty
work of politics.... But whatever else he does in the service of his party,
he should never write for it.... And he should be able to act co-oper-
atively while, if he chooses, completely rejecting the official ideology"
(*CEJL*, 4:412).

Orwell himself did not remain long in the party—in the left wing of
the Labourites (though he voted for them until the end). On the left,
he often felt uncomfortable, vexed, embarrassed. He did not forgive his
socialist friends their snobbery, "dialectics," and "idiotic demands": "He
who said 'a' ought to say 'b'." (Platonov's heroine, Fro, so bright and
so close to Orwell's ideal, replied to such a demand: "And why should
I? Perhaps I don't want to?"). Seeing that he really did not understand
why, having said "a" (socialism), he ought to say "b" (Stalinism), his
friends condescendingly remarked that a great talent is combined with
"the simple-heartedness and naivete of a savage." However, the closest and most penetrating of his friends, Richard Rees, saw something
else in this "childish willfulness in politics" and formulated it, in my
view, brilliantly: He was more progressive than the left and more conservative than the right in his "Promethean arrogance," which grew out
of his "refined and sublimated egoism."[10]

It seems to me that no work of Orwell reveals the essence of his
spirituality so accurately and subtly as a short work written a year
before his death, a review of the English translation of Mahatma
Gandhi's book *The Story of My Experiments with Truth*. Giving due
respect to the achievements of Gandhi—personal courage, honesty, an
understanding of the value of man, energy, organizational talent, seren-
ity, a forgiving nature, faith in the good will of people—Orwell wrote:

> But one should, I think, realise that Gandhi's teachings cannot be
> squared with the belief that Man is the measure of all things, and
> that our job is to make life worth living on this earth, which is the
> only earth we have.... Close friendships, Gandhi says, are danger-
> ous, because "friends react on one another" and through loyalty to

a friend one can be led into wrong-doing. This is unquestionably true. Moreover, if one is to love God, or to love humanity as a whole, one cannot give one's preference to any individual person. This is again true, and it marks the point at which the humanistic and the religious attitudes cease to be reconcilable. To an ordinary human being, love means nothing if it does not mean loving some people more than others.

For Orwell, raised as a religious person, who married, who asked to be buried according to the rites of the English Church, nevertheless "the essence of being human is that one does not seek perfection, that one *is* sometimes willing to commit sins for the sake of loyalty, that one does not push asceticism to the point where it makes friendly intercourse impossible, and that one is prepared in the end to be defeated and broken up by life, which is the inevitable price of fastening one's love upon other human individuals" (*CEJL*, 4:446-67).

Winston and Julia, who were devoted to each other and who fell out of love for each other under torture, took this risk. They were not holy. They were human.

—translated by Lois E. Beekey

Notes

1. Editor's note: The Blairs were neither impoverished nor aristocratic, at least not by any English definition; but this phrase may have been the best way to convey the idea of "lower-upper-middle class" to a Russian audience.
2. Editor's note: This represents a retranslation back into English of Chalikova's Russian translation, but the original text is rather different: "At the time when it happens you do mean it....You *want* it to happen to the other person" (*NEF*, 240).
3. Editor's note: Orwell actually fought for the POUM, an independent Marxist party that did not control any trade unions. Most POUM fighters belonged to the CNT, the anarchist-syndicalist trade union federation, and some CNT members joined the POUM militia, though the CNT had a militia of its own.
4. George Orwell, review of *Baudelaire* by Enid Starkie, *Adelphi,* August 1933, 382-83; and "The Male Byronic," *Tribune,* 21 June 1940.
5. Quoted in William Steinhoff, *George Orwell and the Origins of 1984* (Ann Arbor: University of Michigan Press, 1975), 172.
6. Editor's note: Actually, this quotation is from the 1947 Ukrainian edition of *Animal Farm,* where Orwell called for "the destruction of the *Soviet* myth." That may have been a dangerous thing to say in Russia even as late as 1989, when the failings of communism were still officially blamed on Stalin rather than on the Soviet system.
7. George Orwell, "Marx and Russia," *Observer,* 15 February 1948.

8. Steinhoff, 57.
9. Translator's note: In context, this is the most appropriate rendering of the phrase *tsehh zadorhyj,* which is taken from Pushkin's *Eugene Onegin,* chapter 1, stanza 43.
10. Richard Rees, *George Orwell: Fugitive from the Camp of Victory* (Carbondale: Southern Illinois University Press, 1961), 4, 146.

Rethinking the Modernist Legacy in *Nineteen Eighty-Four*

Alex Zwerdling

George Orwell's *Nineteen Eighty-Four* is the most universally familiar work of fiction published in the twentieth century. It is the *one* novel any literate person will almost certainly have read. It has sold (and continues to sell) millions of copies and has been translated into dozens of languages. It is a required text in most American high schools and many of its colleges, so that anyone who has gone through a conventional education will almost surely have encountered it. In addition, it was from the first and has continued steadily to be a book people read without prompting, even if they have never been required to do so. Its publishing history is as remarkable as the novel itself, and that history raises certain fundamental questions about the audience of modern fiction and Orwell's appeal to such a wide readership. I believe that the extraordinary popularity of *Nineteen Eighty-Four* is no accident, that Orwell worked hard to achieve exactly the kind of universal response he succeeded in producing, and that the choices he made in writing the book were largely determined by his wish to reach the widest possible audience. Why did he need to do this and exactly how did he manage it?

Anyone familiar with the earlier works of Orwell's career will know that he did not begin as a popular writer. *Homage to Catalonia*, the factual narrative describing his participation in the Spanish Civil War, seems to me the masterpiece of his first decade as a writer. But it sold less than a thousand copies from its publication in 1938 to Orwell's death more than a decade later and was only published in America

13

after his last novel made him famous.[1] His other fictional and discursive works of the 1930s were a little more successful, but they never sold more than a few thousand copies and could not be said to have had a mass readership.[2] His political fable *Animal Farm* (published in 1945) was far more popular, of course, but it did not have the impact of *Nineteen Eighty-Four*. Writing it was perhaps a necessary transition from the very limited appeal of Orwell's earlier work to the mass appeal of his last novel. But I very much doubt that the word "Orwellian" would have entered our vocabulary if *Animal Farm* had been his final work. In order to reach beyond the wide readership of *Animal Farm* to the almost universal literate audience of *Nineteen Eighty-Four*, Orwell had to think differently both about his own purposes as a writer and about the fictional methods he was willing to adopt.

The best guide to understanding Orwell's purposes in *Nineteen Eighty-Four* is his own explanation, which has often been quoted but seldom been analyzed. In his public statements about the book, issued because he felt reviewers had distorted his aims, he emphasized the difference between imagining a contingent and an inevitable future: "I do not believe that the kind of society I describe necessarily *will* arrive," Orwell assured one correspondent, "but I believe...that something resembling it *could* arrive" (*CEJL*, 4:502). And, in a closely related statement, he writes: "The moral to be drawn from this dangerous situation is a simple one: *Don't let it happen. It depends on you*" (quoted in *GO*, 395). These statements raise certain obvious questions. What is the missing step between "*could* arrive" and "*will* arrive"? How can the coming of the nightmare world be prevented? And who exactly is the "you" referred to in the sentence "*It depends on you*"?

The idea that separates "*could* arrive" from "*will* arrive" is surely "unless vigorously resisted." And the "you" who must resist includes everyone, at least in countries that still work by the consent of the governed. Orwell's novel is intended as a form of mass inoculation. By giving his readers a small dose of the disease, he hoped to build up their resistance—their immunity—to it. By making them sensitive to the mental and psychological atmosphere of totalitarianism, he hoped to alert them to its first incursions, as health officials try to spot and isolate the carriers of any dangerous illness. But there is one thing wrong with this analogy. In Orwell's mind, the officials are not to be trusted; they are likely to be carriers themselves. A novel of more limited appeal, addressed to the intellectuals who read highbrow fiction and who dominate the social and political institutions of the country, will not serve the purpose because such people cannot be relied upon to resist. They have something to gain, after all: they will become the members of the Inner Party—the O'Briens—of the future. From Orwell's perspective, the core of the resistance would have to come from "the common man," or—in literary terms—from the common reader. This is the underlying reason for his decision to write a book that would have universal appeal, that would bridge the gap between popular and elitist culture.

In trying to write for such a wide and diverse readership, Orwell was going against the grain of the literary culture of his time. By the 1940s, the split between the different audiences of fiction had become an accepted fact both in England and America. There was said to be an unbridgeable gap between "high culture" and "mass culture." A writer was expected to sign up with one brigade or the other, since the two cultures were felt to be at war and crossovers were treated as betrayals.[3] The universal literate audience of a Charles Dickens or a Harriet Beecher Stowe—which in the nineteenth century had combined high and low, intellectuals and common readers, old and young, men and women—had apparently disappeared forever, to be replaced by a number of specialized audiences which did not read the same books. It is clear that Orwell was aware of, yet regretted, this fact. He notes that Kipling was "the only popular English writer of this century who was not at the same time a thoroughly bad writer" (*CEJL*, 1:159). And he laments the disappearance in modern literature of works like *Uncle Tom's Cabin*, "an unintentionally ludicrous book, full of preposterous melodramatic incidents [yet] deeply moving and essentially true" (*CEJL*, 4:22).

The cultural fissure Orwell saw was really the logical culmination of the whole modernist movement that began around 1900—a movement that deliberately idealized a coterie audience for literature as a necessity of the serious writer's intellectual survival. Ezra Pound wrote, "It takes about 600 people to make a civilization."[4] Virginia Woolf noted in her diary that she often felt she was writing for "half a dozen instead of 1500."[5] And D. H. Lawrence expressed his contempt for the idea that the voice of the people is the voice of God in this bitterly sarcastic passage from an essay: "We have to leave everything to the majority, everything to the majority, everything to the mob, the mob, the mob. They know what is obscene and what isn't, they do. If the lower ten million doesn't know better than the upper ten men, then there's something wrong with mathematics. Take a vote on it! Show hands, and prove it by count! *Vox populi, vox Dei.*"[6] In such ways, the most influential writers of the modernist movement defined themselves and their work in opposition to popular culture and the mass audience. They established and perfected a highbrow art—difficult, demanding, and distinguished, but essentially inaccessible to the "untrained'" reader. Reading became a form of work; it had nothing to do with relaxation or entertainment and demanded a strenuous, unremitting analytic attention. Obviously the only kind of reader who could give it such attention was the trained professional, the intellectual for whom reading was a life's work.

This was a vision of culture Orwell never really learned to accept, though he understood and admired the achievements of writers like Lawrence, James Joyce, and T. S. Eliot, who worked in the modernist idiom.[7] He was a cultural egalitarian on principle, though the prevailing literary elitism of his time often made him adopt the language of highbrow writers. His most ambitious essays, for example, were written for an intellectual audience and published in such mandarin journals as *Horizon* and the *Partisan Review*. And even in his early fiction, there are attempts to write according to modernist formulas—as in the Trafalgar Square episode of his novel *A Clergyman's Daughter*, a direct imitation of Joyce's difficult "Circe" chapter in *Ulysses*. There was, then, a split in Orwell himself, a wish to address both a mass and a class audience, and, until *Nineteen Eighty-Four*, no way for him to combine the two tendencies.

In order to achieve his purposes in that last book, Orwell would have to find a way to attract not only a larger but a more heterogeneous audience. This was the problem that faced him: how to write a novel that would be understood by the common reader and yet be of interest to highly educated ones, that would be read both by the "Winstons" of his society and by the "Smiths." In his essay "Poetry and the Microphone," Orwell discusses the possibility of once again making poetry appeal to the common man. A sentence from that essay should help us understand both his need to bring the two cultures together and the way he thought about the task: "It is difficult to believe," he writes, "that poetry can ever be popularised again without some deliberate effort at the education of public taste, involving strategy and perhaps even subterfuge" (*CEJL*, 2:334). The problems facing the modern fiction writer differed only in degree. The serious novelist also needed to educate the public taste, and to use both strategy and subterfuge.

A great deal of shrewd strategic thinking went into the creation of *Nineteen Eighty-Four*, and the aim of this careful planning was to hold two very different audiences: the intellectuals and the common readers. Orwell once described genuine lovers of the novel form as neither highbrows nor lowbrows but "elastic-brows" (*CEJL*, 1:254). The first problem he had to solve in trying to recreate such elasticity of response was to find a hero who would not alienate either set. And so Winston Smith is made into a composite of opposing qualities, as his name suggests. He is 39 years old—neither very young nor very old, with some of the passionate impatience of youth and some of the weight of mature experience. He is neither lower class (a prole) nor upper class (a member of the Inner Party). He is not brilliant, but neither is he slow-witted, so that he presents no threat either to the highly educated or to the minimally educated reader. He is not exactly a hero, someone strikingly above the level of the average person; yet he has enough courage to challenge an oppressive system. He is a sexual rebel but not a sexual athlete; indeed, he has to be roused to passion by Julia and reassured before he can make love. He can understand the nature of the society he lives in, but only when he has been instructed by Goldstein's book and O'Brien's words. In all these ways, Winston Smith is made into a character with whom most readers can sympathize, so that his fate will matter to them. He is an artful construct, not a version of the author himself, who seems to me to have been a great deal more confident, intelligent, and authoritative than his fictional creation.

The same strategic thinking went into Orwell's decisions about the fictional technique and the language of *Nineteen Eighty-Four.* A novel designed for a popular audience must have a strong plot, a sense of suspense, a single continuous narrative line that eventually reaches a conclusion. Most readers read to find out *what happens,* how it comes out. They will resent the interruptions of a philosophic novel in which ideas are unapologetically discussed in abstract language. Such passages in a fictional work impede the action and interrupt the urgency of the narration. On the other hand, intellectual readers have considerable contempt for a work that does not allow them the leisure to think, that moves along too breathlessly and appeals to their child-like eagerness to find out what happens next. Such books are dismissed as "page turners" or as "sensational," acceptable perhaps when the day's work is done and one wants to relax, but not a form of reading that can be taken seriously. Orwell's solution to this problem is to write his novel in two different fictional languages that are, in effect, interlarded in the text. There is the strong narrative line focusing on Winston's and Julia's rebellion, capture, and interrogation; and there is the cool analytic line concerning the principles of the regime expounded in the two extracts from Goldstein's book and in the appendix on the Principles of Newspeak.

Orwell insisted on keeping these analytic essays in *Nineteen Eighty-Four* even when the Book of the Month Club threatened to turn the novel down unless he cut them. His principled refusal could easily have cost him dearly. His publisher wrote that a Book of the Month Club selection was worth at least £40,000 to an author (*GO*, 386); Orwell had earned less than that from *all* the works he had written over the previous twenty years. Eventually the Club came to its senses and agreed to publish the text as Orwell had written it, but in a way his strategy of presentation made this decision possible. There is a good deal of subterfuge in Orwell's way of including what one might call the intellectual meat of the novel. Though the Goldstein expository passages about the regime are in the book, they come rather late in the narrative. And Orwell's decision to compress them into relatively short, self-contained sections and to allow Julia to fall asleep as Winston is reading these extracts to her in effect licenses the reluctant reader to skip. The same can be said for the decision to turn the discussion of "The Principles of Newspeak" into an appendix rather than a part of the plot. In such ways, Orwell made his book appeal at different moments to the intellectual and the non-intellectual reader, though these decisions may have made the novel structurally imperfect.

A similar attempt to appeal to the tastes of his two audiences determined what we might call the level of obscurity in the novel. The modernist movement had created a canon of important works that made the most extraordinary demands on the reader from the first page. The opening paragraphs of Joyce's *Ulysses*, for example, make virtually no sense to the unprepared reader. It is worth looking at them closely to get a sense of how difficult a confident modernist like Joyce makes it for us to enter the world of his novel:

> Stately, plump Buck Mulligan came from the stairhead, bearing a bowl of lather on which a mirror and a razor lay crossed. A yellow dressinggown, ungirdled, was sustained gently behind him by the mild morning air. He held the bowl aloft and intoned:
> —*Introibo ad altare Dei.*
> Halted, he peered down the dark winding stairs and called up coarsely:
> —Come up, Kinch. Come up, you fearful jesuit.
> Solemnly he came forward and mounted the round gunrest. He faced about and blessed gravely thrice the tower, the surrounding country and the awaking mountains. Then, catching sight of Stephen Dedalus, he bent towards him and made rapid crosses in the air, gurgling in his throat and shaking his head. Stephen Dedalus, displeased and sleepy, leaned his arms on the top of the staircase and looked coldly at the shaking gurgling face that blessed him, equine in its length, and at the light untonsured hair, grained and hued like pale oak.
> Buck Mulligan peeped an instant under the mirror and then covered the bowl smartly.
> —Back to barracks, he said sternly.
> He added in a preacher's tone:

—For this, O dearly beloved, is the genuine Christine: body and soul and blood and ouns. Slow music, please. Shut your eyes, gents. One moment. A little trouble about those white corpuscles. Silence, all.

He peered sideways up and gave a long low whistle of call, then paused awhile in rapt attention, his even white teeth glistening here and there with gold points. Chrysostomos. Two strong shrill whistles answered through the calm.

—Thanks, old chap, he cried briskly. That will do nicely. Switch off the current, will you?

He skipped off the gunrest and looked gravely at his watcher, gathering about his legs the loose folds of his gown. The plump shadowed face and sullen oval jowl recalled a prelate, patron of arts in the middle ages. A pleasant smile broke quietly over his lips.

—The mockery of it, he said gaily. Your absurd name, an ancient Greek.[8]

What are we to make of all this? Is Buck Mulligan a central character of the novel? (It turns out that he is not.) Is there really another character called Kinch, and is he a Jesuit? (We learn that this is not his name, and that he is no Jesuit.) Readers unfamiliar with the Catholic mass will be able to make no sense of "*Introibo ad altare Dei*" nor understand Mulligan's parodic version of Holy Communion. And where are we, anyway? Why in a tower with a gunrest? Why the reference to barracks? Are these soldiers? (It turns out that they are not.) And what are we to make of Mulligan's tone, and of the relationship between him and Stephen Dedalus? By this time, unprepared readers are likely to be thoroughly confused; our decision to continue reading becomes very much an act of faith, made in most cases because we have been assured that all this trouble is worth it and that if only we are patient our confusion will eventually be cleared up. The reader who reads simply for immediate pleasure will surely have shut the book.

Joyce both knew and welcomed this fact. His style is a deliberate attempt to separate the sheep from the goats. The serious reader will be willing to tolerate the state of suspended understanding for a good long time, will work hard to make sense of the text, and will perhaps even welcome the difficulty of the task. Such a reader has been trained to think, as Orwell put it in "Poetry and the Microphone," that "there must be something wrong" with a literary work "whose meaning can be taken in at a single glance" (*CEJL*, 2:331). In order to be "interesting," modernist writing had to be disturbing, disorienting, unfamiliar: almost impossible to understand immediately. This becomes the credo of the modern intellectual reader, who seems to glory in delayed gratification. For the common reader, on the other hand, a book had to offer more instant rewards and provide an access route early on that tells him where he is, to whom he should pay attention, exactly what is happening, that gives him his bearings and roots him in a world he knows or can easily recognize. These needs seem to be antithetical— either for the familiar or the unfamiliar, either for the easily interpretable or the obscure. How did Orwell succeed in satisfying these conflicting demands simultaneously?

If we look closely at the opening passage of *Nineteen Eighty-Four* we will find the answer:

> It was a bright cold day in April, and the clocks were striking thirteen. Winston Smith, his chin nuzzled into his breast in an effort to escape the vile wind, slipped quickly through the glass doors of Victory Mansions, though not quickly enough to prevent a swirl of gritty dust from entering along with him.
>
> The hallway smelt of boiled cabbage and old rag mats. At one end of it a coloured poster, too large for indoor display, had been tacked to the wall. It depicted simply an enormous face, more than a meter wide: the face of a man of about forty-five, with a heavy black mustache and ruggedly handsome features. Winston made for the stairs. It was no use trying the lift. Even at the best of times it was seldom working, and at present the electric current was cut off during daylight hours. It was part of the economy drive in preparation for Hate Week. The flat was seven flights up, and Winston, who was thirty-nine, and had a varicose ulcer above his right ankle, went slowly, resting several times on the way. On each landing, opposite the lift shaft, the poster with the enormous face gazed from the wall. It was one of those pictures which are so contrived that the eyes follow you about when you move. BIG BROTHER IS WATCHING YOU, the caption beneath it ran.
>
> Inside the flat a fruity voice was reading out a list of figures which had something to do with the production of pig iron. The voice came from an oblong metal plaque like a dulled mirror which formed part of the surface of the right-hand wall. Winston turned a switch and the voice sank somewhat, though the words were still distinguishable. The instrument (the telescreen, it was called) could be dimmed, but there was no way of shutting it off completely. He moved over to the window: a smallish, frail figure, the meagerness of his body merely emphasized by the blue overalls which were the uniform of the Party. His hair was very fair, his face naturally sanguine, his skin roughened by coarse soap and blunt razor blades and the cold of the winter that had just ended. (*NEF*, 5-6)

Such a beginning seems to me a highly ingenious solution to the problem of satisfying the conflicting demands of different kinds of readers. Despite the fact that Orwell thrusts his first readers without preliminaries into the unknown world of the future, many elements in this passage are reassuring. It immediately introduces us to the main character and describes him in considerable detail; it tells us something about where he lives in images that would have been perfectly familiar to an average reader in post-war Britain: the smell of cabbage and old rag mats in the hallway, the power cuts, the coarse soap and the scarcity of razor blades, even the sight of gigantic posters and the sounds of an official voice reading out production statistics. We seem to be in a known or at least easily knowable world.

Nevertheless, from the very first sentence, which tells us that the clocks are striking thirteen, an opposite kind of appeal is being made. Many of the details in these three paragraphs must have seemed incomprehensible to the novel's first readers: Why is a face on a British poster being measured in meters rather than in feet? What could the caption "BIG BROTHER IS WATCHING YOU" possibly mean? What might something called Hate Week be? What is the Party and why does Winston wear its uniform? And finally, what is this strange instrument in one's home that can be dimmed but never completely turned off? The first page of *Nineteen Eighty-Four* is a carefully worked amalgam of the reassuring and the incomprehensible. It gives readers just enough familiar information to make almost anyone feel a sense of recognition; but at the same time it introduces a number of important elements for which no explanation is yet offered. The level of obscurity is precisely calibrated to intrigue the reader trained in modernist techniques without scaring the common reader away. Orwell's choices—word by word and sentence by sentence—are consistently strategic.

But all of these choices—of Winston Smith as hero, of action balanced by analysis, of a style that merges the familiar and the obscure—are relatively superficial. There is a deeper reason why Orwell's novel has successfully appealed to different kinds of readers, one that is connected with the underlying principles of modernism as an artistic movement. That the nineteenth-century universal audience for fiction had split into two camps in the twentieth century was due finally to a quarrel about values. The spirit of modernism is the spirit of rebellion against authority. As Lionel Trilling puts it is his well-known essay on Orwell, "The prototypical act of the modern intellectual is his abstracting himself from the life of the family...from the ordinary life of the tribe."[9] The major fiction and drama of the period regularly idealizes a struggle between the outsider and conventional society. Joyce's Stephen Dedalus abandons his country, his family, and his church. Ibsen's Nora walks out of the doll's house of conventional marriage. Camus' Stranger commits a gratuitous murder. Mann's hero in *Death in Venice* gives in to his homoerotic desire. Ellison's Invisible Man expresses his contempt for the whole white establishment of his society. Twentieth century literature is filled with such characters— the angry young men and women who will not play the game by the rules, who experiment with their lives in dangerous ways, who refuse to settle down and accept what they take to be the limitations of conventional life. The freshness and originality of modernism owes much to the energy of revolt.

At the same time, such literature cannot fail to alienate readers who have made more conventional life choices, have accepted the familiar rules and traditions, and have "settled down." The kind of serious novel that reaches the top of the best-seller list rarely challenges the moral assumptions by which its readers live. Rebellious characters are punished or reformed or are contained. Conflicts are resolved within the existing social structure. The basic institutions of the society—the family, the law, the standards of success and failure—are not fundamentally challenged. The received ideas of how to live are directly or indirectly ratified by the author and the work.

This chasm between mainstream and modernist literary assumptions would seem to be unbridgeable. But in *Nineteen Eighty-Four*, Orwell managed to find a way to build such a bridge. He hit on the ingenious idea of combining these two traditions by writing a novel about an essentially conservative rebel pitted against a society which has abandoned the values by which we live. Winston and Julia are certainly rebellious characters; but they rebel in order to *restore* the old order, the ideals of privacy, familial loyalty, heterosexual love, freedom of choice, individual human dignity, even of an unforced love for one's country and respect for its leaders. It is the regime, the society of 1984, that has abandoned these conventional ideals, not the novel's major characters. By reconceptualizing the idea of rebellion against authority in this way, Orwell invented a novel that could draw on the hostile energy of modernism (and appeal to the readers who had acquired that taste) while assuring the more conventional readers that the values by which they lived were worth preserving. It was his most innovative solution to the problem with which he began, how to write a single work for audiences that come to a novel with radically different expectations.

I believe that most of these strategic choices were deliberate, and that their cumulative effect was to give *Nineteen Eighty-Four* the diverse and extraordinarily wide readership it has had. In his essays, Orwell had often shown his awareness of the differences between popular and elite forms of writing. But I do not want to suggest that there was something manipulative and cynical in his methods. They were means to an end, and the end was associated both with his political purpose in writing this book and with his own deepest wishes and needs. He was an intellectual who wanted to reach beyond coterie culture because his instincts were firmly democratic. Dickens was much closer to his ideal of a great writer than Joyce, as his well-known essay on the earlier novelist makes clear, and Dickens had made similar compromises in order to reach his own wide audience. Furthermore, Orwell genuinely believed that unless a movement of popular resistance could be developed in democratic countries, they might well go the way of the totalitarian states. And finally, as many readers have sensed, his fundamental values were simultaneously radical and conservative: he had a vision of a new and better world which kept the shape and feel of the old. It was only because these contradictory elements all had deep roots in Orwell's own complex nature that he was able, finally, to go beyond his own special dialect and speak the language of every man.

Notes

1. Christopher Hollis, *A Study of George Orwell: The Man and His Works* (London: Hollis and Carter, 1956), 107.
2. A notable exception was *The Road to Wigan Pier* (1937), a selection of the 50,000-member Left Book Club in the inexpensive orange paperback edition that was the Club's trademark. Such works were not really *chosen* by its members, however; they merely arrived every month. For statistics on the sales of Orwell's works, see John Rodden, *The Politics of Literary Reputation: The Making and Claiming of "St. George" Orwell* (New York: Oxford, 1989), 42-49.
3. On the important contribution of the influential British journal *Scrutiny* to the creation of this cultural climate, see Rodden, *Politics*, 227. Its characteristic tone can be suggested by Q. D. Leavis's dismissal of Orwell's fiction: "Mr. Orwell must have wasted a lot of energy trying to be a novelist—I think I must have read three or four novels by him, and the only impression these dreary books left on me is that nature didn't intend him to be a novelist." (Reprinted from *Scrutiny* in *George Orwell: The Critical Heritage*, ed. Jeffrey Meyers [London: Routledge & Kegan Paul, 1975], 188.)
4. *The Letters of Ezra Pound*, ed. D. D. Paige (New York: Harcourt, Brace, 1950), 221.
5. *The Diary of Virginia Woolf*, ed. Anne Olivier Bell (London: Hogarth, 1978), 2:107.
6. D. H. Lawrence, "Pornography and Obscenity," in *Phoenix: The Posthumous Papers*, ed. Edward R. McDonald (New York: Viking, 1968), 170.

7. These three were the only modern authors he included in his short list of "the writers I care most about and never grow tired of" (*CEJL*, 2:24); and Joyce, he notes, "interests me so much that I can't stop talking about him once I start" (*CEJL*, 1:128).
8. James Joyce, *Ulysses* (New York: Vintage, 1961), 2-3.
9. Lionel Trilling, "George Orwell and the Politics of Truth," in his *The Opposing Self* (New York: Viking Compass, 1959), 163.

Composing
Nineteen Eighty-Four:
The Art of Nightmare

Sue Lonoff

My new book is a utopia in the form of a novel. I ballsed it up rather...but I think some of the ideas in it might interest you.

George Orwell to Julian Symons (1949) [1]

Check the commentary on *Nineteen Eighty-Four* and you will find support for Orwell's modest judgment. Indisputably, the book is a *dys*topia—a term that came into currency after, and partly because of, his narrative. But four decades of scholarly study have yet to yield consensus on its literary aspects: its genre, its consistency, its rendering of character, the quality of the execution. To some readers, it seems not to be a novel at all; it is a fantasy or satire or tract for the times, a history lecture done up as a prophecy. [2] Even those who place it in the novel tradition find flaws in every phase of execution. The segment on Goldstein's book interrupts the narrative. The characters are weak or "rudimentary." The third part is implausibly melodramatic. Room 101 projects a schoolboy's fantasies. Orwell's very language, the prose he took such pride in, has been attacked on the one hand for betraying signs of haste and on the other for revealing too much effort. [3]

You can do what Irving Howe did when he challenged its detractors—hold the book exempt from mere aesthetic judgment: "The last thing Orwell cared about when he wrote *Nineteen Eighty-Four*, the last thing he should have cared about, was literature." [4] But Orwell would have disagreed—emphatically: "...I could not do the work of writing a book, or even a long magazine article, if it were not also an aesthetic experience" (*CEJL*, 1:6). In *Animal Farm*, he had tried (successfully, he thought) "to fuse political purpose and artistic purpose into one whole" (*CEJL*, 1:7). He had hoped for fusion of this kind in its successor, but his final effort left him disappointed.

Yet as Bernard Crick notes, Orwell's discontent was chronic; *Animal Farm* alone met his high standards (*GO*, 384). And against his allegation that he "ballsed up" the writing, there is evidence of long-term care and craftsmanship: an outline done five years before the typescript was completed; notes toward a revision of the first draft; an interim manuscript, dense with corrections; and remnants which support Peter Davison's argument that Orwell composed the novel in six stages—seven, if you include the proofs.[5] Wretched health increased the burden of revision. He had to rush the last draft. He could not get a typist, so he did it in his bedroom over two or three weeks, fighting weakness and the constant threat of relapse. But if tuberculosis sapped his physical strength, it did not impair the vigor of his narrative. The adjectives repeatedly invoked to describe the book—"urgent," "haunting," "terrifying," "brilliant"—attest to its continuing power.

Does its power stem from the fusion Orwell thought he had failed to achieve, or is it powerful despite flawed execution? These questions lead backward and forward: back to versions that precede the final draft, and forward to speculation on its status now that 1984 is past. Strangely, the closer you get to answers, the more you become aware of paradox: this book that attacks totalitarian control is itself more controlled, rhetorically and structurally, than critics have been able to realize.[6] Even so, Orwell felt (with some justice) that he had not made his aims completely clear. If he had, though, he might also have reduced the complexity that takes the book so far beyond the topical. But before going further, I want briefly to consider what he meant when he talked about artistry.

Before he finished his first novel, *Burmese Days*, he spelled out what he thought a novel ought to do. The first and simplest thing was "to display or create character." The second was "to make a kind of pattern or design," as distinct from merely turning out a story. And the third, the one he seems to have cared most about, was "to produce *good writing*." Typically, he added an analogy: writing was to novels what the quality of brush-strokes, the "*texture*," was to really good painting (*CEJL*, 1:126).[7]

In the fifteen years between that book and *Nineteen Eighty-Four*, Orwell revised his priorities. The age, he felt, did not permit a leisurely pursuit of art; politics had to be paramount. Increasingly, he wrote to give insight into power, to examine political corruption. Ideas launched his efforts. He meant to move his audience. "All art is propaganda," he insisted, though "not all propaganda is art" (*CEJL*, 1:448). To crank out propaganda was to sacrifice integrity and publish work devoid of lasting value. Even as a pamphleteer, Orwell took pains. As for fiction, instead of giving up his old criteria, he meshed them with political objectives. Character became less important than subject—or rather, he subsumed the development of character under that of issue, theme, and message. Design remained significant. He cared about the plot *as* plot; beyond that, he cared about symmetry, tempo, the balance to be struck between dialogue and narrative, arrangement of episodes and images. Above all, he retained his pleasure in good writing and his faith in the potential of language. Barbarity and falseness threatened that potential, as they threatened human freedom and sound government.[8] In his own books, preeminently *Nineteen Eighty-Four*, he would attack those interlocking perils. Hence his need to control the words that paint a world in which control is inescapable and lethal.

The governing metaphor and palpable reality of *Nineteen Eighty-Four* is the nightmare. (The word runs consistently through Orwell's notes and drafts, from his first outline to his last response to critics.) It is not the kind of nightmare you associate with Kafka, whose characters and actions seem to emanate directly from the raw, chaotic force of the subconscious. Orwell's political and sexual distortions have a motive, an articulated logic. He does not consistently avoid extravagance or keep subconscious forces from intruding. But even at its most grotesque the novel keeps its balance. Its horrors mount in sequence; dreams and omens create patterns; the issues converge on one another. Most chilling and pervasive are the intricate connections between public and personal pathology. This attack upon a system evolves as one man's story; nothing private can exist that's not political. The point is made repeatedly, and even if it were not, its consequences would be obvious from the action.

Less plain is the extent to which "nightmare" is the key to the structure and progression of the narrative.[9] Perhaps that is because Orwell deliberately cast it "in the form of a naturalistic novel" (*CEJL*, 4:330). From the opening windblast to the last two tears on Winston's nose, this is a world made oppressively factual, too dustblown to be phantasmagoric. But as actual nightmares conflate disparate elements— memories, projections, sensations real and fantasied—so a book that approximates a nightmare can integrate elements drawn from any other mode: naturalism, satire, fable, parody, the Gothic. And since the term connotes two kinds of experience, terrifying dream and terrible reality, it tends to blur distinctions between them. "Nightmare situation" could describe Winston's daily life; the context—a society governed by the Party; the real-world threat that drove Orwell to write; and the totalitarian ethos that he satirizes. If a single term can encompass all these elements then it is likely, as well, to offer clues to the literary aspects of the novel. Those are the aspects I want to consider now, exploring them in terms of Orwell's criteria—form and structure, character development, writing—to answer questions about fusion, control and the art of *Nineteen Eighty-Four*.

* * * * *

That Orwell planned to unify politics and artistry is evident from his preliminary outline for the book he called "The Last Man in Europe." Newspeak, the party slogans, Ingsoc, world geography, the Two Minutes Hate, the lonely hero and his diary—all were conceived by the start of 1944 and listed in the pages of his notebook. Big Brother was foreshadowed in the phrase "Leader-worship," doublethink in "Dual standard of thought" (*GO*, 407-9). The atmosphere of nightmare, the systematic lying, the altering of history, the torture, the insanity—these basic ingredients of *Nineteen Eighty-Four* were on his mind before he wrote a page of manuscript. But they were not just items in a memo. From the outset, he viewed them as components of a structure, which he held to with remarkable fidelity.[10]

The book he envisioned was to have two major parts: a "build up" in six "long chapters," a climax and denouement in three. Later, he divided his manuscript in three parts: a section that establishes the terms of Winston Smith's life, a section that develops his relationship with Julia, and a section after their arrest at Mr. Charrington's, in which O'Brien carries out the torture. But in some ways the book remains a two-part structure—first the build-up that culminates in Winston's arrest, then everything that happens to him after he is captured—with a hinge in the middle and an epilogue. The hinge is Goldstein's book, or rather, Winston's reading of it; the Newspeak Appendix is its complement.

Orwell's plan is at once complex and elegantly simple. In Part One, Winston is essentially alone, though we are made aware of Julia and O'Brien ("The writer's approaches to X & Y," Orwell had noted in his outline.) In Part Two, Winston's primary relation is with Julia, though O'Brien comes to the foreground in two chapters. In Part Three, Winston's primary relation is with O'Brien, though Julia comes to the foreground in two chapters. Not coincidentally, "*the book*" within the book is also divided into three parts, though Winston never gets to read its middle chapter. Even "The Principles of Newspeak" has three sections—on the A, B, and C vocabularies. But again, there are underlying patterns of two: Newspeak is explicitly contrasted with Oldspeak; its grammar has "two outstanding peculiarities"; words like "duckspeak" have two opposing meanings.

Could Orwell have played games or created balanced forms to gratify a sense of aesthetics? The very notion insults the spirit of his work. Yet intricate patterns, based on twos, threes, and even fours, proliferate in the text and in his notebooks:[11] three Party slogans comprised of linked opposites ("War is Peace, Freedom is Slavery, Ignorance is Strength"); three super-states, which form shifting alliances; three stages in Winston's "reintegration"; 101, an integer consisting of three numerals but hinting at a binary sequence. Symmetry can also be observed on the sentence level. Consider the openings of the first and last chapters:

It was a bright cold day in April, and the clocks were striking thirteen.	The Chestnut tree was almost empty. A ray of sunlight slanting through a window fell yellow on dusty tabletops. It was the lonely hour of fifteen.[12]

As Winston Smith enters his building (and the novel) he is isolated—in this draft, at any rate. An earlier version has him talking to "the aged prole who acted as porter and caretaker" (*Ms*, 3). But Orwell cut the caretaker, leaving Smith by himself except for the poster of Big Brother. Again, as the novel closes, Winston is alone, except for the internalized Big Brother. In between he travels a boomerang's course, from the solitude which leads to self-awareness to that which marks the loss of his identity.

But if the narrative follows a trajectory, how can it also be hinged? To answer, we might start by examining the changes between the outline and the finished novel. Most of those changes affect the story's politics, rather than its structure. Orwell dropped allusions to "the Trusts" and "Bakerism" and subdued the allusions to Jews and Roman Catholics;[13] in this dystopia, Ingsoc would supplant all other systems, as the worship of Big Brother would supplant all other faiths. He seems to have enlarged the role of X (O'Brien), but again, the change would not require a major shift in structure, since he had only to establish connections between two consecutive items in his outline: "Conversation with X" (I.vi) and "The torture and confession" (II.i).

Virtually all the later structural changes—especially the revision from two parts to three—can be traced back to a single item in the first version of the layout: "The brief interlude of the love affair with Y" (I.j). This "interlude," subservient to the politics in outline, expanded to fill the middle section of the novel and run over into "torture and confession." Perhaps Orwell always meant to give Y (Julia) a larger role. Certainly, by filling in the details of their meetings, the contrasts in their outlooks, and the dangers that confront them, he added a romantic dimension to the plot—and a motive for Winston's rebellion. But more than that, he provided the book with a profounder, more engaging dialectic.

The outline and earliest versions of the manuscript suggest the basic terms of the conflict. On one side there is the Party, a nightmare system whose horrors include the worship of power, constant surveillance, denial of the past and of objective reality. On the other side there is Winston, fighting for sanity, for memory and truth, for self and sexual expression. But these are not the only forces in conflict. Another set of terms emerges in Part Two as Winston discovers the supreme importance of uncomplicated human love and loyalty.[14] This female side of *Nineteen Eighty-Four*—female in that its agents are Julia, Winston's mother, his sister, and the prole washerwoman—contrasts with the male side embodied in the Party and its agents, O'Brien and Charrington. In Part Three, the dialectic is predominantly male again; O'Brien's arguments counteract Winston's and tragically overcome them. But without the addition of love—in all its aspects—the ending would be less complete and chilling. Winston as "the last man" isn't nearly so alone before he forms the ties with Julia and recovers buried memories—*his* history, the truth about his own life. Enlightened, he can reach beyond himself, beyond Julia, to the woman in the yard and proles everywhere. Then he is literally arrested by the Thought Police and borne back to unalterable solitude. In a grim perversion of Hegelian synthesis, love becomes the proof of his subjection to Big Brother, loyalty becomes a constant shifting of belief, and sanity becomes untenable.

In America, the Book of the Month Club felt uneasy about the chapter I have called the hinge and sounded Orwell out on cuts and alterations. Orwell was adamant: "A book is built up as a balanced structure and one cannot simply remove large chunks here and there unless one is ready to recast the whole thing" (*CEJL*, 4:483). He had already done his recasting. He had drafted Goldstein's book (perhaps in 1946) and then thoroughly revised and rearranged it (*Ms*, xiv). He had made substantial alterations in the chapters that precede Winston's reading of the volume, frequently removing the transitional passages that smooth the narrative flow. For instance, in rough draft Winston puts on his overalls, tells Julia that he is going to O'Brien, and accepts her decision to accompany him. When they rejoin each other inside O'Brien's building, she takes charge of getting them admitted. After the encounter Julia leaves before Winston, but she violates O'Brien's orders and waits for Winston outside, where she embraces him and plans their next meeting (*Ms*, 130-75). All of this (except her exit) disappears from the final draft. The story cuts from Winston's thoughts, in the room above the junk-shop, to their entry in the room where O'Brien sits dictating; at the end of the encounter it cuts again, from Winston's thoughts about O'Brien's "interrupted" Party business to his weary walk to Charrington's, eleven days later, with the unopened book in his briefcase.

The removal of these episodes compresses the action; perhaps less positively, it reduces Julia's role and shifts the focus from her feminine affection to the specious understanding between men. But that, I think, was not Orwell's objective in revising, at least, not on any conscious level. Plot elaboration at these junctions is distracting—if you are writing a novel of ideas. He had already made the love affair sufficiently explicit; he had shown that, in this system, sex itself becomes political. By omitting transitions he could subtly emphasize the arbitrary, disconnected nature of his nightmare-state, where sudden shifts in policy and sudden disappearances are the very stuff of daily life.

On the other hand, he could not omit the explanation that would make these lives and policies plausible. He had to interpolate "*the book*." To maximize its impact on the narrative, he placed it between the aftermath of Hate Week and Winston's beatific vision at the window. In that position, even as it halts the story's progress, it works as an ideological pivot or hinge between the rising action and the denouement. Turning (or returning) to origins and causes, Goldstein's book suggests why Winston's story takes a tragic course and why his efforts are about to boomerang. Winston thinks he understands it but miscalculates its message—as he misconstrues O'Brien and Charrington. Because he fails to grasp the pervasive power of doublethink, the basis of the system's "controlled insanity," he also fails to realize that "*the book*" portends defeat and closure, rather than eventual liberation. ("Among ourselves we call it the Book of the Dead," O'Brien announces in the draft [*Ms*, 167]).

O'Brien, complex as a character and theorist, exemplifies the fusion of art and politics that Orwell wanted to achieve. He is doublethink made palpable. Dual in all aspects of language and behavior, he maintains schizoid standards with a singleness of purpose that demonstrates the madness of the system. His duality, evident in Winston's first impressions, becomes more pronounced with every subsequent encounter—and, at the same time, more insidious. O'Brien's form is "bulky" yet oddly graceful; his manner is "urbane" yet sympathetic. Powerfully constructed, manifestly intellectual, he reminds Winston of a prizefighter and nobleman, roles to which he adds those of ally and tormentor, rationalist and zealot, lethal guardian. His gestures—the way he manipulates his spectacles, the handshake so hearty that it crushes Winston's bones—are singular as well as symbolic. Even his name suggests doubleness. "O'Brien" is both common and Irish, belying his high position in the Party and setting him apart from Smith, Syme, Charrington, and Parsons, whose names are all distinctly English.

I am tempted to believe that Orwell knew those six letters could also be divided differently: "*ob*," the Latin preposition "from" or "out of," is followed by "*rien*," the French word for "nothing" whose root is the Latin "*rem*" or "thing."[15] In any case, the name is implicitly Catholic, and therefore consistent with the priestly role of this sinister apostle and betrayer.

O'Brien's words, above all else, convey his duality. Orwell carefully worked and reworked them, revising to emphasize the ironies implicit in O'Brien's ideology and actions. For instance, Orwell first had Winston dreaming that O'Brien says, "Sooner or later you will come to me" (*Ms*, 67). But he changed that phrase in draft to the luminous and vatic, "We shall meet in the place where there is no darkness" (*Ms*, 69). Later, the draft has O'Brien proposing a toast "to the day when two & two make four" (*Ms*, 167), words that Winston could hardly misinterpret or ignore as an allusion to his diary (*NEF*, 69). Perhaps for those reasons Orwell cut it from the novel, leaving the dialogue suitably ambiguous, so that when Winston proposes drinking "to the past," O'Brien agrees "gravely": "The past is more important" (*NEF*, 146). The impact of this statement only becomes clear when you see what Winston's future entails. Still later in the draft, Winston thinks he hears O'Brien say,

> For seven years I have watched over you, Winston. Seven years ago I saw the seed of evil in your face. I watered it & nursed it till it was a thriving plant. And now that it has reached full growth I tear it out by the roots, & you will be made perfect, even as I am perfect. (*Ms*, 257-59)

But Orwell removed the allusion to Blake,[16] as he removed superfluous details elsewhere; he also made the theology less blatant, so that while the lines retain their biblical aura, their irony is chillingly political:

> Don't worry, Winston; you are in my keeping. For seven years I have watched over you. Now the turning point has come. I shall save you, I shall make you perfect. (*NEF*, 201).

Rereading O'Brien's speeches, you discover the extent of their duplicity. Although he rarely lies to Winston and Julia, his words are designed to deceive them: "Do you understand that even if [Winston] survives, it may be as a different person?" (*NEF*, 143). You also get a sense of the convolutions entailed in reality control. Did he collaborate in writing Goldstein's book, as he claims, or is the claim another Party fabrication?

Against such pervasion and unshakable doublethink, Winston's integrity is futile. "What a man," Winston says to himself in the draft, as he leaves O'Brien's building in darkness (*Ms*, 175). In fact, as O'Brien and the early title indicate, Winston is the last remaining man in this dystopia, the only advocate of humanistic values in a system bent upon destroying them.[17] Despite Party pressures, he insists on his identity, insists on seeking answers to his questions; despite his anxieties, he moves toward integration, combining the "male" qualities he so admires—courage, independence, strength of conviction—with the "female" ones he often dreads as weakness. In contrast, O'Brien is both more and less than human. Textual allusions link him with a pantheon of powerful male figures: God, the devil, the Grand Inquisitor, a sadistic schoolmaster, a punishing father, the brother who turns on his sibling.[18] In any guise he is a character immune to doubt, exempt from fear. Not even morality dismays him.

O'Brien unmans Winston—in the text's words, gets inside him—by making him cast off his love and faith. Winston's ultimate torturers are literally man-eaters, "enormous rats" whose teeth and muzzles loom before the victim sitting strapped and masked and impotent before them. Orwell later conceded to Julian Symons that "the 'Room 101' business" was vulgar (*CEJL*, 4:502-3). But its "schoolboy" melodrama produces effects that are consistent with his aims throughout this section. The victims of Room 101 surrender the last vestige of control over reason and autonomy. As terror repressed by the conscious mind takes over, their nightmares become their realities. To bring that terror home, Orwell shifts away from plainstyle. Prose and sanity degenerate together.

Winston's loss (of self and Julia) can be seen as a regression that culminates in premature senility. When he first rebels against the system, he is driven by anger and defiance, characteristics traditionally connected to an adolescent phase of development. By the end of Part Two he has matured, but his maturity is hard-won and precarious. It is also contingent on recall of his younger self; through memory and dream, he has relived and come to terms with his betrayal of his mother and sister. When O'Brien exerts his power over Winston, he reverses the process of development. As he puts his victim through what he terms the learning phase—in other words, as Winston is relentlessly tortured—Winston becomes more and more like a child, still defiant, yet requiring approval. As he enters the phase O'Brien terms understanding—that is, as mind and body are totally degraded—he becomes as dependent as a baby. He is given a respite to recover flesh and strength; then, abruptly, to insure his acceptance, he is plunged into O'Brien's inversion of the primal scene, reduced to the helpless terror of an infant confronting "the worst thing in the world."[19]

The process of regression is depicted in language that itself lapses from maturity. Through Part Three, the dialogue resounds with stage effects; the physical descriptions are hideous:

> He seized one of Winston's remaining front teeth between his powerful thumb and forefinger. A twinge of pain shot through Winston's jaw. O'Brien had wrenched the loose tooth out by the roots. He tossed it across the cell.
> "You are rotting away," he said; "you are falling to pieces. What are you? A bag of filth." (*NEF*, 224)

Perhaps these sections got beyond Orwell's control, despite considerable efforts at revision. Or perhaps he believed that only extreme language could convey these extremes of experience. I think he meant to imitate aspects of pulp fiction, the kind he analyzes in "Boys' Weeklies," out of a conviction that such "blood-and-thunder stuff" retains a hold on those who think they have outgrown it (*CEJL*, 1:482, 484). But here, crude effects serve sophisticated ends; they give the reader a "bellyfeel" of totalitarian brutality.

There is also a political dimension to Orwell's choice of rats as Winston's torturers. The system that sustains them engenders human beings who resemble beetles, rodents, and vermin. The Party itself is a devouring monster, a Cronos determined to annihilate chronology by forcing the present into stagnant circles and continually altering the past. Winston feels he has been rescued from the horror when he hears the cage door closing. But as the narrator says, it "had clicked shut and not open" (*NEF*, 236), phrasing that drives Winston's destiny home "like the final tap to a nail."[20]

Orwell was as thoroughly committed to "good writing" as he was to history and politics. His narrative contravenes the principles of Newspeak, extending the reader's range of thought and experience through language that is neither as barren as his vision nor radically inconsistent with it. He renders the gritty greyness of a world that relentlessly assaults the pleasures of the senses in phrases which thrust impressions at the reader, impressions of smells and tastes and colors. Similes coexist with clinical analysis: promiscuity is both a symptom of revolt and "like the sneeze of a horse that smells bad hay" (*NEF*, 102). Strategic repetition of ominous phrases and graphic descriptions of the implements of tyranny conduce to "fantasmagoric effect[s]," an expression that recurs twice in his outline. He breaks up the narrative with nursery rhyme and doggerel, verse that is at once nostalgic and prophetic, a link to the past and the future. He modulates to lyric prose for scenes in the country and Winston's last reverie at the window. And of course he employs the satirist's arsenal: irony, invective, innuendo.[21]

Yet in reading the novel you are far more aware of consistency than of variation. It is unified, not just by his political vision, but also by the method and angle of narration, which he seems to have determined quite early. The "lay-out" of 1943 (or 1944) begins as an objective list of items; its perspective is implicitly omniscient:

PART I   Build up of
           a. The system of organized lying...
           b. The ways in which this is done...
           c. The nightmare feeling caused by the disappearance of
               objective truth....

But even before this version concludes, the protagonist's consciousness is coming into prominence, and in the second version, which follows it directly, the standpoint shifts to the diarist:

[II...]
               i.   The torture & confession
            ii.   Continuation of diary, mentally.
          iii.   Recognition of own insanity. (*GO*, 408)

Orwell had mixed feelings about first-person novels. (Of his own six, only *Coming Up for Air* is narrated by its protagonist.) He knew the form was useful for getting at the inner mind, for treating emotion and sex honestly. But he felt it tied the author too closely to the teller and narrowed what the teller could plausibly perceive and feel.[22] Nonetheless, he needed a spokesman for his views, an individual who, in looking outward and inward, would illuminate the evils of a system. So although he kept the story in the third person, he wrote it from Winston's perspective.

Winston is the filter for nearly everything that happens in *Nineteen Eighty-Four*. His activities compose the action of the novel. He overhears or joins in the dialogue. The details are those that impress themselves upon him: the woman in the film, with the child held against her; the crimson of Julia's sash, tight about her waist; O'Brien waving four extended fingers while his other hand prepares to press the lever. Of course, he is not wholly distinct from his creator. He shares Orwell's propensities in small and large matters: his love of dace and bluebells, his hatred of Party lies, his need to set ideas down on paper. He has the same eye for telling bits of color: the rat's pink hands, the diary's creamy pages. He has the same memory for commonplace lyrics. Most important for the texture of the prose, he is given Orwell's compulsion to describe, or perhaps I should say he is the agent of impressions which the narrative ascribes to his consciousness.

Orwell also uses Winston to achieve flexibility within the larger context of confinement. Winston moves, not only through the streets and rooms of Airstrip One, but also through a kind of inner space. There is no question as to which provides more latitude: his dreams sustain connections that the Party would obliterate; his memories reanimate the past. Though he gains information piecemeal, his identity is constant—until it is destroyed in the last chapter. The narrative voice is correspondingly consistent, so long as it's identified with Winston. Orwell varies the style by including prole dialect, the songs, the journal entries, bits of Newspeak, Julia's idiom, and O'Brien's later tirades. Only in the pages given over to "*the book*" is there a shift to an omniscient perspective. To mark that change (and possibly, to imitate Trotsky's prose[23]), the words become more Latinate and the syntax becomes more convoluted. Yet even here, the limited perspective casts its shadow. Winston's choice of chapters determines what the reader sees; "*the book*" breaks off abruptly when he stops.

In important ways, however, the narrative dissociates Winston's perspective from the reader's. Orwell plays with time and continuity, moving freely in and out of Winston's consciousness, shifting between action and reflection. He also creates distance through parody and satire, enabling the reader to draw conclusions that are far beyond the reach of any character.

Both dissociation and the angle of narration contribute to the atmosphere of nightmare, an atmosphere sustained by his control of tone and image—in broader terms, the texture of the writing. Here, for example, the Party's men have just broken into the room above the shop:

> There was another crash. Someone had picked up the glass paperweight from the table and smashed it to pieces on the hearthstone.
>
> The fragment of coral, a tiny crinkle of pink like a sugar rosebud from a cake, rolled across the mat. How small, thought Winston, how small it always was! There was a gasp and a thump behind him, and he received a violent kick on the ankle which nearly flung him off his balance. (*NEF*, 183-84)

This is reportage, and yet each bit of observation draws you in and makes you feel for the observer. The words are terse and plain—a man like Winston would use them—but their plainness does not preclude complexity. Delicate images are balanced against harsh ones; the simile compounds the violation. Details stir the senses, while onomatopoeia intensifies the message of destruction: "crash," "smashed," "gasp," "thump," "flung." Psychologically as well, the text is complex. The paperweight had symbolized beauty and the past. Now, like Winston's world, it lies shattered. It is also metonymic, a sexual surrogate. The tiny pink crinkle is devalued and ruined as Julia writhes helpless on the floor. The ankle reference adds to the imagery of impotence; Winston has a varicose ulcer. Then there is the site of destruction, the hearthstone, an allusion that recalls both the couple's domesticity and Winston's lost mother, dispenser of chocolate. Counterpointing the elements of loss and invasion is a subtle undercurrent of detachment. Winston's reaction—"How small...how small it always was!"—momentarily puts the terror at a distance, while two uses of the impersonal "There" and the inexplicit "Someone" generalize the agents of destruction.

That in fact such lucid prose was the product of great effort is clear from Orwell's letters and, more specifically, from remnants of earlier versions. Though less than half the text survives in manuscript facsimile, those pages suggest how the draft he called "a ghastly mess" developed into publishable writing (*CEJL*, 4:404). Predictably, he worked to cut away the fat, eliminating details not germane to the story and adjectives that cluttered his sentences. You can see these trends in the opening line:

<pre>
                                        the clocks
            bright   ~~innumerable clocks~~
//It was a / cold ~~blowy~~ day in ~~early~~ April, and ~~a million radios~~...
</pre>

But economy—or even that broader goal, "good writing"—did not motivate all of the changes. Orwell seems to have corrected with several aims: to bring out ideas, tighten up the story, add items that would reinforce pattern and motif, and produce lean, vivid sentences. Sometimes, propaganda and art were at cross purposes; more often, the tension was productive.

Consider the draft of the section in which O'Brien first enters Winston's cell:

<pre>
              The shock of the sight had driven all discretion
    Winston sprang to his feet. ~~All discretion had gone~~ out of him.
For the first time in years he forgot the presence of the telescreen.
    "They've got you too!" he cried.
              long
    "They got me ~~years~~ ago," said O'Brien. "My name is Watson.
              by
Nosy Watson is the nickname ~~under~~ which you have been
taught to call
~~known~~ me, I believe."
</pre>

> He stepped aside. The stumpy guard with the gorilla-like face
> appeared from behind him.... (*Ms*, 241)

From this passage, you can understand why Orwell rarely bothered to
save his notes and drafts. He must have had some purpose for
O'Brien's clumsy alias. "The most hateful of all names in an English
ear is Nosey Parker," he had written in "The Lion and the Unicorn"
(*CEJL*, 2:59). He had also noted that Holmes and Dr. Watson exem-
plify aspects of an "ancient dualism," the split between soul and body
(*CEJL*, 2:163). But whatever his intentions, the nickname is a howler,
and (like Julia's last name, Vernon) it got cut:

> Winston started to his feet. The shock of the sight had driven
> all caution out of him. For the first time in many years he forgot
> the presence of the telescreen.
>
> "They've got you too!" he cried.
>
> "They got me a long time ago," said O'Brien with a mild, almost
> regretful irony. He stepped aside. From behind him there emerged
> a broad-chested guard with a long black truncheon in his hand.
>
> "You knew this, Winston," said O'Brien. "Don't deceive your-
> self. You did know it—you have always known it." (*NEF*, 197)

The changes here suggest that Orwell wrote by the rules he set in
"Politics and the English Language." He hones his prose to give more
point to the encounter; the new lines add meaning, not filler. They also
improve the rhythm of the passage and the balance between dialogue
and narrative. Plain, short words of native origin predominate. Images
gain particularity. Now the barbarisms are intrinsic in the plot and not
a byproduct of style or execution. But the contrast isn't only in the pol-
ish. The second version amplifies the power of the Party and the terror that lies in wait for Winston. While the first guard is simply an
atavistic brute, his successor wields an instrument, a black one. O'Brien
too becomes more sinister. His "mild, almost regretful irony" signals the
change in his relations with his victim yet preserves his consistent duality. He admits—indirectly—to deceit and entrapment, yet his very confession is accusing: Winston knew. And Winston assents to the charge
of self-deception: "Yes, he saw now, he had always known it."

How are we to take this statement? It fits into a pattern; all through
the novel there are references to doom and fatality. "The end was contained in the beginning," Winston says in resolving to visit O'Brien.
"We are the dead," each major character repeats, before the "iron
voice" confirms the allegation. Winston and Julia cannot make love
without remembering that someday they will be destroyed. But Julia,
the hedonist, makes light of retribution until she is tortured and

converted. Winston is more complex. He rebels against the system yet virtually invites it to destroy him. Why, when he hopes "to keep the inner heart inviolate," does he boast to O'Brien, "I have not betrayed Julia"? Why, as he undergoes O'Brien's vicious baiting, does he think, "Perhaps one did not want to be loved so much as to be understood"? Is this part of Orwell's satire? Or part of something else that the narrative could not contain or fuse?

There may be several answers, several ways of construing the recurrent allusions to fatality. Viewed as part of the design, they are fully consistent with the circular structure of the narrative. For in a way, Winston's first rebellion *is* his last, the determinant of everything that follows. From the time he purchases the diary and pen—for seven years, if you reckon from his first dream of O'Brien—he moves inexorably toward the Chestnut Tree Café and the "victory over himself." Images of dust and water reinforce the theme of inescapable defeat and dissolution. Dust invades all surfaces: the cracks of people's faces, the floor of the belfry where Julia draws her map, the tabletop where waiters set his liquor. Water both sustains and engulfs him. He feels like a wanderer at the bottom of the sea, "lost in a monstrous world where he himself was the monster" (*NEF*, 25); he dreams of his mother, "drowning deeper every minute," yet continuing to gaze at him through "darkening water" (*NEF*, 135). Finally, he sinks his consciousness in alcohol. Victory Gin becomes "the element he swam in"; its scent pervades his penitential tears (*NEF*, 241).

Orwell also provides him with a background that makes an obsession with death plausible. The absence of his father, his mother's disappearance, the whole thrust of the system toward acceptance and conformity, suggest that when he does rebel each impulse toward fulfillment will exact its toll in self-recrimination. Long before O'Brien gets him, Winston tortures Winston: "It was as though [he and Julia] were intentionally stepping nearer to their graves" (*NEF*, 116). He hopes only to postpone the day of capture, and after that, to die with hate intact. Instead, he abandons even his hatred in his "blissful" surrender to Big Brother.

A few critics have complained that there is something spurious in Winston's reactions under pressure.[24] While no one says the story should have ended optimistically, Winston's masochism strikes some readers as exaggerated, willed by Orwell for propaganda purposes instead of evolving from the action. It also tends to erode the opposition between enforced compliance and autonomy. Orwell postulates a system that is closed and a "lost man" who searches for an opening. If the character himself is predestined or preprogrammed, what becomes of this crucial antithesis?

I would answer that Orwell chose to undercut it, to increase the sense of nightmarish reality. "*I understand HOW*," Winston writes in his diary. "*I do not understand WHY*." O'Brien tells him why the Party is so obsessed with power, why it thinks it has control over reality and history, and why it is so sure that it's invincible. Winston knows these "reasons" are profoundly irrational, but knowing just exacerbates the torture. He himself is confident of few things. One is that the forces of destruction lie in wait for him. Another is that sanity, which never was "statistical," can only be maintained by stubborn vigilance. If he were convinced that he was always sane and rational, the novel's oppositions would be simpler. But the forces of unreason inhere within him, too. They contravene his efforts to maintain his independence; they complement the madness of the system. And certainly, that is part of Orwell's message. Decency is always being menaced, he lets us know, threatened from without and from within. Even Winston kicks a hand into the gutter.

Above all, Winston's fatalism sets in relief the issue Orwell cared most about: survival. It was a subject he knew something about—after Paris and pneumonia, Spain and a bullet wound, increasingly severe tuberculosis. I do not mean to read the author's fate into the character's; Orwell's letters on his illness, and reports from those who knew him, make it plain that he expected to recover.[25] But he was pessimistic about the fate of Europe and desperate to make his contemporaries realize what totalitarianism might portend. Gravely ill and driven, he was writing with two purposes: to warn the world and leave *his book* in testament.

Nineteen Eighty-Four concludes by satirizing the conventions of the comic ending: love, reunion, happiness. Winston is no longer "a flaw in the pattern." Big Brother has won out, and Winston loves him. There is a terrible rightness about the conversion scene, a rightness about the whole last chapter. Though Winston's life is shattered and his mind reduced to fragments, the narrative is strikingly coherent. Scarcely a facet of life in Oceania, scarcely a motif or significant image, is not reinvoked and set in place. The sequence of the book's three parts is also recapitulated in this section. First there are the details of Winston's life, its ambiance. Then his thoughts move back to Julia and his mother, though he dismisses both as faulty memories. Finally, he is left with the "enormous face" above him and the prospect of a bullet in his brain.

Thus in formal terms the novel ends in closure, its loose threads tied, its hero's future settled. In other terms, however, it stays open. Its political vision is still trenchant. The horror story grips new generations. That which is slated for oblivion within its boundaries haunts the reader's memory beyond them. This, I think, is proof that Orwell did not botch the task he found so urgent. As he himself said (in an analysis of Dickens), "There are no rules in novel writing, and for any work of art there is only one test worth bothering about—survival."[26]

_____

Notes

1. *CEJL*, 4:475; see also *CEJL*, 4:448.
2. The classifications into parody, satire, fantasy, and so forth have appeared in so many articles and chapters that attributing them to single sources seems pointless—though attention should be paid to Bernard Crick's long argument on the book's "Seven Satiric Thrusts" (George Orwell, *Nineteen Eighty-Four*, ed. Bernard Crick [Oxford: Clarendon, 1984], 55-92); to Denis Donahue's assertion that the book is a political fable (*"Nineteen Eighty-Four:* Politics and Fable," in *George Orwell and Nineteen Eighty-Four*, [Washington, D.C.: Library of Congress, 1985], 59-60); and to Irving Howe's claim, following Northrop Frye, that the book is a Menippean satire ("The Fiction of Anti-Utopia," in *Orwell's Nineteen Eighty-Four: Text, Sources, Criticism*, ed. Irving Howe [New York: Harcourt, Brace, 1963], 197). More recently, Howe has modified that definition, suggesting that the book is "a mixture of genres, mostly Menippean satire and conventional novel, but also bits of tract and a few touches of transposed romance" ("1984: Enigmas of Power," in *1984 Revisited*, ed. Irving Howe [New York: Harper, 1983], 7-8). The mixed genre position has also been taken by Lynette Hunter in her reader-oriented study of the narrative (*George Orwell: The Search for a Voice* [Milton Keynes: Open University Press, 1984], 192 and, more broadly, chap. 7).
3. For a summary of arguments as to whether or not the book is a novel, see Robert A. Lee, *Orwell's Fiction* (Notre Dame: University of Notre Dame Press, 1969), 129-30. For an early listing of the novel's flaws, see Bruce Bain, "After the Bomb," *Tribune*, 17 June 1949, 17-18. By 1956, Howe finds it necessary to refute the "complaint one often hears...that there are no credible or 'three-dimensional' characters in the book" ("Orwell: History as Nightmare," in *Politics and the Novel*, 2d ed. [New York: Avon, 1970], 241. Julian Symons is among the critics who label the third part melodramatic ("Power and Corruption," *Times Literary Supplement*, 10 June 1949, 380). V. S. Pritchett also criticizes the torture scenes and the Ministry of Love ("Books in General," *New Statesman and Nation*, 18 June 1949, 646, 648). To some extent, these assumptions remain current; see, for example, Michael Orange, *"Nineteen Eighty-Four* and the Spirit of Schweik," in *George Orwell*, ed. Courtney T. Wemyss and Alexej Ugrinsky (New York: Greenwood Press, 1987), 51-54 (although Orange seems to respect "the intertextual density of [*NEF's*] texture," 56). Isaac Deutscher (whose comments have often been disputed) accuses Orwell of a narrow imagination, derivative plotting, and "crude" symbolism ("*1984*—The Mysticism of Cruelty," reprinted in *Twentieth-Century Interpretations of 1984*, ed.

Samuel Hynes [Englewood Cliffs, N.J.: Prentice-Hall, 1971], 30). There has been astute and favorable work on the literary aspects, as my notes will suggest. Still, opinion persists that *Nineteen Eighty-Four* is not well written. Consider Alfred Kazin's comment: "Orwell was an efficient novelist not particularly interested in fiction; he used it for making a point" ("'Not One of Us,'" in *George Orwell and Nineteen Eighty-Four*, 71). Bernard Crick has consistently maintained that the novel does not represent Orwell's best writing. But unlike the critics who think he dashed it off, Crick thinks Orwell tried too hard for effect and created conflicting layers of satire (*Nineteen Eighty-Four*, 132-33).

4. Since Howe first made this judgment in 1956 ("Orwell: History as Nightmare," 230), he has moved steadily toward an appreciation of Orwell's craftsmanship: "Reading through these four large volumes [of *CEJL*] has convinced me that Orwell was an even better writer than I had supposed....He was, I now believe, the best English essayist since Hazlitt, perhaps since Dr. Johnson" (*Harper's Magazine*, quoted on the back covers of the HBJ/Harvest edition). See also his analysis of "formal means" in "The Fiction of Anti-Utopia," 180. But he seems still to prefer the essayist to the novelist. Hugh Kenner makes more accurate comments on the strategic effects of Orwell's fictive language; see the conclusion to "The Politics of the Plain Style" in *Reflections on America, 1984: An Orwell Symposium*, ed. Robert Mulvihill (Athens, Ga.: University of Georgia Press, 1986), 64-65.

5. The outline, now in the Orwell Archive, has been printed as Appendix A in Crick's *George Orwell* (407-9) and his edition of *Nineteen Eighty-Four* (137-38). The notes toward revision (1948), from a notebook also in the Orwell Archive, have been printed as Appendix C in his *Nineteen Eighty-Four* (141-43). Davison's introduction to the facsimile establishes the evidence for the six stages. And several of Orwell's own letters suggest the amount of effort he put into the book—for instance, "a novel has to be lived with for years before it can be written down, otherwise the working-out of detail, which takes an immense amount of time and can only be done at odd moments, can't happen" (*CEJL*, 4:497).

6. Hunter (*Search for a Voice*, 212-14) is the only other critic I have found who connects the creator's control over his fiction with the party's control within it.

7. As Ian Watt notes, Orwell's "attitude to language is old-fashioned" (as are many of the views on art I cite here). Nonetheless, it was genuine and "central" ("Winston Smith: The Last Humanist," in *On Nineteen Eight-Four*, ed. Peter Stansky [New York: W. H. Freeman, 1983], 111).

8. The obvious source is "Politics and the English Language," especially the second half (*CEJL*, 135-140). On links between art and propaganda, see also *CEJL*, 2:126, 130, and 240-41. Orwell's comments on aesthetics are scattered through *CEJL*. See especially "Why I Write," "Charles Dickens," "Inside the Whale," "Politics vs. Literature," "The Prevention of Literature," and his reviews of Henry Miller's, Jack London's, and George Gissing's work.

9. Mark Crispin Miller takes a similar position: While the book has lost its topical immediacy, it will keep its grip on readers because it is "a work...that

deliberately evokes the state of perfect nightmare" ("The Fate of *1984*" in *1984 Revisited*, ed. Irving Howe, 22; see also 19-46). Though Jeffrey Meyers challenges the "cliché" that *Nineteen Eighty-Four* is a "nightmare vision," in reading it realistically he demonstrates connections between craft and idea (*A Reader's Guide to George Orwell* [London: Thames and Hudson, 1975], chap. 8).

10. Joseph Slater comments incisively on the novel's form in "The Fictional Values of *1984*," in *Essays in Literary History Presented to J. Milton French*, ed. Rudolf Kirk and C. F. Main (New Brunswick, N.J.: Rutgers University Press, 1960), 254-57. Langdon Elsbree also discusses its structure in "The Structured Nightmare of *1984*," *Twentieth Century Literature* 5 (October 1959): 135-41; but I do not accept his argument that its form is a function of its "subrational" elements—its dreams, reveries, and symbols.

11. For instance, here are some of the entries under "Chap. VI" in "Notes of 1948 Towards a Revision of the First Manuscript..." (Crick's *Nineteen Eighty-Four*, 141-43):

    The war, & the Eurasian advance in W. Africa, 3 times (4?)
    Gin (3 times at least)
    Two or three refs. to the _____ (never named)?
    Picture of B.B. (3 or 4 times, & introduce early).

12. Miller (see n. 9) indicates another kind of symmetry. In its revised form, "the sentence (nearly) breaks apart into a neat pair of old-fashioned trimeter phrases" reminiscent of an English ballad; but "thirteen" disrupts the rhythm, as it disrupts our expectations (22-23).

13. Though they are less blunt than they would have been if Orwell had followed his outline, references to Catholics and Jews remain. For analyses of them, see Crick's *Nineteen Eighty-Four*, 39-41; Melvyn New, "Orwell and Antisemitism: Toward *1984*," *Modern Fiction Studies* 21 (Spring 1975): 81-105; and, for a larger perspective, John Rodden, "Orwell on Religion: The Catholic and Jewish Questions," *College Literature* 11 (1984): 44-58.

14. My interpretation implicitly takes issue with Daphne Patai's (*The Orwell Mystique* [Amherst: University of Massachusetts Press, 1984], 239ff.). Patai is astute about the games that Orwell plays (220-38), but too one-sided about his "Androcentrism." A more objective assessment of Orwell's attitude toward women is Leslie Tentler's "'I'm Not Literary, Dear': George Orwell on Women and the Family," in *The Future of Nineteen Eighty-Four*, ed. Ejner J. Jensen (Ann Arbor: University of Michigan Press, 1984), 47-63. On the connection between mother-love and feeling, it is also useful to compare this version with the more emphatic passage in the early draft, *Ms*, 129-31.

15. In 1931-1932, Orwell sought work as a translator, claiming that he could manage modern and old French—"at least anything since 1400 A.D." (*CEJL*, 1:78).

16. The implications and the phrasing of the cancelled lines recall "A Poison Tree" (*Songs of Experience*). Orwell knew Blake's work from early childhood; he suspected that his own first poem, dictated at age four or five, was plagiarized from Blake's "Tiger, Tiger" (*CEJL*, 1:1).

17. Watt makes a strong case for Winston's humanism (*On Nineteen Eighty-Four*, ed. Stansky, 107-8); he also takes account of its limits and the charges

that Orwell failed at characterization (ibid., 110-13). Patrick Reilly also considers its defeat in *"Nineteen Eighty-Four:* The Failure of Humanism," *Critical Quarterly* 24 (Autumn 1982): 19-30. An argument that contradicts Watt's (and mine) is James Connors, "Do It to Julia," in *Nineteen Eighty-Four to 1984,* ed. C. J. Kuppig (New York: Carroll & Graf, 1984), 231-41. Connors assembles textual evidence to show that Orwell makes Winston "a shadow-man" in service to the party, rather than a full "human being"; if space and time permitted, I would argue that he misreads the evidence, ignoring the subtler shadings of the passages that bring out Winston's humanistic values.

18. Allusions to these roles recur throughout Part Three, in chaps. 2, 3, and 5. Additionally, O'Brien functions as a surgeon, a perverse healer of the spirit. He is capable of containing Winston, mirroring his thoughts, and getting inside him, acts whose erotic implications Paul Robinson explores ("For the Love of Big Brother: The Sexual Politics of *Nineteen Eighty-Four*" in *On Nineteen Eighty-Four,* 155-58).

19. Philip Rahv makes more politically oriented comments on "the psychology of capitulation" ("The Unfuture of Utopia," *Orwell's Nineteen Eighty-Four,* ed. Howe, 313). For more intensive studies of the novel's psychoanalytic and mythic aspects, see Marcus Smith, "The Wall of Blackness: A Psychological Approach to *1984,*" *Modern Fiction Studies* 14 (1968): 423-33; Richard I. Smyer, *Orwell's Development as a Psychological Novelist* (Columbia: University of Missouri Press, 1979), 142-59—speculation that goes too far; and Alex Zwerdling, "Orwell's Psychopolitics," in *The Future of 1984,* ed. Jensen, 87-110.

20. *CEJL,* 4:221. In this passage from "Politics vs. Literature," Orwell cites the effect of one of Swift's sentences; more broadly, he argues that the literary quality of *Gulliver* cannot be divorced from its world-view. On possible sources for Orwell's rat episode, see Crick's *Nineteen Eighty-Four,* 442-43. Meyers traces other allusions in his work (*Reader's Guide,* 149-50). Judith Wilt, implicitly refuting the "schoolboy" charges, analyzes Orwell's use of rats and its modernist implications ("Behind the Door of *1984,*" in *Modernism Reconsidered,* ed. Robert Kiely and John Hildebidle [Cambridge: Harvard University Press, 1983], 247-62).

21. I have omitted from this hasty summary allusions to techniques that have already been analyzed—for example, Orwell's use of the boot image. Slater (see n. 10) deals briefly yet cogently with style, dialogue, interior monologue, imagery, and Orwell's use of lyrics (a subject that warrants closer study).

22. For samples of Orwell's comments on point of view, see *CEJL,* 1:126-28, 154-55, 495, and *CEJL,* 4:512. The impact of this perspective becomes clearer when you contrast it with the omniscient narration of Huxley's *Brave New World* and the first-person narration of Zamyatin's *We.*

23. Deutscher (in *Twentieth Century Interpretations,* ed. Hynes) was one of the first to make this claim, which Meyers also supports (*Reader's Guide,* 146-47).

24. For instance, Symons and Pritchett. While Patai does not claim that they are spurious, she views Winston's reactions as symptomatic of Orwell's flawed values (*Orwell Mystique,* 232-33, 263).

25. In many letters from this period he talks about his illness, but as frequently he talks about recovery. He qualifies the sole allusion to his death, which appears in a letter to his publisher, Warburg: "If anything should happen to me I've instructed Richard Rees, my literary executor, to destroy the MS without showing it to anybody, but it's unlikely that anything like that would happen. This disease isn't dangerous at my age, and they say the cure is going on quite well, though slowly...." (*CEJL*, 4:404).

26. *CEJL*, 1:455, and cf. *CEJL*, 4:302. John Rodden, to whose comments on this article I am deeply indebted, points out that Orwell never fully acknowledged the effect of extra-literary factors on a book's reputation: "Survival is an institutional and political matter, as much as a literary/aesthetic one."

Fourteen Types of Passivity: Suppressing Agency in *Nineteen Eighty-Four*

Daniel Kies

The linguistic criticism of *Nineteen Eighty-Four* has focused primarily on Newspeak as a language[1] and on Orwell's ideas about the relationship between language and thought.[2] It has largely ignored, however, the literary language Orwell used in writing *Nineteen Eighty-Four*. Indeed, the few critical remarks about Orwell's use of language have generally been negative—sometimes attributing the dull, monotonous, dry writing style to Orwell's career as a journalist[3] or to the phlegmatic topic of his novel. Irving Howe, for example, writes that

> the style of *1984*, which many readers take to be drab or uninspired or "sweaty," would have been appreciated by someone like Defoe, since Defoe would have immediately understood how the pressures of Orwell's subject, like the pressures of his own, demand a gritty and hammering factuality. The style of *1984* is the style of a man whose commitment to a dreadful vision is at war with the nausea to which that vision reduces him. So acute is this conflict that delicacies of phrasing or displays of rhetoric come to seem frivolous—*he has no time, he must get it all down*. Those who fail to see this, I am convinced, have succumbed to the pleasant tyrannies of estheticism; they have allowed their fondness for a cultivated style to blind them to the urgencies of prophetic expression. The last thing Orwell cared about when he wrote *1984*, the last thing he should have cared about, was literature.[4]

Those critical responses to Orwell—including Howe's defense of his style—are wrong-headed, as Sue Lonoff has also argued in the previous chapter. Orwell asserted that one of his primary motives for writing was

> aesthetic enthusiasm. Perception of beauty in the external world, or, on the other hand, in words and their right arrangement. Pleasure in the impact of one sound on another, in the firmness of good prose or the rhythm of a good story. Desire to share an experience which one feels is valuable and ought not to be missed. The aesthetic motive is very feeble in a lot of writers, but even a pamphleteer or a writer of textbooks will have pet words and phrases which appeal to him for non-utilitarian reasons; or he may feel strongly about typography, width of margins, etc. Above the level of a railway guide, no book is quite free from aesthetic considerations. (*CEJL*, 1:3-4)

The Orwell who wrote that "What I have most wanted to do throughout the past ten years is to make political writing into an art.... I could not do the work of writing a book, or even a long magazine article, if it were not also an aesthetic experience" (*CEJL*, 1:6) could not have been indifferent to literary artistry, including literary style. In fact, Orwell's writing style is a carefully constructed complex of various linguistic devices that contribute importantly to the central themes of *Nineteen Eighty-Four*.

One of those themes is the powerlessness of the individual under a totalitarian government. Orwell illustrated that futility through the fate of Winston Smith; however, it is not at the level of plot that the reader can best appreciate that powerlessness. Rather, it is through the language that Orwell used to describe Winston, to narrate his actions, and to develop his character that the reader perceives not only the futility of struggle but also Orwell's sensitivity to both the use and meaning of language. Specifically, Orwell manipulated the expression of agency so that Winston Smith is never seen as active or in control of any situation.

Agency is one of the most widely used techniques to control a literary theme in a text.[5] It can be expressed (or suppressed) by a number of syntactic constructions, and Orwell employed them all to establish the complete abolition of human freedom. Many of the examples below come from one scene in the novel, the end of Part Two, Section III, in which Winston and Julia feel some satisfaction in their lives, in their physical relationship, and in their loving protection of each other. It is interesting to note that just at the one point in the novel when the reader might expect these characters to be active and in control, Orwell used language that continually undercuts any sense of Winston or Julia as an agent, a conscious initiator of an action. Central among the linguistic features that undercut agency is passive voice.

Orwell was keenly aware of the potential that passive voice held for manipulating a hearer/reader: it allows the speaker/writer to hide the agent by neglecting to mention the agentive *by*-phrase. Orwell's fourth rule for clear writing was "Never use the passive where you can use the active" (*CEJL*, 4:139). Yet just two years after writing that rule, Orwell seemed to revise his thinking. In "Politics and the English Language" he was acutely aware of the subtleties of meaning afforded by changes in syntax; but in *Nineteen Eighty-Four* he seemed to incorporate the thematic, informational flexibility afforded by passive voice syntax into his writing. (This was not the only reversal in Orwell's thinking about language. As Arthur Eckstein will reveal, Orwell came to realize that the Anglo-Saxon word stock that he had championed in "Politics and the English Language" might supply the vocabulary for Newspeak, whereas Latinate English allowed greater scope for linguistic [and thereby human] freedom.)

Specifically, Orwell exploited fourteen syntactic devices:

1. PASSIVES
   a. Bill hit John   [active voice]
   b. John was hit (by Bill)   [passive voice]

Passives are among the most common grammatical devices to undercut agency in English, allowing the agentive noun phrase to occur out of thematic, sentence initial position in an optional agentive *by*-phrase at the end of the sentence.[6] By writing in the passive voice, eliminating the agentive *by*-phrase, Orwell was able to suggest that his characters are not conscious initiators of action:

> She described to him, almost as if she had seen or felt it, the stiffening of Katharine's body as soon as he touched her, the way in which she still seemed to be pushing him from her with all her strength, even when her arms were clasped tightly around him. (*NEF*, 110)

> The instrument (the telescreen it was called) could be dimmed, but there was no way of shutting it off completely. (*NEF*, 6)

2. NOMINALIZATIONS
   a. Free radicals oxidize cell membranes quickly.
   b. The oxidation of cell membranes (by free radicals) was quick.
      [nominalization of the verb *oxidize*]

Nominalized verbs undercut agency in that they can occur without any overt mention of agency (again supplied through the optional presence of an agentive *by*-phrase).[7] Orwell was able to describe Katharine's reaction to Winston's touch almost as if her stiffening were a physical process beyond Katharine's conscious control:

> She described to him, almost as though she had seen or felt it, the stiffening of Katharine's body as soon as he touched her.... (*NEF*, 110)

Notice also how Winston has a *sensation* (rather than *senses*) in this description of drinking Victory Gin:

> The stuff was like nitric acid, and moreover, in swallowing it, one had the sensation of being hit on the back of the head with a rubber club. (*NEF*, 8)

3.   INTRANSITIVES
     a. John dropped the bag.   [transitive pattern]
     b. The bag dropped.   [intransitive pattern]

Intransitive uses of verbs allow a writer to suggest that events arise or occur in the story beyond the control of characters by suppressing any explicit mention of human agents, as is usually required by the transitive uses of verbs.[8] Orwell seems to rob Winston of control over his own thoughts and perceptions by using an intransitive verb in the main clause:

> Actually the idea had first floated into his head in the form of a vision of a glass paperweight mirrored by the surface of the gate-leg table. (*NEF*, 114)

> The hallway smelt of boiled cabbage and old rag mats. (*NEF*, 5)

4.   PATIENTS AS SUBJECTS
     a. John sent a package.
     b. John got a package.

Verbs like *get*, *see*, and *hear* (as opposed to *send*, *look*, and *listen*) undercut agency in that they imply that the grammatical subject of the sentence is not the initiator of the activity described by the verb, but is rather a patient affected by that activity. Notice Orwell's undercutting of Winston's agency in the following sentences, the second of which also demonstrates the use of an atypical passive construction:

> ...the rule was not strictly kept, because there were various things such as shoelaces and razor blades which it was impossible to get hold of.... (*NEF*, 9)

> If you're happy inside yourself, why should you get excited about Big Brother and the Three-Year Plans and the Two Minutes Hate and all the rest of their bloody rot? (*NEF*, 111)

> ...look, I got a little packet of tea as well. (*NEF*, 117)

5. DEPERSONALIZATION
    a. John spoke.
    b. John's voice spoke.
    A voice spoke.
    [Both sentences in (b) represent a depersonalizing/
    dehumanizing metonymy]

Depersonalization depends on metonymy, where a part of a person (often a voice—the least physical and hence least agentive feature of a person) is used to represent, figuratively, the whole person:

> The youthful body was strained against his own, the mass of dark hair was against his face...her youth and prettiness had frightened him...The girl picked herself up and pulled a bluebell out of her hair. (*NEF*, 100)

> The telescreen barked at him to keep still. (*NEF*, 191)

> ...a yell from the telescreen bade them be silent. (*NEF*, 191)

> His froglike face grew calmer,....[where the face is metonymical for the whole person] (*NEF*, 192)

> "Smith!" yelled the voice from the telescreen. (*NEF*, 193)

6. PERFECT ASPECT
    a. John wants to go.
    [present tense expression of agent's desire]
    John wanted to go.
    [past tense, but still agent's desire is relevant]
    b. John had wanted to go.
    [perfect aspect, agent's desire no longer relevant to the present]

The perfect aspect of the verb suggests completed activity, that all action was finished in the remote past, undercutting any sense of action—even past action—that might have any relevance to the activity of the present. Orwell shifted to the perfect aspect to underscore the characters' sense of powerlessness and impotence:

> ...and it was possible that his features had not been perfectly under control. (*NEF*, 54)

> She had clasped her arms around his neck, she was calling him darling, precious one, loved one. He had pulled her down onto the ground, she was utterly unresisting....(*NEF*, 100)

> Unlike Winston, she had grasped the inner meaning of the Party's sexual puritanism. (*NEF*, 110)

7. NEGATION
   a. John hit Bill.   [positive assertion of agency]
   b. John didn't hit Bill.   [negated assertion]

Negation undercuts agency most directly, highlighting the agent's limited abilities:

> Unfortunately, he could not remember whether she had already been at that table when he arrived.... (*NEF*, 54)

> He still had not the courage to approach her. (*NEF*, 99)

> In this game we're playing, we can't win. (*NEF*, 112)

8. STATIVE VERBS/RESULTIVE VERBS
    a. John stopped.   [ordinary intransitive verb]
    b. John was stopped.   [statal passives or resultive verbs
                              suggest an "outside" agency]

Verbs that suggest the existence of a state or a result of some other agent can also undercut any sense of immediate agency on the part of its associated grammatical subject. Notice in the following examples that even cognitive activities such as remembering (in themselves suggesting less agency than physical activities) seem static rather than dynamic processes for Winston:

> Katharine, in any case, had long ceased to be a painful memory and become merely a distasteful one. (*NEF*, 110)

> There had been times when consciousness...had stopped dead....(*NEF*, 198)

9. PRESENTATIONAL *THERE* STRUCTURES
    a. A man with a briefcase sat down.   [agentive subject]
    b. There sat down a man with a briefcase. [agentive subject
                                              is de-emphasized in
                                              sentence medial
                                              position]

Michael Halliday illustrates the significance of the sentence initial position in organizing the clause as message.[9] The sentence initial position is significant, he reminds us, because it serves to introduce the "theme" of discourse. Similarly, Randolph Quirk and others highlight the significance of sentence final position in organizing the information structure of a clause.[10] The sentence final position becomes important in English since it serves as the locus of "new" information in the clause (and discourse). Hence, if one wished to use sentence position alone to downplay the agency of a particular noun phrase, sentence medial position would seem ideal since it keeps that particular noun phrase out of thematic or informationally prominent positions within the sentence. Sentences with presentational *there* subjects allow speakers and writers to de-emphasize agentive grammatical subjects by burying them in sentence medial position, as Orwell did:

> There was nobody of whom they could ask the way. (*NEF*, 111)

(Also notice Orwell's use of negation in the grammatical subject above to further undercut any sense of agency.)

> In a place like this, the danger that there was a hidden micro-
> phone was very small, and even if there was a microphone it
> would only pick up sounds. (*NEF*, 112)

(Presentational *there* undercuts agency above since the agent, pre-sumably the Thought Police, goes unmentioned.)

10. SUBJUNCTIVE MOOD
   a. I became a millionaire.   [indicative mood = real
                                                world activity with real
                                                world consequences]

   b. If I became a millionaire,....   [subjunctive mood =
                                                possible world only with no
                                                necessary suggestion of
                                                action in the real world]

The subjunctive mood allows us to discuss possible worlds, and any sense of agency is understood as only hypothetical, unreal. Consider Winston's musing over the possible actions that he "would have" taken if his world had turned out differently. Orwell understood how the subjunctive mood would make Winston's bold assertions ring hollow, suggesting that Winston would likely fail in his struggle to gain some degree of empowerment:

> I would have [given Katharine a "good shove" over the cliff], if I'd
> been the same person then as I am now. Or perhaps I would—
> I'm not certain. (*NEF*, 112)

The subjunctive mood undercuts agency not only in character devel-opment but also in the narration of the story as a whole:

> And it was exactly at this moment that the significant thing hap-
> pened—if, indeed, it did happen. (*NEF*, 18)

11. LINKING VERBS LIKE *SEEM*
    a. John broke the window.   [transitive verb with
                                           agentive subject]
    b. John seems to have broken the window. [linking verb,
                                           casting doubt
                                           on the agency of
                                           the grammatical
                                           subject]

Linking verbs like *seem* and *appear* add a hedge, a sense of doubt, to any assertion into which they are incorporated. Just when Orwell could have described the physical encounter between Winston and Julia as the dynamic, life-affirming act it was, he chose instead to undercut the assertion by using a linking verb:

> Her body seemed to be pouring some of its youth and vigor into his. (*NEF*, 113)

> All this he seemed to see in the large eyes of his mother and his sister.... (*NEF*, 29)

12. IMPERSONAL *ONE* IN POINT-OF-VIEW SHIFTS
    b. I now can conclude that....   [first-person personal
                                           pronoun clearly indicates
                                           agency and responsibility]
    b. One now can conclude that....   [impersonal third-person
                                           pronoun undercuts a
                                           clear sense of agency
                                           and responsibility for
                                           any conclusions]

Orwell employed the third-person singular personal pronouns *he/she* and the impersonal pronoun *you* throughout most of the novel. The occasional shift to the impersonal *one* allowed Orwell another grammatical device with which to downplay any sense of his characters' agency, as in this passage describing Winston's reaction to drinking Victory Gin. Note how this device generalizes and dilutes our sense of any direct personal reaction on Winston's part:

> Instantly his face turned scarlet and water ran out of his eyes. The stuff was like nitric acid, and moreover, in swallowing it one had the sensation of being hit on the back of the head with a rubber club. (*NEF*, 8)

Note the same shift, with the same effect, in these passages describing the torture of Winston. (These passages also exploit many of the stylistic features discussed earlier: passive voice, nominalization, depersonalization, perfect aspect, negation, subjunctive mood, and the linking verb *seem.*)

> Winston's heart sank.... He had a feeling of deadly helplessness. If he could have been certain that O'Brien was lying, it would not have seemed to matter. But it was perfectly possible that O'Brien had forgotten the photograph. And if so, then already he would have forgotten his denial of remembering it, and forgotten the act of forgetting. How could one be sure that it was simple trickery? (*NEF,* 204)

> A needle slid into Winston's arm. Almost in the same instant a blissful, healing warmth spread all through his body. The pain was already half-forgotten. He opened his eyes and looked up grate-fully at O'Brien. At the sight of the heavy, lined face, so ugly and so intelligent, his heart seemed to turn over. If he could have moved he would have stretched out a hand and laid it on O'Brien's arm. He had never loved him so deeply as at this moment, and not merely because he had stopped the pain. The old feeling, that at bottom it did not matter whether O'Brien was a friend or an enemy, had come back. O'Brien was a person who could be talked to. Perhaps one did not want to be loved so much as to be under-stood. (*NEF,* 208)

13. MODALITY SHIFTS
    a. John slapped the table.   [ordinary, agentive transitive]

    b. John $\begin{Bmatrix} \text{would} \\ \text{should} \\ \text{could} \\ \text{ought to} \\ \text{needs to} \\ \text{might} \\ \text{tried to} \end{Bmatrix}$ slap the table

    [the modal or quasi-modal auxiliary undercuts the agency of the transitive verb]

As with the judicious use of impersonal *one,* Orwell carefully used the modal auxiliary. Modals allowed him to hedge on the assertions made by transitive verbs; modals suggest obligation, necessity, willingness, or attempts to act, but they do not necessarily imply successfully com-pleted action:

> He [Winston] tried to squeeze out some childhood memory.... But it was no use, he could not remember. (*NEF,* 7)

> The old man had grown noticeably more cheerful after receiving the four dollars. Winston realized that he would have accepted three or even two. (*NEF,* 81)

14. EXISTENTIAL *IT* and other CLEFT SENTENCES
  a. John mailed the letter yesterday   [ordinary, agentive
                                                transitive]
  b. It was yesterday that John mailed the letter.
     It was the letter that John mailed yesterday.   [a cleft sentence,
     for example using the existential *it* as grammatical subject in the
     main clause, allows for an information focus on one constituent,
     effectively undercutting the agency of the grammatical subject
     in the more usual, unmarked sentence pattern, as in 14(a)]

Orwell could, in essence, lessen the suggested agency of certain con-
cord subjects by using a clefted sentence pattern. A cleft sentence
focuses on some peripheral part of a clause, such as an adverbial or
adjective, and thereby demotes the agentive element to a subordinate
clause:

> When one knew that any document was due for destruction, or
> even when one saw a scrap of waste paper lying about, it was an
> automatic action to lift the flap of the nearest memory hole and
> drop it in....(*NEF*, 35)

> It was true that he had no memories of anything different. (*NEF*, 52)

In concert, these fourteen stylistic features allowed Orwell to establish a limited third person narrator whose mind style is restricted to
Winston's point of view and Winston's perceptions.[11] Such limited narration takes the reader into Winston's mind without creating a first person narrative. A first person narrative would not effectively promote
the theme of passivity, since first person narrators are (by nature) too
agentive; they are always doing, saying, and thinking. Conversely, an
omniscient third person narrator could not adequately convey the terrifying uncertainty of living in a totalitarian society. With a limited third
person narrator, Orwell effectively prevents the reader from knowing
anything that Winston does not know but allows readers to experience how truly passive Winston is.

In his personal relationships, Winston is rarely, if ever, the initiator
of action. The sexual aggressors in *Nineteen Eighty-Four* are Katharine
("the frigid little ceremony that Katharine had forced him to go through
on the same night every week" [*NEF*, 110]) and Julia. Although Winston
is endlessly curious about the Brotherhood, he does little to learn
about it on his own; rather, O'Brien has to initiate him: "He knew that
sooner or later he would obey O'Brien's summons. Perhaps tomorrow,
perhaps after a long delay—he was not certain" (*NEF*, 132).

His passivity extends even into his relationships with minor
characters. It is Parsons who approaches and converses with Winston;

it is Mrs. Parsons who must ask for neighborly help (Winston does not offer it). Syme approaches Winston in the canteen seeking a lunch companion.

Finally, Winston does not take much initiative or imagination to his work. He does not give the fictitious Ogilvy the Order of Conspicuous Merit because of the necessary cross-referencing that it would entail. In other words, he has ideas, but he will not act on them unless invited or ordered to do so.

The novel does present at least two moments in which Winston seems strongly agentive: in his memories of his childhood and in his opening a diary. Nevertheless, those moments also are suffused with language that undercuts Winston's agency. Significantly, those two moments of agency are also moments at which Winston feels profoundly guilty, and the horrible guilt that Winston associates with those two moments of agency reveals perhaps the psychological source of his passivity. For example, Winston remembers such aggressive acts as fighting for more food or stealing chocolate as a youth. Orwell's narration, however, downplays Winston's agency through the use of subjunctive mood, depersonalization, modality shifts, passive voice, presentational *there*, nominalizations, patient subjects, negations, and the perfect aspect all in one passage:

> Suddenly, as though he were listening to someone else [subjunctive mood], Winston heard himself demanding in a loud booming voice [depersonalization] that he should [modality shift] be given [passive voice] the whole piece. His mother told him not [negation] to be greedy. There [presentational *there*] was a long, nagging argument [nominalization] that went round and round, with shouts, whines, tears, remonstrances, bargainings [nominalizations]. His tiny sister, clinging to her mother with both hands, exactly like a baby monkey, sat looking over her shoulders at him with large mournful eyes. In the end his mother broke off three-quarters of the chocolate and gave it to Winston, giving the other quarter to his sister. The little girl took hold [patient subject] of it and looked at it dully, perhaps not [negation] knowing what it was. Winston stood watching her for a moment. Then with a sudden swift spring he had snatched [perfect aspect] the piece of chocolate out of his sister's hand and was fleeing for the door. (*NEF*, 134-35)

Likewise, when Winston commits himself to opening a diary, Orwell's narration erases Winston's agency:

> The thing that he was about to do was to open a diary [cleft sentence]. This was not illegal (nothing was illegal, since there [presentational *there*] were no [negation] longer any laws), but if

detected [subjunctive mood] it was reasonably certain that it would [modality shift] be punished [passive voice] by death, or at least by twenty-five years in a forced labor camp [cleft sentence]. Winston fitted a nib into a penholder and sucked it to get the grease off. The pen was an archaic instrument, seldom used [passive voice] even for signatures, and he had procured [perfect aspect] one, furtively and with some difficulty, simply because of a feeling [nominalization and depersonalization] that the beautiful creamy paper deserved to be written on [passive voice] with a real nib instead of being scratched [passive voice] with an ink pencil. Actually he was not [negation] used to [passive voice] writing by hand. (*NEF*, 9-10)

Indeed, the pivotal act that sets the whole plot in motion—Winston's purchasing of the blank book to use as a diary—seems involuntary:

He...had [perfect aspect] been stricken [passive voice] immediately by an overwhelming desire [nominalization and depersonalization] to possess it.... At the time he was not [negation] conscious of wanting it for any particular purpose. (*NEF*, 9)

The facsimile edition of the manuscript of *Nineteen Eighty-Four* reveals how Orwell frequently revised his prose to enhance the passivity of his language. For example, he extensively reworked the passage above describing Winston's opening of a diary to include presentational *there*, subjective mood, modality shifts, perfect aspect, and additional passive voice verbs. In the manuscript passage below, notice how each clause but one in his earlier draft contains agentive active voice verbs:

As soon as he set eyes on it he had known that in just such a book he could write the diary he dreamed of—a diary that should be simply a transcript of the interminable monologue that went on and on inside his skull.... He dipped his pen in the ink and began to write. No mark appeared on the paper: instead, next moment, a huge blob of ink flopped off the nib and ruined the front page.... The pen was an archaic instrument, seldom used even for signatures. Normally one either used an ink-pencil or dictated into the speakwrite....(*Ms*, 23)

Likewise, note Orwell's revision in two very different sections of the novel, each revision reaching for greater passivity in language. The manuscript clause "Private ownership has given way to group ownership" in Goldstein's book is revised to employ a passive voice verb: "Private property has been abolished" (*Ms*, 211). Orwell further enhanced the passive voice with nominalizations and depersonalization:

> Wealth and privilege are most easily defended [passive voice] when they are possessed [passive voice] jointly. The so-called 'abolition [nominalization] of private property' which took place in the middle years of the century meant, in effect, the concentration [nominalization] of property in far fewer hands [depersonalization] than before.... (*NEF*, 170)

Also, the following clause describing Winston's experience in his cell at Miniluv originally read, "...whereas they [the Thought Police] ordered the political prisoners about like dogs" (*Ms*, 213). That clause was revised to eliminate the agency of *they ordered*: "...even when they were obliged to handle them roughly" (*NEF*, 187).

Indeed, the whole of Oceania becomes such a regimented society that even the police have no agency. They follow orders ("are obliged to handle them roughly") and become as thoroughly passive as their victims.

Howe, more than other critics, is sensitive to the thematic import of the loss of agency:

> Oceanic society may evolve through certain stages of economic development, but the life of its members is static, a given and measured quantity that can neither rise to tragedy nor tumble to comedy. Human personality, as we have come to grasp for it in a class society and hope for it in a classless society, is obliterated; man becomes a function of a process he is never allowed to understand or control.[12]

Orwell's style is not the dry language of a hurried work. Rather, it demonstrates the best in literary art, a merger of grammatical form with meaning and theme. Orwell was sensitive to this iconic merger of form with function in literature:

> When I was sixteen I suddenly discovered the joy of mere words, i.e., the sounds and associations of words.... I wanted to write enormous naturalistic novels with unhappy endings, full of detailed descriptions and arresting similes, and also full of purple passages in which words were used partly for the sake of their sound. (*CEJL*, 1:1-2)

Orwell's revisions reflect a conscious attempt to create a particular syntactic stance. That stance enabled him to progress systematically through several levels of passivity:

style > narration > character development > plot

Orwell conveyed the horrifying futility of life in a totalitarian regime not only through the overt passivity that readers can readily discover in plot and dialogue, but also through the covert passivity of Winston's mind style, as reflected in narration and character development.

Notes

1. Madelyn Flammia, "Beyond Orwell: Clarity and the English Language," in *George Orwell*, ed. Courtney Wemyss and Alexej Ugrinsky (New York: Greenwood Press, 1987), 28-33; Roy Harris, "The Misunderstanding of Newspeak," in *George Orwell: Modern Critical Views*, ed. Harold Bloom (New York: Chelsea House Publishers, 1987), 113-19.

2. Gunther Kress and Robert Hodge, *Language as Ideology* (London: Routledge & Kegan Paul, 1979), 144-50.

3. Hakan Ringbom, *George Orwell as Essayist: A Stylistic Study* (Abo, Finland: Abo Akademi, 1973), 11-12; Peter Petro, *Modern Satire: Four Studies* (Berlin: Mouton, 1982), 95; Harold Bloom, "Introduction," in *George Orwell: Modern Critical Views*, ed. Harold Bloom (New York: Chelsea House Publishers, 1987), 1-2.

4. Irving Howe, "*1984*: History as Nightmare," in *Orwell's Nineteen Eighty-Four*, 2d ed., ed. Irving Howe (New York: Harcourt Brace Jovanovich, 1982), 321.

5. Anne Cluysenaar, *Aspects of Literary Stylistics* (New York: St. Martin's Press, 1975), 63-65; George Dillon, *Language Processing and the Reading of Literature* (Bloomington: Indiana University Press, 1978), 9-21; William Empson, *Seven Types of Ambiguity*, 3d ed. (London: Chatto and Windus, 1963), 1-47; Nils Enkvist, *Linguistic Stylistics* (The Hague: Mouton, 1973), 115-18; Michael Halliday, "Linguistic Function and Literary Style," in *Literary Style: A Symposium*, ed. Seymour Chatman (London: Oxford University Press, 1971), 330-65; Geoffrey Leech and Michael Short, *Style in Fiction: A Linguistic Introduction to English Fictional Prose* (London: Longman, 1981), 189-91.

6. George Curme, *A Grammar of the English Language,* vol. 2, *Syntax* (Essex, Conn.: Verbatim, 1931), 443-47; Randolph Quirk, Sidney Greenbaum, Geoffrey Leech, and Jan Svartvik, *A Comprehensive Grammar of the English Language* (London: Longman, 1985), 159-71.

7. Daniel Kies, "Some Stylistic Features of Business and Technical Writing: Nominalization, Passive Voice and Agency," *Journal of Technical Writing and Communication* 25 (1985): 199-208.

8. For an interesting discussion of syntactic and thematic tension that can arise through the manipulation of transitivity patterns in the language of literature, see Timothy Austin, "(In)transitives: Some Thoughts on Ambiguity in Poetic Texts," *Journal of Literary Semantics* 16 (1986): 23-38.

9. Michael Halliday, *An Introduction to Functional Grammar* (London: Edward Arnold, 1985), 38-67.

10. Quirk et al., *Comprehensive Grammar*, 1356-57.

11. For an extensive discussion of mind style, see Leech and Short, *Style in Fiction*, 187-208.

12. Howe, "History as Nightmare," 324.

Psychomachia versus Socialism in *Nineteen Eighty-Four*: A Psychoanalytical View

Laurence M. Porter

In almost striking contrast to the public who received *Nineteen Eighty-Four* with enthusiasm, many influential critics have attacked the novel as an ineffectual political statement. These critics have pursued three main lines of argument. They have assailed the novel for its political naiveté; they have condemned it as counterrevolutionary; and they have found it hopelessly subjective, claiming that emotional problems spawned by Orwell's own unhappy childhood recur obsessively in what should have been a political statement, overmastering the intended message.[1] Critics who choose the last of these attacks claim that the focus on Winston's subjectivity in *Nineteen Eighty-Four* is a disguised form of autobiographical confession that distorts the attempt to present a plausible political order in the novel. No doubt Orwell drew upon his personal experience of being bullied and tormented in public school—as he drew upon his five years' experience as an oppressor in the colonial police—to help him more vividly imagine a totalitarian state. The issue is whether he was blinkered by his experience or whether, in Irving Howe's suggestive words, "The private nightmare, if it is there, is profoundly related to, and helps us understand public events."[2]

The hostile critics' discontent can be placed in sharper focus if one situates *Nineteen Eighty-Four*, composed between August 1946 and December 1948, in the apocalyptic tradition, inspired by the Nazi takeover of Europe, that emerged in Western literature after the war.

This international tradition encompasses works such as Albert Camus's *The Plague*, Günter Grass's *The Tin Drum*, Thomas Mann's *Doctor Faustus*, Michel Tournier's *The Ogre*, and Kurt Vonnegut's *Slaughterhouse-Five*. In most such works, an element of hope subsists, because the hero differentiates himself from the surrounding chaos through (physical or mental) escape (Vonnegut), resistance (Camus), or both (Grass). Even Tournier's protagonist, throughout much of his novel an effective collaborator with the Nazis, dissociates himself from them via a delusional transcendence at the end. Thomas Mann's composer is engulfed, but leaves a legacy of genius. Orwell's mediocre hero, in contrast, is engulfed and leaves nothing. The most salient difference between *Nineteen Eighty-Four* and the other works just mentioned, however, is that Orwell's novel presents a detailed program for political repression. A committed socialist, Orwell analyzes the establishment of an evil, totalitarian power that is seized and monopolized rather than shared as socialist power ideally would be shared. His dystopia consists of a ruthless, apparently invincible state that has perfected thought control so as to maintain the oligarchy of the Inner Party. For a generation, *Nineteen Eighty-Four* exercised enormous influence as an impassioned warning against the potential abuses of collectivism, of a socialism gone sour, abuses exemplified under the regimes of Hitler and Stalin.

The pessimism of his generation was aggravated in Orwell because he had lost his wife to cancer in March 1945, and because he knew that he himself was dying of tuberculosis.[3] Moreover, he, unlike the other apocalyptic novelists just mentioned, was primarily inspired by Stalinist rather than fascist totalitarianism, and at the time the former (unlike the latter) showed no signs of ending. Such explanations, however, beg the crucial political questions: Can one effectively espouse a cause such as socialism while depicting its defeat? Can one advocate an ideal by denouncing its perversion? Does Orwell authentically accept the socialist ideal of a classless society? And even if we answer these three questions in the affirmative, does the masochistic debasement of Winston, through its excess, nevertheless mark *Nineteen Eighty-Four* as a political manifesto? Placing the novel in the generic traditions of the allegory and the psychomachia (the latter previously unrecognized as one of Orwell's major models) can mitigate the objections implied by the first three questions; psychoanalytic speculation concerning the historical author can elucidate—if not ward off—the last.

What particularly generates socialist and communist readers' dissatisfaction with Orwell's novel today are the two contradictory roles assigned in it to the proles. From Winston's (as from Marx's) perspective they represent hope for the future, a source of energy for social reform. From the psychodynamic perspective, an undercurrent in the novel, they represent a reserved area (analogous to that of dreams and fantasies in everyday life) where relatively free expression of the id may be possible (one recalls the untamed peoples beyond the Green Wall in Orwell's main model, Zamyatin's *We*). As the Party slogan has it, "Proles and animals are free."

In the individual psyche, we try to protect ourselves from the painful clash of id impulses and superego prohibitions by compartmentalizing them, by busily erecting the barriers of ego defenses between them. In the political order, such compartmentalization is complicated by hierarchy. The oligarchy justifies its rank and prerogatives by appealing to its ascetic self-denial. The basis of legitimacy of the medieval knights was that they risked their bodies in war, in the defense of the non-aristocratic noncombatants. The latter, in theory, could indulge themselves: the well-fed, well-rested monk of the medieval fabliau was notoriously a more vigorous lover than the war-weary, battered knight. And in *Nineteen Eighty-Four* (unlike in real totalitarian societies, where indoctrination of the workers is all-important), the proles are segregated from the ascetic priests of the superego, the Inner Party, through a systematic policy of apartheid.

Orwell does not, then, found or describe a revolutionary praxis in *Nineteen Eighty-Four*. He simply incites one. This absence of a specific political program is no reason to denounce him as a counterrevolutionary, any more than one should denounce Marx for not having drawn a blueprint for implementing the dictatorship of the proletariat.[4] Marx proposed the myth of an inevitable historical process in the course of which the institutions of the capitalist state, individual ownership of the means of production, and the unequal distribution of wealth would wither away. When Lenin decreed the necessity of a militant party elite in order to accelerate that process, he created the theoretical paradox of a privileged class that was required to ensure the abolition of privilege. Orwell explores and dramatizes the consequences of this paradox, which could be paraphrased by the key question in Plato's *Republic*: "Who will watch the watchmen themselves?"

To the extent that we readers take this theme as part of the mimetic rather than the allegorical dimension of *Nineteen Eighty-Four*, it does seem dismissive, condescending, and reactionary, because no counterstatement validating the proles as political beings is offered. To the extent that we understand it as an implied summons to the workers to raise their political consciousness, it echoes the impassioned call to action that concludes *The Communist Manifesto*.

The relationship between the public and the private dimension becomes clearer, and in a way that vindicates Orwell's achievement, once one understands the particular allegorical tradition within which he worked to create *Nineteen Eighty-Four*. He is writing a non-Christian psychomachia with both personal and collective implications. The term "psychomachia," meaning "battle within the soul," comes from the title of a work by the fourth-century Latin Christian poet Prudentius, who described a war between the virtues and the vices personified as female soldiers. More recent examples would be John Bunyan's *Pilgrim's Progress* or the Jungian-inspired novels of Hermann Hesse, such as *Steppenwolf* or *Narcissus and Goldmund*. Within the sphere of allegory, Orwell draws upon personal experiences in order to obtain materials for dramatizing the interpenetration of the individual and the collective superego.[5] The result returns full circle to political relevance as an analysis of what makes the individual vulnerable to totalitarian oppression.[6] *Nineteen Eighty-Four* reveals how authoritarian regimes usurp the place of the individual's parents and family as the focus of loyalty.

One can make a shrewd guess as to where Orwell derived the inspiration to give the struggle between individual and state a psychoanalytical cast. His first wife Eileen Maud (*née* O'Shaughnessy) was a lay psychotherapist when Orwell met her, and she had completed all but the dissertation for the M.A. in psychology at University College, London (*GO*, 173). Her conversation probably stimulated his interest in Freudian concepts. Orwell himself mentions Freud three times (*CEJL*, 2:193n, 3:224, and 4:158); the first and last of these references accuse pro-Communist intellectuals—those whom Orwell feared might rule the world in 1984—of unconsciously suppressing or misattributing politically heterodox thoughts. In other words, Orwell uses Freud's discovery that slips of the tongue or pen in everyday life are unconsciously motivated to explain the unthinking Doublethink of the political unconscious that provides the basis for unswerving party loyalty. And the third reference associated Freud and Machiavelli with the power-worshipping gangster oligarchy of detective fiction. Within *Nineteen Eighty-Four* itself, the psychic mechanism of sublimation is keenly analyzed by Orwell's Julia in what are essentially Freudian terms, when she explains how sexual urges are rechanneled into patriotic hysteria (*NEF*, 110-11).

Any interpretation of *Nineteen Eighty-Four* as a quasi-Freudian psychomachia, specifically, as the engulfment of the ego by the superego, certainly cannot explain the entire novel. Such a reading will of necessity remain in places inaccurate, self-contradictory, and incomplete, because it cannot account for the aesthetic demands of the novel form as a progressive structure. But if we identify one level of Orwell's novel as the outward and visible manifestation of an inner, intangible struggle between ego and superego, we can better explain the inverisimilitude of certain episodes. To be sure, the Freudian model seems archaic in the face of feminist, Lacanian, and object-relations psychoanalysis. I do not claim that it is the most adequate psychological model for explaining Orwell as a historical personage. My intent, however, is quite different. I am investigating (with a few biographical asides, not essential to my argument) what Orwell as implied author of *Nineteen Eighty-Four* appears consciously to have known about the unconscious, specifically about the structure and dynamics of the psyche. In the 1940s, the Freudian model was by far the most prominent one available to him, and it neatly fit the glorification of the father-figure in German and Italian fascism.

The role of the powerful father is filled in the protagonist Winston's imagination (seen as a partial reflection of Orwell's) by the projected image of Big Brother, toward whom the fictional hero feels powerful ambivalence. The dehumanizing engulfment of both id and ego by the superego as the final resolution of this ambivalence is suggested at the end of the novel by Winston's inability to solve a chess problem (in that most Oedipal of games); compare the useless chessboard beside the disgraced, abject three traitors at The Chestnut Tree.

On the psychic as opposed to the social plane, the condition of an individual living in 1984—especially when he, like Winston, is the only individual whose inner life is represented—reflects the condition of the ego confronted by the excessively punitive superego. Brainwashing and propaganda are known to have debilitating effects on the autonomy of the ego.[7] Orwell represents the permeability of the weakly defended ego by the superego by depicting the constant invasion of private, inner space (itself symbolic of the individual identity) by public, outer space. He rewrites the initial description of Winston's apartment building to include in the entrance hall a poster with the huge face of Big Brother, "too large for indoor display" (*Ms*, 3). Orwell's revision of the description of Winston's room adds another portrait of Big Brother over the telescreen, and posters all over the walls outside (*Ms*, 5). Big Brother's eyes seem to follow you when you pass by. So great is Orwell's concern with depicting the violation of inner space by the alien observer that he includes the implausible detail of a police spy helicopter hovering outside the windows to watch what is going on within (*NEF*, 6). The two-way telescreen in every room continues this motif. Orwell's vacillations during revision regarding the telescreen reflect his difficulty in deciding how overt to make the psychodynamic as opposed to the mimetic dimension of his novel. Originally he said that the spyscreen was turned on continuously; later he wrote that transmissions ceased for six hours in twenty-four (*Ms*, 5). This detail reflects the understanding that psychic censorship relaxes during sleep, so that disguised contents of the id can emerge into consciousness. And, indeed, we eventually learn that even Parsons, Winston's sweatily compliant neighbor, has committed thoughtcrime in his dreams. But in the definitive version, the screen once again transmits all the time. Orwell ascribed special importance to the idea that police spies might be watching the inhabitants of Oceania at any time; he revised the passage in question five times (*Ms*, 7, 9). O'Brien dramatizes the situation much later by proclaiming that "No one dares trust a wife or a child or a friend any longer" (*NEF*, 220). Private loyalties and pleasures have become suspect.

From the perspective of the accusatory, punishing superego confronting the always-guilty id (for no constructive aspects of the superego as a teacher, guide, or protector are presented in Orwell's work), any private space, physical or psychic, must be the theater of transgression. If such space is tolerated by the superego, then it functions only as a snare. Thus the unusual configuration of Winston's room, which features an alcove unobserved by the telescreen, not only allows him a place safely to write his subversive diary, but inspires him with the idea of doing so (*NEF*, 9). And the furnished room above Mr. Charrington's shop, where Julia and Winston take refuge and make love, will be revealed as a trap set by the Thought Police, the better to allow the guilty couple to inculpate themselves.

Typically for most fiction, the protagonist's first attempts at differentiation are artificially delayed. Winston waits till his 30s to experience an adolescent identity crisis. When the novel begins, he has thoroughly introjected the collective totalitarian superego. He loves his work, and is playing the classic psychic censor's role as a handmaiden of suppression on behalf of the collective superego of political orthodoxy. He rewrites and erases the past in such a way that all party predictions come true, and all party promises are realized. Records of unwelcome facts are thrown into an incinerator called the "Memory Hole," a collective counterpart of what Freud called the individual preconscious.

Winston's personal drama begins when he attempts to achieve autonomy from his political masters. He purchases forbidden knickknacks that recall a past before Ingsoc. He begins a diary, inaugurating an illegal, unpatriotic "ownlife" of self-expression. And he allows himself to be drawn into a furtive affair, although only married sex for procreation is allowed.

None of these activities poses any threat to the state. Indeed, they even lead to Winston's becoming a more effectual Outer Party member, since he redoubles his diligence in order to conceal his inward disaffection. Why then should the all-powerful Thought Police observe the obscure, ineffectual Winston for seven years "like a beetle under a microscope" (*Ms*, 281)? Why should the masterful O'Brien consecrate months of his time to Winston's conversion? Although admiring of Orwell, the critic Philip Rahv objected that "O'Brien's...motivation in the psychological economy of the novel remains unclear."[8] O'Brien himself says that Winston must be wondering "why the Ministry of Love should expend so much time & trouble on [him]" (*Ms*, 307; cf. 305). No definitive answer is given. A solution can be found, however, in the conventions of the genre of the psychomachia, which brings one or two entire alien orders (i.e., the non-ego portions of the psyche) to bear upon the individual consciousness. A lack of verisimilitude similar to that of *Nineteen Eight-Four* is found in stories of the Christian tradition where a tempting Devil devotes years to seducing just one soul—a labor-intensive enterprise, no matter how choice that soul may be. C. S. Lewis's *Screwtape Letters* proposes the solution of assigning lesser souls to lesser, apprentice tempters. Even so, however, Lewis's Hell seems not only a particularly nasty corporation, but a singularly inefficient one.

The pre-Oedipal harmony of impulse and the ego is represented by the little room that Winston and Julia rent in the proles' quarter. There they can retreat from responsibility to bed, and to be loved. This motif of nostalgia returns in the details of the nursery rhymes that Winston loves, in the antique rubbish in Mr. Charrington's shop, and in Winston's choice to toast to the past when he visits O'Brien. For the regressive part of Winston's psyche, the dream of inner harmony recurs in his dream of the Golden Country, where he can rest happily in the sun with his mother, with Julia, and eventually with O'Brien as well. For the progressive part of Winston, inner harmony is symbolized by the mythical rebel leader Goldstein (literally "gold-stone"), whose emblematic name evokes the philosopher's stone of personal wholeness and, in context, the integrity of self-assertion in the face of tyranny.

As an adult, Winston cannot maintain his regressive refuge indefinitely. The insects that assail him and Julia stand for younger siblings in archetypal symbolism (Winston's last memory of his family consists in his stealing a piece of chocolate from his starving little sister), for competing obligations that interfere with the exclusivity of self-gratification. A rat, representing his deepest fears, emerges in the rented room just after he has made love to Julia there for the first time, as if exercising psychic censorship and prohibiting his pleasure (*NEF*, 119–20; note, incidentally, that a euphemized version of the devouring rodent or threatening paternal phallus appears even in the Golden

Country, whose fields are "rabbit-bitten"). And it is in his refuge that Winston formulates the decision to accept O'Brien's invitation to visit him, and to commit himself to the struggle to overthrow Big Brother.

With that covert act the struggle begins. The intermittent connection between O'Brien and the individual superego, curiously at variance with the depiction of him as a hard-headed, cynical, ruthlessly efficient political leader, appears in his prudish remark about Julia's "dirty-mindedness" (*NEF*, 216), that is, her unrestrained sexuality. That detail, together with the motif that the Party wanted to eliminate the orgasm and permit intercourse only for the purpose of procreation (*NEF*, 110–11) seems more a parody of the Catholic Church than of Communism. More obviously, O'Brien's national origin also suggests the Catholic Church; the meeting with Julia and Winston in his flat parodies a communion service; and he catechizes Winston, under torture, to believe in a geocentric universe and miracles such as levitation. Ingsoc is a generic target for satire. The improbable details of O'Brien's conversion of Winston impart psychodynamic resonances to *Nineteen Eighty-Four* which weaken the novel as a socialist statement while adding a dimension of psychological truth related to the insight of Freud's *Civilization and Its Discontents*: one cannot create any social order without frustrating some basic instincts.

An interpretation in the subjective mode provides an obvious answer to the puzzle of why O'Brien is bound to Winston and shares his thoughts. He embodies part of Winston's mind, the superego. If the Thought Police and O'Brien in particular are taken as representations of the superego, of the censorious inner observer, the mimetic implausibilities disappear. In the psychodrama that we all experience, the superego originates in the child from the judgments and commands of significant others in the child's life. Eventually these verbal directives become internalized and are no longer recognized as something alien to the self, although they continue to generate inner conflicts. Indeed, the agony of *Nineteen Eighty-Four* is essentially internal: even if Winston had committed no forbidden act, he would have committed "the essential crime that contained all others in itself. Thoughtcrime" (*NEF*, 19).

The enigmatic core of the novel is the uncanny bond between Winston and O'Brien. O'Brien claims to feel an affinity with Winston; he says he considers Winston worth taking pains over; but to accept such an explanation is to beg the question. It does not account for how O'Brien can apparently not only read Winston's mind, but also know the ancient dreams that had dropped out of Winston's consciousness into the repository of the preconscious. Winston had earlier thought that "with all their cleverness they [the Thought Police] had never mastered the secret of finding out what another human being was thinking" (*NEF*, 138). In fact, O'Brien never professes to be able to read people's minds in general, only Winston's.

From the beginning, Winston is curiously drawn to O'Brien and senses a mysterious communion with him. His rebellion is oddly mingled with submission. Part of the explanation is, of course, that O'Brien (carefully made five years older than Winston rather than the same age, as originally [*Ms*, 39]) functions as a father surrogate for the orphaned Winston. Winston desires even a punitive intimacy with this figure, because a bad object is better than no object at all. But many details of the text show that O'Brien can become plausible only as part of Winston's self. The suggestion that O'Brien plays the characteristic role of the superego is introduced by Orwell's revision of the moment of O'Brien's first appearance (*Ms*, 35), from just before Julia's entrance to just after. In the definitive version, in other words, temptation elicits repression rather than the reverse. Again, when first glimpsed in his home by Winston, O'Brien is busy dictating judgments of a proposal into a "Speakwrite." What is decreed is then registered, again in the mode of superego prohibition. Illogically, Winston immediately, and with only the vaguest understanding of his own motives, blurts out a full confession of his intent to overthrow Big Brother (*NEF*, 140), as if to reflect the ego's total vulnerability to the superego.[9]

The unspoken intimacy between O'Brien and Winston, according to the latter, began in a dream (*NEF*, 24). Winston feels that he has been carrying on an imaginary conversion with him for years (*Ms*, 95). "All through his interrogation," moreover, "although he had never seen him, he had had the feeling that O'Brien was at his elbow, just out of sight. It was O'Brien who was directing everything.... He was the tormentor, he was the protector, he was the inquisitor, he was the friend" (*NEF*, 201). This one observation alone could be explained as the phenomenon of "identification with the aggressor" common among prisoners and other victims. But elsewhere it is clear that O'Brien knows intimately even the unconscious contents of Winston's mind: "Do you remember thinking once, that..." (*Ms*, 301) he asks. "Do you remember," O'Brien says again in Room 101, "that moment of panic that used to occur in your dreams?" the explanation of which Winston himself suppressed from conscious awareness (*NEF*, 233). O'Brien says his mind and Winston's resemble each other (*NEF*, 213). The explanation is, of course, that in psychoanalytic theory the superego belongs to the domain of the unconscious, where all impressions are preserved. Again, O'Brien's statement that "the more the Party is powerful, the less it will be tolerant" (*NEF*, 221) applies perfectly to the punishing superego.

Where the novel appears to run out of control, even as an allegorical statement, is in its depiction of Winston's masochism, which seems
to have been affected by the intrusion of autobiographical elements.
From a pragmatic standpoint, the detailed account of the protracted
tortures that Winston endures helps us as readers to identify with him
and to feel similarly oppressed. From a thematic standpoint (one which
Orwell underlines several times by saying that Winston has foreseen
everything), the punishments seem a magical result of Winston's
masochistic desire for attention from a father figure. Moreover, he may
be unconsciously seeking destruction at the hands of Big Brother to
expiate his crime of having, in his own role as greedy big brother, contributed to the death of his little sister during his childhood.[10]

Winston's possible guilt and exaggerated sense of responsibility for
the fantasized death of his little sister (he doesn't really know what
happened to her, but he feels survivor guilt), and his certain guilt over
betraying his lover Julia appear to converge in Room 101 with the historical Orwell's guilt over his wife. In *Nineteen Eighty-Four*, the
dreaded Room 101 symbolizes the original personality ("1") annihilated
("0") and then replaced with another ("1") totally subordinated to the
Party, like the "unifs" of Eugeny Zamyatin's *We*, or more immediately
like Winston's teeth that rot or are yanked out by O'Brien to be
replaced by new ones. But the number can also be deciphered as "I
owe one (life)." Consider that Orwell believed he was probably ster-
ile, but desperately wanted a child. For that reason, and because he
begrudged the expense of an operation, he ignored his wife's symptoms of uterine cancer—abdominal pain, internal bleeding, and
fatigue—and seems to have opposed her having a hysterectomy.
Adding insult to injury, because those very symptoms made having sex
difficult, Orwell had at least several affairs during the last years of the
war. Finally, oblivious to his wife's precarious health, he placed her
under additional physical strain by adopting a son so that his own life
could be symbolically perpetuated. Eileen died on the operating table
while Orwell was off in Paris (*GO*, 264, 319-36). The paperweight that
Winston treasures in *Nineteen Eighty-Four*, and in which a small piece
of pink crinkled coral is embedded, may well memorialize Orwell's
feelings about this disaster. The submerged invisible growth (the coral
reef) that assumes monstrous proportions and wrecks ships could figure the fear of cancer, magically transformed into the lovely, benign,
and wished-for internal growth of the fetus—a hope smashed by the
Thought Police of guilt.[11] The prefix of O'Brien's name links him as a
vehicle of guilt with Orwell's wife O'Shaughnessy. It reappears irrepressibly, once again associated with guilt and with Ireland, in a review
written by Orwell only a few months after Eileen's death (28 October

1945). Complaining there of the rabid nationalism of Sean O'Casey's *Drums under the Windows (CEJL,* 4:13-15), he says that Ireland is the bad conscience of the English people: "It is difficult to object to Irish nationalism without seeming to condone centuries of English tyranny and exploitation."

O'Brien is and is not a figuration of the superego. He is, in his role as the teacher who incites massive efforts at suppressing disloyal impulses; as a fanatic, he becomes a self-betraying, involuntary spokesperson for the implied author. Unlike the true superego, however, he is proactive rather than merely reactive; and in his humorous and ironic modes, he, unlike a superego, remains detached. The aesthetic requirements of the novel necessitate the transformation of O'Brien from an unconscious figment into a credible representation of a person; lead to ascribing to him traits that a pure incarnation of the superego could not have; and change his behavior from reactive (called into play by the emergence of inadmissible impulses) to proactive (encouraging the development of political heresy in Winston and then leading him into entrapment).[12] Later, during the protracted scenes of torture and interrogation, O'Brien's maieutic function satisfies the aesthetic and thematic needs of the story and distinguishes him from a superego figure proper. His role is transformed so that he can move the plot and expound the theories of the totalitarian state. But he still incarnates the enslaver, and he has the last word.

The collective and the individual motifs of Orwell's novel blend in the figure of O'Brien. In Oceania as in other totalitarian states, the author implies, the state wishes to assume the role of a collective superego and maintain its subjects in a state of childlike dependency throughout life. The absurdities of totalitarian doctrine are so enormous, however, that only a few fanatics like O'Brien can ever interject them permanently.[13] For others, state dogma must be continually reinforced from the outside. Orwell's Outer Party collectively figures the embattled ego, torn between impulse and prohibition under the glare of conscience.

Politically speaking, *Nineteen Eighty-Four* has, as many have observed, a Trotskyesque tinge. We should not forget that the most profound, calculated, devious betrayal in *Nineteen Eighty-Four* is O'Brien's betrayal of Winston. O'Brien is to Winston as the Soviet state was to the Russian Revolution. In each instance, a surge of political individuation was thwarted by betrayal, leading to the reengulfment of the ego (in its function as the cutting edge of individuality) by another part of the self, the superego (or, in history, by a corrupt Communist Party). From this perspective the action of *Nineteen Eighty-Four* can be summed up in one short clause. Winston is prevented from becoming an independent person. From the historical perspective, the name "Big Brother" reenacts the Russian Revolution, insofar as it contains in itself both the promise and the denial of equality. Or, in microcosm, Winston is tempted into and then prevented from becoming a political being. In his psyche, loving Big Brother is tantamount to the death of the adult, individuated self because it entails regression to an undifferentiated, pre-Oedipal state via the oral gratifications of alcoholism. The prospect that the Party will execute Winston, a now totally devoted follower, is implausible from a practical standpoint, but it reflects the psychological truth of a dependency that stifles maturation.

An analysis that ended here would be incomplete from a psychological perspective. Many novels, and particularly those that portray a psychic drama, provide two separate endings, one for the protagonist and the other for the implied author (the personality considered to be coextensive with the text, and which can be inferred from it). Often the protagonist is destroyed, after which the implied author seems to turn to exit from the text with a gesture that dissociates him or her from the protagonist. For example, after the marvelous Marquise de Merteuil has prevailed throughout Choderlos de Laclos's *Liaisons dangereuses*, in a brief epilogue she is stricken with disfiguring illness, financial ruin, and social disgrace. Having complaisantly contemplated her demonic games, the implied author appears to be saying: "That looks like fun...but I probably couldn't get away with it." And he then reaffirms traditional sociocultural values against the chaos of unbridled egotism triumphant in the central story; he resurrects the claims of the collectivity to quash those of the evil individual. (At the same time, the historical Laclos thus evades the possibility of real censorship.) In Orwell's masterpiece, the appendix on "The Principles of Newspeak" (*NEF*, 246-56) serves a similar function of thematic differentiation, but this time it is individuality that is affirmed against the evil collectivity triumphant in the central narrative. Winston has been erased as an independent being, but his protest lives on in the novel devoted to his misfortunes. In the last paragraph of the appendix, *Nineteen Eighty-Four* retrospectively joins the masterpieces of Shakespeare, Milton, and others that were being translated into Newspeak so as to preserve for Ingsoc culture the aura of prestige that those works of the past had retained. The task of reducing these unique, resistant masterpieces to uniformity was so arduous that its projected completion and, with it, the consummation of the reign of Newspeak had been postponed into an indefinite future. Thus, Orwell optimistically restates the commonplace that the pen—his, if not Winston's—will prove mightier than the sword.

Notes

1. On Orwell's "naiveté" see Isaac Deutscher's influential "*1984*—The Mysticism of Cruelty," in *Russia in Transition*, rev. ed. (New York: Grove, 1960), 250-65: "At heart Orwell was a simple-minded anarchist" (262). And see Wyndham Lewis, "Climax and Change," in *Nineteen Eighty-Four to 1984: A Companion to the Classic Novel of Our Time*, ed. C. J. Kuppig (New York: Carroll & Graf, 1984), 180-86. Fredric Jameson calls *Nineteen Eighty-Four* a "counterrevolutionary tract" in *The Political Unconscious: Narrative as a Socially Symbolic Act* (Ithaca, N.Y.: Cornell University Press, 1981), 268. For the idea of a tortured, neurotic Orwell venting his obsessions in his fiction, see Deutscher, 263 ("his political reasoning struck me as a Freudian sublimation of persecution mania"); and Richard Rees, *George Orwell, Fugitive from the Camp of Victory* (Carbondale: Southern Illinois University Press, 1962), 107-8. For correctives to these views, demonstrating Orwell's political acuity and the authenticity of his commitment to socialism, see Mark Reader, "The Political Criticism of George Orwell," (Ph.D. diss., University of Michigan, 1966); William Steinhoff, *The Road to Nineteen Eighty-Four* (London: Weidenfeld & Nicolson, 1975), 193-215; and Lionel Trilling, "Orwell on the Future," *New Yorker*, 18 June 1949, 158-64.

2. Irving Howe, "*1984*: History as Nightmare," in *Orwell's Nineteen Eighty-Four: Text, Sources, Criticism*, ed. Irving Howe, 2d ed. (New York: Harcourt Brace Jovanovich, 1982), 323n.

3. See Otto Friedrich, "George Orwell," in *Companion*, ed. Kuppig, 106.

4. Orwell offers a detailed social program in the concluding pages of his unduly neglected essay, "The English People" (ca. 1944), *CEJL*, 3:30-38. His letter of 11 April 1940 to Humphry House (*CEJL*, 1:529-32) contains another noteworthy clarification of his social views.

5. For interesting reflections on this topic see Philip G. Zimbardo, "Mind Control: Political Fiction and Psychological Reality," in *On Nineteen Eighty-Four*, ed. Peter Stansky (New York: W. H. Freeman, 1983), 197-215

6. A relatively close parallel is found in Eugène Ionesco's play *Rhinocéros*.

7. On the autonomy of the ego in psychoanalytic theory see David Rapaport, "The Theory of Ego Autonomy: A Generalization," *Bulletin of the Menninger Clinic* 22 (1958): 25-35; and Heinz Hartmann, *Ego Psychology and the Problem of Adaptation*, trans. David Rapaport (New York: International Universities Press, 1958). For the application of the concept to the study of the individual under totalitarian oppression, see Gordon W. Allport, "Personality under Social Catastrophe," in *Personality in Nature, Society, and Culture*, ed. Clyde Kluckhohn and H. A. Murray (New York: Knopf, 1949), 185-225. For these references I am indebted to an unpublished paper on "The Autonomy of the Ego in Women" by Laurel Porter, ACSW, presented to the Michigan Society for Psychoanalytic Psychology.

8. Philip Rahv, "The Unfuture of Utopia," in *Orwell's Nineteen Eighty-Four*, ed. Howe, 315.

9. An anomalous word in O'Brien's Newspeak at this juncture suggests his censoring function. He condemns one point in the proposal to which he is responding as "verging thoughtcrime" instead of the plainer "near (or, close to) thoughtcrime." The Oldspeak word evokes the French word "la verge" or penis (literally, "wand")—Orwell knew French, and perhaps here he juxtaposes the symbolic transgression with its denunciation.

10. Here and at many other points I am deeply indebted to Jonathan Rose, whose inspired suggestions greatly enhanced the coherence and substance of this essay.

11. In Winston's masochism, which appears excessive and overdetermined, biographically oriented critics have found their most convincing avenue for extrapolating from the protagonist to the historical author. The most thorough psychoanalytic study of the novel to date speculates that five years of "traumatic overstimulation" at St. Cyprian's provoked in Eric Blair a rage that had no outlet, and that led in turn to fears of retaliation. In Orwell and in Winston, as in certain analysands, such feelings take form as a morbid dread of rats (see *GO*, 216). The school staff was needed by the child as surrogate parents, but they were sadistic. To preserve his image of them as good, the child had to assume their guilt: he felt a strong unconscious need for punishment that would shelter him from his own aggressive impulses, confirm his status as bad, and thereby justify the "parents," who as a result could be fantasized as adequate protectors. The adult Orwell would have perpetuated his scapegoat role by identifying himself with workers and derelicts subject to economic victimization and helplessness. At the same time, maternal figures would be imagined as protecting the childlike self by interposing their own bodies between him and his persecutors. (To several obvious examples in *Nineteen Eighty-Four*, of which "Do it to Julia" is only the most notorious, I would add that just she and not Winston is struck by the guards when they are arrested together.) To the unpublished paper summarized above, by Dr. Martin D. Capell, on "George Orwell: The Child-Scapegoat," I served as respondent at the April 1986 meeting of the Michigan Society for Psychoanalytic Psychology in East Lansing.

12. In his depiction of O'Brien as a superego figure, Orwell eliminates the vestiges of the Christian countermythology of God and the Devil (the latter is mentioned in the manuscript, *Ms*, 91), but traces of the Devil persist in an obsessive use of the word "sulphurous" (*Ms*, 185 [twice], 197) and in a detail added in the final version when Winston says he is ready to throw sulphuric acid in a child's face (*NEF*, 142).

13. Explicit thematic evaluation of the rulers in *Nineteen Eighty-Four* through authorial intervention is avoided; O'Brien's words speak for themselves. But the *cupiditas* of the lust for power was linked in Orwell's mind to the elemental pig-like greed of the exploiters in *Animal Farm*. The description "pug"-faced or "puggy" applied to O'Brien in the typescript and then suppressed (*Ms*, 145, 281) is a link to *Animal Farm*, as Peter Davison points out in his introduction (*Ms*, xvii). This link does not disappear: it returns irrepressibly in the textual juxtaposition of the first description of Big Brother's portrait with statistics about "pig-iron" (*NEF*, 5-6).

Eric Blair's School Days

Jonathan Rose

Bernard Crick began his biography of George Orwell with a warning:

> I believe that many English biographers have unnecessarily per-
> plexed themselves by trying to demonstrate that the child is always
> father to the literary man, when on any cool appraisal of first pub-
> lications we must be as astonished at the unpredictable disconti-
> nuities from childhood as with the few slender analogues. We have
> not yet emancipated ourselves either from literary Freudianism or
> from the cultural belief of the English upper middle classes that
> school-days are necessarily crucial.

Crick's exasperation is understandable. He found the field of Orwell
scholarship cluttered by "many theories about his mature work based
upon thinly supported surmises about his childhood and particularly
his schooling." Before Crick produced his biography, critics tried to
piece together Orwell's life from his fiction (read too literally as autobiography), from "Such, Such Were the Joys" (often treated as a memoir, though it should be reclassified as fiction), and from the unverified
recollections of acquaintances and relatives. The results, Crick complained, were often so inaccurate that he "had to spend a dispropor-
tionate amount of time" scotching myths and misconceptions that had
attached themselves to Orwell (*GO*, xxvii). Consequently, Crick did not
try to fit Orwell into any psychological or literary theories; he concentrated on the more difficult and necessary job of getting the facts
straight.

Those facts, however, point directly to the very conclusion that Crick tried to steer his readers away from. Orwell's schooldays were crucial, after all: they deeply colored his politics, his literary tastes, his life goals, and his philosophical temperament. Of course, he was not a finished product when he left Eton, but most of his adult writing was in some critical way rooted in his childhood. When Eric Blair departed for Burma at age nineteen, much of George Orwell had already been roughed in. He had developed some general ideas about socialism, revolution, war, and totalitarianism that he would build upon in this later literary career. He had even written a school story that crudely but distinctly anticipated *Nineteen Eighty-Four.*

Later in life, Orwell was gripped by a boyhood nostalgia reflected in what he wrote and what he chose to write about. He was no J. M. Barrie: he never refused to grow up, and he disdained the "permanent adolescence" that so many English authors of his generation were mired in. Nevertheless, he always enjoyed a remarkably close rapport with children, and he never let go of the special personal pleasures of his childhood. It was a fairly happy childhood, contrary to what many critics have assumed. With the exception of "Such, Such Were the Joys," Orwell generally wrote quite fondly about that period of his life, and he doggedly tried to recover its vanished delights.

Authorship itself was, for Orwell, the realization of a boyhood plan. "From a very early age," he recalled in 1946, "perhaps the age of five or six, I knew that when I grew up I should be a writer" (*CEJL*, 1:1-3). That is indeed an extraordinarily early age to embark on a literary career, and Orwell may have been exaggerating his precocity. But certainly by early adolescence he was telling his closest friends about his plans to become "a famous author." He even selected the bindings for his collected works: disliking anything "ostentatious," he settled on dark blue covers.[1] Thirty years later he would request that his actual uniform edition be "very chaste-looking & preferably dark blue" (*CEJL*, 4:406). From age ten to twenty-five (roughly), he concocted in his head "a continuous 'story' about myself, a sort of diary existing only in the mind" (*CEJL*, 1:2), and in one sense he never broke that habit. Orwell-like characters—and Orwell himself—would play leading roles in most of his fiction and reportage, to the point where one could splice together a selection of his works and create something approximating an autobiography. And in 1943 he got as far as making notes for an abortive novel modeled on his own childhood, "The Quick and the Dead" (*GO*, 262).

As a student, young Eric also churned out light verse, skits, short stories, mysteries, long dramas in the styles of Shakespeare and Aristophanes, some florid Georgean poetry, and a superabundance of awful schoolboy humor. These early drolleries reveal no trace of talent and no hint of the grim pessimist that Orwell would eventually become. There is, in fact, nothing in them to suggest that the author was unhappy.

The notion that Orwell had a miserable childhood is based almost entirely on "Such, Such Were the Joys," where he remembered himself as a pariah, despised by his classmates at St. Cyprian's and persecuted by the couple who ran the school ("I had no money, I was weak, I was unpopular, I had a chronic cough, I was cowardly, I smelt"). But Orwell admitted that his memories, set down after thirty years, were not clear (*CEJL*, 4:334, 361-62), and he may have projected the unhappiness of his adult life on his past. He could also have been following a literary bandwagon: as Noel Annan quipped, the interwar years were "the age of Almamatricide," when authors competed to produce ever more devastating exposes of their old public schools. Arnold Lunn's *The Harrovians* (1913) and Alec Waugh's *The Loom of Youth* (1917) began a torrent of debunking school novels ("In 1922 six, in 1926 five, in 1930 five, in 1934 four").[2] Orwell was imitating that well-established literary genre when he wrote "Such, Such Were the Joys"; and, like *Down and Out in Paris and London*, he wrote it as autobiographical fiction cast in the form of documentary, not literal fact.

Crick's biography and an assortment of memoirs have made it clear that the man who was capable of writing *Nineteen Eighty-Four* was also capable of magnifying the horrors of school life. St. Cyprian's was, at times, an ordeal, but it was not a Dickensian hell. The proprietors were strict, snobbish, and sometimes violent with the students, but they were not quite the ogres described by Orwell. Cyril Connolly, who published his own diatribe against the couple in *Enemies of Promise*, recanted completely when he discovered that they had taken "immense trouble...to help me win my scholarship to Eton"; he concluded that he had "read mercenary motives into much that was just enthusiasm."[3] Orwell himself conceded that the school had its compensations: late night swimming, cricket, caterpillar hunting, butterfly collecting, nature walks, and early mornings spent reading favorite authors (*CEJL*, 4:344-45). And he was able to relax at Eton, where he had a room to himself, did no more work than he absolutely had to, and enjoyed what he later described as a "tolerant and civilized atmosphere which gives each boy a chance of developing his own individuality."[4]

His sister Avril and his friend Jacintha Buddicom both remembered Eric as a generally contented, resilient, self-reliant child, not the terrorized outcast of "Such Were the Joys." Avril Blair and Humphrey Dakin (Orwell's brother-in-law) even described him as rather spoiled.

Granted, they did not know him in his school environment, but Eric only attended St. Cyprian's for a bit over five years, and much of that time he was on vacation at his home outside Henley, where he enjoyed a comfortable Edwardian childhood that resembled something out of an Edith Nesbit story. He was close to his sisters, and he had a pleasant, uncomplicated, intellectual friendship with Jacintha Buddicom. With them and a few close friends, he spent his holidays hunting, fishing, hiking, collecting eggs, visiting neighbors, exploring haunted attics, enjoying the cinematograph, devouring penny candy, and talking endlessly about books. They cooked hedgehogs in clay, manufactured and exploded homemade bombs, and constructed a whisky still (which also detonated) on the kitchen stove. They played cards, croquet, "Snakes and Ladders," and ingenious word games that involved making up new words, something that came easily to the future inventor of Newspeak.[5]

Orwell continued to indulge in these pastimes even as an adult. Probably the only job he ever thoroughly enjoyed was a brief stint as a tutor to three young boys with whom he constructed bombs, went hunting and fishing, and discussed books and politics. One of his charges, Richard Peters, described him as

> a mine of information on birds, animals, and the heroes of boys' magazines. Yet he never made us *feel* that he knew our world better than we knew it ourselves.... He entered unobtrusively into our world and illuminated it in a dry, discursive sort of way without in any way disturbing it. He never condescended; he never preached; he never intruded. (*GO*, 127-30)

Later, when he taught at a wretched day school of the type described in *A Clergyman's Daughter*, he treated "the boys as friends" (according to one of his pupils) and spent much of his free time teaching them hobbies and taking them on nature walks (*GO*, 138-39). Fredric Warburg, his publisher, recalled that even at age forty, Orwell still enjoyed placing pennies on railway tracks to be flattened by passing trains.[6] During the cold winter of 1945-46, amid universal shortages, Orwell reminisced fondly about the rifle and toy cannon he had owned as a boy, and he recommended them as Christmas presents. "One of the advantages of being a child thirty years ago was the light-hearted attitude that then prevailed towards firearms," he wrote (*GO*, 41-42). Angling was another of his youthful dissipations, and when Malcolm Muggeridge visited Orwell just before he died, he found him keeping a fishing rod by his hospital bed. "Towards the end of his life he increasingly reverted to his origins," Muggeridge recalled. "The little boy lived again in the middle-aged writer, as did the countryside he'd roamed over, the streams he'd fished in."[7]

All this suggests that Peter Stansky and William Abrahams were wrong to conclude that Orwell became a writer as a "way of avenging [himself] for an unhappy childhood" (*UO*, 16). For Eric Blair, writing was one of the joys of a mainly pleasant childhood; for George Orwell, it was a means of recalling the time "When good King Edward ruled the land, / And I was a chubby boy" (*GO*, 4-5). In *Coming Up for Air*, George Bowling steals away from his middle-aged responsibilities to visit the town he grew up in, which is clearly Henley. Bowling insists that the world before the Great War "was a good world to live in," a world of hunting, fishing, penny candy, outings with the gang, and (importantly) the only sexual liaison in the entire body of Orwell's fiction that is pleasant, not sordid, and never punished. Bowling has not forgotten the underside of prewar England:

> You saw ghastly things happening sometimes. Small businesses sliding down the hill, solid tradesmen gradually turning into broken-down bankrupts, people dying by inches of cancer and liver disease, drunken husbands signing the pledge every Monday and breaking it every Saturday, girls ruined for life by an illegitimate baby.... And yet, what was it that people had in those days? A feeling of security, even when they weren't secure. More exactly, it was a feeling of continuity.... Whatever might happen to themselves, things would go on as they'd known them. (*CUA*, 36, 43-44, 66-76, 86-102, 119, 122-26, 237-39)

Although Orwell grew up in a middle-class home, he had some early experiences of deprivation that left a mark on his writing. He once admitted, with some shame, that his most vivid memory of the First World War was "margarine": "By 1917 the war had almost ceased to affect us, except through our stomachs" (*CEJL*, 1:537). In addition to suffering through wartime rationing, Jacintha Buddicom recalled, he "complained bitterly about the school food."[8] Orwell may have embellished all the other evils of St. Cyprian's, but his classmates confirm that the food was absolutely vile (*GO*, 28). Both there and at Eton, students were underfed as a matter of school policy, on the theory that a little hunger was good for the constitution and stimulated scholarly activity. As a consequence of this and his later experiences of poverty, scrounging for food became a preoccupation in Orwell's novels and nonfiction. His *Collected Essays, Journalism, and Letters* contain 59 references to civilian shortages during and after the Second World War, and those shortages are deliberately and perpetually maintained by the

regime in *Nineteen Eighty-Four*. All of Orwell's protagonists are poorly
nourished, even when they are paid well. In *Burmese Days* John Flory
lives mainly on whiskey because his native servants cannot properly
prepare European meals. And thanks to modern food processing,
George Bowling is served frankfurters made of fish and marmalade
containing "a certain proportion of neutral fruit juice" ("This started
me off...talking about the neutral fruit-trees"). Again, only in the lost
Edwardian paradise of *Coming Up for Air* does everyone have enough
to eat: Bowling remembers sitting down to huge prewar feasts of
"boiled beef and dumplings, roast beef and Yorkshire, boiled mutton
and capers, pig's head, apple pie, spotted dog and jam roly-poly"
(*CUA*, 9, 26-27, 97).

"The world of today is a bare, hungry, dilapidated world compared
with the world that existed before 1914," we are told in *Nineteen
Eighty-Four* (*NEF*, 155). Winston Smith may drink "to the past"; he
may try to reconstruct history from Victorian artifacts and the muddled
recollections of old men; but in the end he succeeds in dredging only
one happy image out of his memory—a remembrance of himself, as
a boy, playing "Snakes and Ladders." The old children's rhymes sprinkled throughout the novel were more important to Orwell than most
critics imagine: while he was working on *Nineteen Eighty-Four*, he also
considered writing an entire book on nursery rhymes.[9] Childhood nostalgia was one of the few indulgences that Orwell, the harsh realist
and ascetic, freely allowed himself, and he refused to apologize for it:

> There is now a widespread idea that nostalgic feelings about the
> past are inherently vicious...and [that] if one thinks about the past
> at all it should be merely in order to thank God that we are so
> much better than we used to be. This seems to me a sort of intel-
> lectual face-lifting, the motive behind which is a snobbish terror
> of growing old. One ought to realize that a human being cannot
> continue developing indefinitely, and that a writer, in particular, is
> throwing away his heritage if he repudiates the experience of his
> early life. In many ways it is a grave handicap to remember that
> lost paradise "before the war."... In other ways it is an advantage.
> Each generation has its own experience and its own wisdom,
> and...one is likelier to make a good book by sticking to one's early
> acquired vision than by futile effort to "keep up." (*CEJL*, 4:445-46)

Excepting his ephemeral journalism, the better part of what Orwell
wrote was in some important way inspired by the books he had read
as a boy. His descents into the slums, the first-hand accounts of poverty
in *Down and Out in Paris and London*, *A Clergyman's Daughter*,
"Clink," and "The Spike," are all indebted to Jack London's *The People*

of the Abyss, which Orwell read at Eton, as well as to his first tramping adventure, undertaken at age seventeen (*GO*, 66). *Love and Mr. Lewisham* by H. G. Wells, one of Orwell's favorite boyhood authors, has the same basic plot as *Keep the Aspidistra Flying*: a young, marginally employed intellectual postures as a social rebel but fails to deal realistically with the problem of earning a living until he becomes a father, whereupon he drops his angry-young-man pose and buckles down to his family responsibilities. Wells's *The History of Mr. Polly*, in which a thoughtful petty bourgeois escapes a suffocating suburb and a nagging wife, is clearly the model for *Coming Up for Air*, as Orwell half-admitted (*CEJL*, 4:422).

The most obvious source of both *Animal Farm* and *Nineteen Eighty-Four* is *Gulliver's Travels*, which had been one of Orwell's best-loved books since the age of eight. Swift anticipated mind control, rewritten history, machine-written literature, shorthand languages like Newspeak, and "what would now be called totalitarianism," Orwell wrote in 1946, just as he was beginning work on *Nineteen Eighty-Four*. "He had an extraordinarily clear prevision of the spy-haunted 'police state,' with its endless heresy-hunts and treason trials, all really designed to neutralize popular discontent by changing it into war hysteria" (*CEJL*, 4:213-14, 220). Of the many other possible sources of *Nineteen Eighty-Four*, there are several that Orwell probably or certainly read as a boy: Jack London's *The Iron Heel*, Hilaire Belloc's *The Servile State*, and H. G. Wells's *When the Sleeper Wakes* and *A Modern Utopia* (*CEJL*, 2:205; 3:55-56; 4:162-63). Jacintha Buddicom remembered that Eric was particularly fascinated by the last of these: "He said he might write that kind of book himself."[10]

In addition, eighteen of Orwell's essays (nearly half of his serious criticism) focus on his boyhood reading. These include his two pieces on Kipling ("the storyteller who was so important to my childhood"), "Charles Dickens" ("when I say I like Dickens, do I simply mean that I like thinking about my childhood?"), "Wells, Hitler, and the World State" ("I doubt whether anyone who was writing books between 1900 and 1920...influenced the young so much"), "Boys' Weeklies," "Prophesies of Fascism," "Charles Reade," "In Defense of P. G. Wodehouse," "Raffles and Miss Blandish," "The Art of Donald McGill" (Eric was a collector of "saucy postcards"), "Politics vs. Literature" (on Swift), "Oysters and Brown Stout" (on Thackeray), "Riding Down from Bangor," "Nonsense Poetry," "Funny, But Not Vulgar," "Good Bad Books," and his introduction to a volume of Jack London stories. When, in 1945, Eyre and Spottiswoode proposed to reprint a series of forgotten Edwardian novels, Orwell welcomed the project ("I rather envy the person whose job it will be to scout round the threepenny boxes, hunting down copies of his boyhood favourites"), and for that series he wrote a preface to Leonard Merrick's *The Position of Peggy Harper* (*CEJL*, 4:19).

As a writer *for* children, Orwell produced his "fairy story" *Animal Farm*, which originated as a tale he spun out with his first wife—who was a child psychologist (*OT*, 171-72). For the BBC, Orwell broad-casted a program on children's poetry and wrote adaptations of "Little Red Riding Hood" and "The Emperor's New Clothes."[11] The last of these, of course, sums up Orwell's mission as a political writer. "The fact is people are fed up with this Russian nonsense," he told Dwight Macdonald in 1946, "and it's just a question of who is the first to say 'The Emperor has no clothes on.'"[12]

Orwell seriously considered the possibilities of using comic books as vehicles for socialist propaganda. Even in his thirties, he was an avid reader of public school stories (*GO*, 170, 260). He realized, how-ever, that Billy Bunter was rapidly losing his audience to cheap sci-ence fiction. English children, he noted in 1939, were devouring American pulp magazines featuring tales like "'When Hell Came to America,' in which the agents of a 'blood-maddened European dicta-tor' are trying to conquer the U.S.A. with death rays and invisible aero-planes." Having seen the future of boys' magazines—"more scientific interest, more bloodshed, more leader-worship" (*CEJL*, 1:475-78, 483-84)—Orwell seems to have followed that trend in *Nineteen Eighty-Four*, which sometimes reads very much like a political comic book. Of course, it is much more than that, but there is a flavor of *Amazing Stories* in its futuristic machinery of terror that many critics have dis-missed as juvenile.[13] *Nineteen Eighty-Four* has always been a popular novel among young adolescents, and Orwell may have been deliber-ately writing to them on a pulp-fiction level.

Orwell did not fully work out his political convictions until the Spanish Civil War, at the earliest, but it was in school that he devel-oped the radically independent turn of mind that would be his great-est strength as a writer. By the time he left St. Cyprian's, he was cool, aloof, and very selective in choosing his friends, a loner by choice rather than the sad outcast of "Such, Such Were the Joys." According to Jacintha Buddicom, he was an

> inveterate individualist, who always thought for himself, and never ran with the crowd.... A fat lot the self-sufficient, self-contained, supercilious Eric would have cared whether he was *popular* or not. What he thought, he thought: what he did, he did—without being *interested* in whether he was liked or disliked for it, or what effect he was creating.... It would really be more accurate to say that other people were unpopular with *him*.[14]

Cyril Connolly remembered him as

> always laughing and arguing and barracking and quibbling with
> people and heckling. And he seemed, like Socrates, to be con-
> stantly questioning everybody in everything they did or said. And
> always with this wheezy laughter. "You think that but, by God, I
> don't think you'd think it in ten years' time...," he was a debunker
> before the word existed...."Two years' time, there won't be any
> Ascot. No—it will be a Chinese Ascot."[15]

Eric revealed that perverse streak at the early age of eleven, when
he introduced himself to Jacintha Buddicom by doing a headstand.
"You are noticed more if you stand on your head than if you are right
way up" was his bland explanation.[16] Already he had mastered the
Orwellian trick of arresting an audience by doing or saying the unexpected, although there was a lemony whimsy in Eric's skepticism that
contrasts sharply with the darkness of Orwell's adult writings. His
friends described him as a "good-humoured cynic" and "a boy of a
peculiar humour—a saturnine perhaps and not wholly benevolent
humour but above all a humourist" (*UO*, 55, 99-100, 105-7).

Eric directed that humor particularly against the privileges of wealth
and class, having noticed the special treatment that boys of good family received at school. "Might have known the jute market had recov-
ered," a St. Cyprian's schoolmate recalled him as saying. "Bones (an
Anglo-Indian boy) is back in favour with the headmistress. His father
must have been able to pay his bill." Denys King-Farlow remembered
him as "an awful bore about money" at Eton (*GO*, 50), where Eric
once acidly observed,

> There are at least six masters on the staff who make a very good
> living out of the Crucifixion. It's worth over £2000 a year between
> them. I've looked out what they get, as chaplains and so on. I
> reckon that must have been the most profitably exploited event in
> history—and they all have to talk as if they wish it hadn't
> happened.[17]

Orwell later claimed he had been admitted to St. Cyprian's at half-
tuition because he "seemed likely to win scholarships and thus bring
credit on the school," and that eventually the proprietors "began
throwing the fact in my teeth" to make him cram harder (*CEJL*, 4:335-
42). This, like almost everything else Orwell wrote about St.
Cyprian's—the favoritism, the flaunting of money, and his own awareness that he was a relatively poor student whose future depended on

winning scholarships—is true but exaggerated. Jacintha Buddicom
recalls that he did complain of favoritism toward the moneyed and
titled but that "he accepted it as a fact of life," with more bemusement
than bitterness.[18] All the same, it is clear that Orwell's preoccupation
with class injustice and the power of money in capitalist society began
in school, however much his later experiences of poverty may have
contributed to it.

That sensitivity to inequality made Orwell into something of a
socialist even before he graduated from Eton. In *The Road to Wigan
Pier* he recalled that, at age seventeen, "I loosely described myself as
a Socialist," albeit without having "much grasp of what Socialism
meant" (*RWP*, 140). Bernard Crick and most other critics assert that
Orwell did not turn to socialism until the mid-1930s, that he tended
to project his adult political views back to his youth (*GO*, 67-68). But
this conclusion may be too hasty. Jacintha Buddicom confirmed that
the Eric she knew between 1914 and 1922 was a socialist, even if his
socialism amounted to little more than a vague equalitarianism.[19] His
aunt, Nellie Limousin, was a keen socialist and Esperantist, and his
mother and grandmother seem to have dabbled generally in the
"advanced" movements of the day (*GO*, 13-14, 97-98, 114-15).

Miss Buddicom also believed that some of Eric's relatives were
involved in the Fabian Society, but her memory was not clear on that
point, and I have not been able to find their names in any Fabian publication or membership list. In any case, we know that Eric was an
enthusiastic reader of Bernard Shaw and H. G. Wells. He was once
taken to meet another Fabian author, Edith Nesbit, and he was bitterly
disappointed when he missed an opportunity to meet Wells.[20]
According to the diary of Kingsley Martin, Eric participated in a socialist conference at Dunsford held 11-13 February 1922, and attended by
a number of Fabian notables, including Sidney and Beatrice Webb.[21]
Eric still possessed a full complement of class prejudices, and he could
not yet sympathize with workers as individuals. But it seems likely that
he was a socialist in the sense that a good many Fabians were socialists—he professed a sincere but nebulous faith in equality without any
clear plan for bringing it about or any preferences among the various
socialist sects. For him, socialism was simply "justice and liberty" (as
he later wrote in *Wigan Pier*), and ideological squabbles among socialists were pointless: "Economic injustice will stop the moment we want
it to stop, and no sooner, and if we genuinely want it to stop the
method adopted hardly matters" (*RWP*, 149).

Orwell's socialism was always tempered by a profound hostility to
modern technology and "mechanical progress," which he repeatedly
denounced as a "swindle" (*CEJL*, 1:121, 526; *RWP*, 191, 203). That

conservatism followed directly from his childhood nostalgia, his refusal to renounce his own past. "By retaining one's childhood love of such things as trees, fishes, butterflies...one makes a peaceful and decent future a little more probable," he wrote in one of his *Tribune* columns, "and by preaching the doctrine that nothing is to be admired except steel and concrete, one merely makes it a little surer that human beings will have no outlet for their surplus energy except in hatred and leader-worship" (*GO*, 303-4). Like every sensitive Georgian schoolboy, Eric Blair loved rural walks and the Shropshire poetry of A. E. Housman (*GO*, 51), and Orwell later irritated readers of the socialist *Tribune* by publishing nature notes that could just as well have appeared in *Country Life*. For that, as for all his other ideological deviations, he was unrepentant:

> I am not able, and I do not want, completely to abandon the world-view that I acquired in childhood. So long as I remain alive and well I shall continue to feel strongly about prose style, to love the surface of the earth, and to take pleasure in solid objects and scraps of useless information. It is no use trying to suppress that side of myself. The job is to reconcile my ingrained likes and dislikes with the essentially public, non-individual activities that this age forces on all of us. (*CEJL*, 1:6)

Orwell vilified those socialists for whom socialism meant technocracy, central planning, and cellophane-wrapped efficiency, "all that dreary tribe of high-minded women and sandal-wearers who come flocking towards the smell of 'progress' like bluebottles to a dead cat." That sort of invective was directed primarily against the Fabians—"the 'progressives,' the yea-sayers, the Shaw-Wells type, always leaping forward to embrace the ego-projections which they mistake for the future" (*RWP*, chaps. 11-12; *CEJL*, 1:520). In fact, many Fabians were more devoted to industrial development than to equality: that is one reason why Shaw and the Webbs embraced Stalin in the 1930s. Even before Eric left school, he began to doubt that Fabian enthusiasm for progress. The marginal jottings in his copy of *Plays Pleasant and Unpleasant* coolly puncture Shaw's forward-looking bromides—his insistence that Ibsen is high art ("Higher than Shakespeare, Homer, Dante, Plato?"), that there is "plenty of good in the world working itself out as fast as the idealists will allow it" ("Indeed?"), that "we should all get along much faster and better" ("Where to?") (*GO*, 62).

Eric's favorite living author may well have been Shaw's intellectual sparring-partner, G. K. Chesterton, that flamboyantly conventional enemy of modernity and skeptic of skepticism. "He was crazy about Chesterton," recalled Jacintha Buddicom, to whom he once presented

a copy of Chesterton's novel *Manalive*.[22] One of Orwell's first published articles appeared in *G.K.'s Weekly*, and as late as 1935 he had
not entirely given up defending the medieval politics of that magazine, which advocated a return to a little England of free peasants and
craftsmen (*GO*, 175). Orwell loathed J. B. Morton, D. B. Wyndham
Lewis, and the whole "silly-clever" school of English Catholic apologists, but he was always more charitable toward Chesterton, whom he
regarded as "a writer of considerable talent who chose to suppress
both his sensibilities and his intellectual honesty in the cause of Roman
Catholic propaganda." Orwell acknowledged that Chesterton was an
anti-Semite and an admirer of Mussolini, but "at least he had courage.
He was ready to attack the rich and powerful, and he damaged his
career by doing so" (*CEJL*, 3:174-75). Even during the Second World
War, Orwell praised Chesterton's opposition to the Boer War: both
authors were enthusiastic English patriots who hated British imperialism. They also shared a hostility to monopoly capitalism, a nostalgia
for an old England of independent shopkeepers, a faith in the decency
of the common man, and a fascination with popular culture ("Good
Bad Books" is a phrase and a concept that Orwell borrowed directly
from Chesterton).

Both Orwell and Chesterton criticized socialist intellectuals in similar terms—as cranks and elitists who despised the masses and were
working to create, not equalitarian democracy, but a bureaucratic dictatorship. Chesterton described a revolt against such a dictatorship in
his 1904 novel *The Napoleon of Notting Hill*; it is not certain that
Orwell ever read it, but he did credit Chesterton with predicting "the
rise of a slave society which might be called either capitalist or
Communist" (*CEJL*, 4:163). Chesterton warned that Bernard Shaw
would trample on the rights of freeborn Englishmen in the name of
progress, and he twitted Beatrice Webb for "ordering about the citizens of a state, as she might the servants in a kitchen."[23] Orwell sounds
very much like Chesterton when, in *The Road to Wigan Pier*, he
protests that

> the underlying motive of many Socialists...is simply a hypertro-
> phied sense of order. The present state of affairs offends them not
> because it causes misery, still less because it makes freedom
> impossible, but because it is untidy; what they desire, basically, is
> to reduce the world to something resembling a chessboard. Take
> the plays of a lifelong Socialist like Shaw. How much under-
> standing or even awareness of working-class life do they display?
> Shaw...can only bring a working man on the stage...as a sort of
> W. W. Jacobs figure of fun—the ready-made comic East Ender, like
> those in *Major Barbara* and *Captain Brassbound's Conversion*. At

best his attitude to the working class is the sniggering *Punch* attitude, in more serious moments (consider, for instance, the young
man who symbolizes the dispossessed classes in *Misalliance*) he
finds them merely contemptible and disgusting. Poverty and, what
is more, the habits of mind created by poverty, are something to
be abolished from *above*, by violence if necessary; perhaps even
preferably by violence. Hence his worship of "great" men and
appetite for dictatorships, Fascist or Communist.... You get the
same thing in a more mealy-mouthed form in Mrs. Sidney Webb's
autobiography, which gives, unconsciously, a most revealing picture of the high-minded Socialist slum visitor. The truth is that to
many people, calling themselves Socialists, revolution does not
mean a movement of the masses with which they hope to associate themselves; it means a set of reforms which "we," the clever
ones, are going to impose upon "them," the Lower Orders. (*RWP*,
178-80)

Orwell's opposition to that sort of Fabian arrogance can be traced
back to his youth, to the Dunsford socialist conference he attended in
1922. There he spoke enthusiastically about democratic, libertarian
forms of socialism, opening a long discussion on the Cooperative
movement. There was also a debate on vocational representation,
"which," according to Kingsley Martin, "Blair took up as a new idea
he'd just found. Beatrice [Webb] lost her temper & bullied Blair."[24]
Vocational representation, under which members of Parliament would
be elected by workers voting by craft, was being championed at the
time by the guild socialists as a form of proletarian democracy. As
such, it was anathema to the Webbs, who much preferred the benevolent paternalism of administrators and social scientists like themselves, the people they liked to call "brainworkers."

One should not make too much of this one incident, but it seems
that Eric, before his nineteenth birthday, was already beginning to
develop an Orwellian distrust of socialist intellectuals from his reading
of Chesterton and from the scolding he received at the hands of
Beatrice Webb. The pigs of *Animal Farm* call themselves "brainworkers" (*AF*, 42), just as the Fabians did, and they use that status to appropriate extra food and privileges until they become a new oppressor
class. (For Geoffrey Gorer, Orwell specifically underscored this point
as the central lesson of the book [*GO*, 339]). Eric Blair wanted to write
a book like Wells' *A Modern Utopia*, and it obviously contributed something to *Nineteen Eighty-Four*, inasmuch as it described a totalitarian
world state governed by an intellectual elite that maintains a card file
for every human being on earth. For Wells, that was a vision of an ideal
society; Orwell transformed it into a nightmare. The Fabians favored
government by a managerial caste, but Orwell—like Chesterton, James

Burnham, and many contemporary conservatives and neoconservatives—saw a threat to freedom in the rise of this "new class," the class
that rules the world in *Nineteen Eighty-Four.*

> The new aristocracy was made up for the most part of bureaucrats,
> scientists, technicians, trade-union organizers, publicity experts,
> sociologists, teachers, journalists, and professional politicians.
> These people, whose origins lay in the salaried middle class and
> the upper grades of the working class, had been shaped and
> brought together by the barren world of monopoly industry and
> centralized government. As compared with their opposite numbers
> in past ages, they were less avaricious, less tempted by luxury,
> hungrier for pure power, and above all, more conscious of what
> they were doing and more intent on crushing opposition. (*NEF*,
> 169)

One extraordinary (and unpublicized) bit of juvenalia in the Orwell
Archive reveals that the germ of *Nineteen Eight-Four* had formed in
Eric Blair's mind while he was still at Eton. It is a fragment of a story
(the first half is missing) titled "A Peep Into the Future," written in
Blair's hand for the June 1918 issue of the *Election Times*, a school
magazine. I do not have permission to quote from the manuscript, but
a summary should reveal that Eric was already toying with some of the
themes he would develop thirty years later.

The story is set in a futuristic Eton, where a revolution has taken
place. Apparently the revolt was not a matter of class struggle, but a
war of the Two Cultures, for the new headmaster is the scientist Sir
Pigling Hill, who has imposed a technocratic dictatorship on the
school. In 1919 Blair would actually briefly study biology under a science master named M. D. Hill: in 1920 he returned to a concentration
in classics (*UO*, 95). (The name "Pigling" may allude to the fetal pigs
commonly used in classroom dissections—and, of course, it just might
be an anticipation of *Animal Farm.*) "A Peep Into the Future" seems
to be a send-up of H. G. Wells: assuming it was Eric's first attempt to
write a book like *A Modern Utopia*, it supports my earlier suggestion
that Blair had learned to distrust Fabian authoritarianism long before
he wrote *The Road to Wigan Pier.*

"A Peep Into the Future" satirically takes off from the liberal ferment
that gripped Eton at the close of the First World War. Cyril Connolly
described the 1916 Election—the class of scholarship students that
included Blair—as "an oasis of enlightenment," a circle of "scholar ath-
letes, animated, unlike the rules of the college, by postwar opinions.
They hated bullying, beating, fagging, the election system, militarism,
and infringements of liberty, and believed in the ultimate victory of

human reason." But, Connolly notes, "Orwell was rather aloof" from that Etonian *éclairissement*.[25] He had already taken up what would be his lifelong position inside the Left: he wanted to scrap the status quo, only he feared that it might be replaced by something worse.

Robert P. Longden was one of the reformers of the 1916 Election: in "A Peep Into the Future" he has been purged by Pigling Hill. For the sake of economy, flowing academic gowns have been reduced to narrow ribbons of black fabric. In a scene that anticipates the Minitrue refectory, the boys of tomorrow's Eton mindlessly consume an unappetizing meal. Saying grace has been abolished, and the dining hall is decorated with propaganda slogans hailing the virtues of science. As in *Nineteen Eighty-Four*, this materialist ideology is brutalizing, tearing apart family ties: James Gibson, another progressive-minded classmate of Blair's, appears in the story with his infant son, whom he cruelly kicks across the room. Prof. Hill conducts a class that reads like a silly spoof of Room 101: to illustrate stimulus and response, he subjects a master to the ultimate form of torture—the racket created by a couple of rowdy pupils. In *Nineteen Eighty-Four* Winston Smith sees hope for liberation in the huge prole woman who sings outside his window. That cockney woman also appears in "A Peep Into the Future," but there she actually brings the regime crashing down around her, and Eton returns to its traditional unscientific curriculum.

Orwell later dismissed his school magazine squibs as "the most pitiful burlesque stuff you could imagine" (*CEJL*, 1:1). That describes "A Peep Into the Future" perfectly: it is a shallow, smirking, unfunny attempt at humor. But it is also, clearly, the smiling embryo of *Nineteen Eighty-Four*. As such, it supports what Anthony West and several other critics have claimed: that the totalitarian world of Ingsoc is really a monstrous magnification of a British public school.[26] At age fifteen, Eric Blair already knew, in a callow way, what George Orwell is supposed to have learned in Catalonia—that revolutions are usually hijacked by tyrants.

This raises an intriguing question: How did young Eric acquire this political wisdom? When he wrote "A Peep Into the Future" he does not seem to have had in mind the Bolshevik Revolution, which was only a few months old and had not yet begun to devour its children. As Orwell later recalled, the upheaval in Russia "made no impression" on Eton (*CEJL*, 1:537). At the time, he never discussed it with Jacintha Buddicom.[27]

But Blair, along with every other public school boy, was familiar with the French and English Revolutions. He briefly studied history at Eton, and although he did not do well in the subject, he may have learned enough to realize the dangers inherent in revolution. We always assume that Big Brother is an amalgam of Hitler and Stalin, but he was also partly inspired by what Eric had learned about Napoleon and Cromwell.

In *Nineteen Eighty-Four* there is a subtle but distinct hint that the Party traces its ideological pedigree back to the Roundheads: just off Trafalgar/Victory Square stands "a statue of a man on horseback which was supposed to represent Oliver Cromwell" (*NEF*, 95). The actual statue is of Charles I. The Puritan Commonwealth, after all, had been England's only experience with a military dictatorship, and it had instilled that traditional English "dislike of standing armies" that Orwell extolled in *The Lion and the Unicorn* (*CEJL*, 2:61). In the 1940s Orwell noted that the struggle between the Puritans and the Cavaliers "distinctly resembled the left-right antagonism of today," and he compared "Cromwell's soldiers slashing Irishwomen's faces with razors" to the modern atrocities committed by Nazis and Communists (*CEJL*, 1:522–23; 3:369–70).

At this point it is worth quoting at some length from Orwell's little-known and never reprinted introduction to a collection of historic British political pamphlets, which include some polemics by Gerrard Winstanley and other seventeenth-century radicals. Published in 1948, the preface clarifies the message Orwell intended to send in *Animal Farm* and *Nineteen Eighty-Four*, and it underscores the fact that both books were inspired by the Roundheads as well as the Bolsheviks:

> ...it is easy to see that the forces represented by Cromwell deserved to win, since they at least offered a hope for the future, whereas their adversaries did not. But, as some observers realised at the time, their victory brought no actual benefit, but merely the promise of one.... The war was hardly over before it became clear that the causes for which the rank and file had believed themselves to be fighting were largely lost. The old tyranny had been overthrown, but neither liberty of opinion nor social equality had been brought much nearer. To-day the whole process seems familiar, like one of the classic openings at chess.[28] It is as though history, while not actually repeating itself, were in the habit of moving in spirals, so that events of hundreds of years ago can appear to be happening at one's elbow. Certain figures, arguments and habits of mind always recur. There is always the visionary, like Winstanley, who is equally persecuted by both parties. There is always the argument that one must go forward or go back, and the counter-argument that the first necessity is to consolidate the position that has been won. There is always the charge that the revolutionary extremist is really an agent of the reactionaries. And once the struggle is well over, there is always the conservative who is more progressive than the radicals who have triumphed.

Though that last sentence refers to Jonathan Swift, it could stand as a perfect description of that incomparable paradox, George Orwell. History taught him at once the futility and the necessity of revolution:

> The most encouraging thing about revolutionary activity is that, although it always fails, it always continues. The vision of a world of free and equal human beings, living together in a state of brotherhood—in one age it is called the Kingdom of Heaven, in another the classless society—never materialises, but belief in it never seems to die out. The English Diggers and Levellers...are links in a chain of thought which stretches from the slave revolts of antiquity, through the various peasant risings and heretical sects of the Middle Ages, down to the Socialists of the nineteenth century and the Trotskyists and Anarchists of our own day....[Winstanley's] essential predicament is that of any intelligent democratic Socialist to-day.[29]

Orwell's distrust of Cromwell appears to have developed before his anti-Stalinism. In 1932 he wrote a school play in which Charles II confounds the Roundheads. The exiled King is, in fact, the only truly *noble* character Orwell ever created in a work of fiction.[30] Richard Peters recalls him saying, in 1930, "that he would have sided with the Cavaliers rather than the Roundheads because the Roundheads were such depressing people.... For temperamentally he was a Cavalier, lacking the fervour and fanaticism of the Puritan" (*GO*, 129). Orwell's anti-Puritanism, partly rooted in his marginal but lifelong attachment to the Anglican Church, clearly blossomed before he displayed any deep hostility to (or interest in) the Soviet system.

We cannot trace Orwell's Cavalier sentiments any earlier than 1930; but there is evidence that, as a schoolboy, Eric had acquired a wary attitude toward the French Revolution, from two sources in particular. One St. Cyprian's teacher annually delivered a thrilling reading of *A Tale of Two Cities,* with magic lantern slides. In 1939 Orwell noted that Dickens' horrific account of the Reign of Terror, though exaggerated, "would apply pretty accurately to several countries today" (*CEJL*, 1:423). In 1927 or 1928—well before he had anything to say about the Russian Revolution—Orwell wrote a play fragment with a setting that suggests Paris during the Terror.[31]

The other possible source was Thomas Carlyle's *The French Revolution.* At St. Cyprian's, Cyril Connolly and Blair consecutively won a prize awarded for the best list of books checked out of the school library. "The books were given out in the evening by Flip herself," Connolly recalled, "and a way by which it was sometimes possible to get back in 'favour' was by taking out or returning one which had caught her eye." Connolly managed that by heading his reading list with *The French Revolution.*[32]

If Airstrip One was indeed St. Cyprian's writ large, then some very revealing parallels emerge from this episode. Like O'Brien, Flip handed out rewards, punishments, and books—Carlyle for Connolly, *Vanity Fair* for Blair (*CEJL*, 4:350). Moreover, *The French Revolution* and *The Theory and Practice of Oligarchical Collectivism* convey much the same message: that revolution ends in war, terror, and tyranny. And there can be little doubt that young Blair would have noted well how his best friend won the favor of the headmaster's wife.

Orwell displayed only a passing interest in Carlyle until 1944-45, when he had just finished *Animal Farm* and was gestating *Nineteen Eighty-Four.* Then he repeatedly attacked Carlyle as "one of the founders of the modern worship of power and success"—a Machiavellian tradition that would culminate in Ingsoc (*CEJL*, 3:7, 100, 222, 368, 375).

One other incident may have prodded Blair along the long road from the French Revolution to *Nineteen Eighty-Four:* on his examination for the Burma Police, Blair was asked to write a history paper on the topic "If Nelson had lost Trafalgar?" (*GO*, 77). Evidently the question stuck in his mind: he would answer it twenty years later in a 1942 radio broadcast. There Orwell compared Hitler to Napoleon and speculated that if Trafalgar had gone the other way, England probably would have been conquered and "Europe would have been given over to a military dictatorship."[33] He began a more elaborate answer the following year, when he started to sketch out *Nineteen Eighty-Four* and wrote *Animal Farm.* The latter, of course, also ends with the triumph of a Napoleon.

This is not to imply that *Animal Farm* is not an allegory of the Soviet Union, or that Orwell's critique of totalitarianism was not a response to Hitler and Stalin. My point is simply that the English and French examples had already taught Eric Blair, while he was still in school, that revolutions usually lead to tyranny. That background helps to explain why Orwell was so quick to recognize the evils of Stalinism: quite simply, he had learned from history.

One other childhood experience had an enormous influence on Orwell's critique of totalitarianism: the First World War. It is often said that *Nineteen Eighty-Four* depicts London in 1944, but in some respects it is more like 1916. Growing up in a liberal and prosperous society, young Eric was suddenly plunged, at a politically impressionable age, into something resembling totalitarianism. England was locked in a seemingly endless war, a war of spy manias and fanatical propaganda, shortages and rationing, concocted atrocity stories indistinguishably mixed up with real atrocities, and the occasional bomb falling on London. In *Nineteen Eighty-Four* letters have been replaced by preprinted postcards, which only permit the sender to cross out the messages he does not wish to send: such cards were actually handed out to British infantrymen in World War One.

The face of Big Brother, with his black mustache and those eyes that follow you everywhere, may be the face of Hitler or Stalin; but the earliest poster of that type was of Lord Kitchener, issuing the ultimate demand of the totalitarian state: "YOUR COUNTRY NEEDS YOU." He got Eric Blair, who won "favor" at St. Cyprian's for writing a memorial poem honoring Kitchener. Although *Nineteen Eighty-Four* did draw on Orwell's World War II work for the BBC, it should be remembered that that was not the first time he had written war propaganda. The roots of Winston Smith can be traced back to St. Cyprian's, where Eric wrote two patriotic war poems printed in the *Henley and South Oxfordshire Standard*—his very first published literary work (*GO*, 36-38). As Jeffrey Meyers recognized, the last words spoken by Winston Smith before his arrest—"We are the dead"—is a quotation from the most famous poem of the Great War:

> We are the Dead. Short days ago
> We lived, felt dawn, saw sunset glow,
>   Loved and were loved, and now we lie
>   In Flanders fields.[34]

The fund drives for Floating Fortresses and the recruitment of children into the Spies may have had their origins in Blair's very first political activities, which he was pressed into even before the outbreak of the War:

> The earliest political slogan I can remember is "We want eight (eight dreadnoughts) and we won't wait." At seven years old I was a member of the Navy League and wore a sailor suit with "HMS *Invincible*" on my cap. Even before my public-school OTC I had been in a private-school cadet corps. Off and on, I have been toting a rifle ever since I was ten, in preparation not only for war but for a particular kind of war, a war in which the guns rise to a frantic orgasm of sound, and at the appointed moment you clamber out of the trench, breaking your nails on the sandbags, and stumble across mud and wire into the machine-gun barrage.

In fact, Orwell added, "part of the reason for the fascination that the Spanish Civil War had for people of about my age was that it was so like the Great War..., a positional war of trenches, artillery, raids, snipers, mud, barbed wire, lice and stagnation." This adolescent romance of war was, however, somewhat let down by Franco's artillery, which did not have enough shells to maintain a serious barrage: "It was so different from the tremendous, unbroken roar that my senses had been waiting for for twenty years" (*CEJL*, 1:538).

Just as Blair's knowledge of the Puritan and Jacobin Revolutions enabled him to see what had gone wrong with the Bolshevik Revolution, so his experience of World War One prepared him to expect the worst in World War Two. Two years before Hitler invaded Poland, Orwell was already warning that the coming "great war 'against Fascism' (cf. 1914, 'against militarism')...will allow Fascism, British variety, to be slipped over our necks" (*CEJL*, 1:276). In 1940 he recalled that the

> truly frightening thing about the war in Spain was not such violence as I had witnessed, nor even the party feuds behind the lines, but the immediate reappearance in left-wing circles of the mental atmosphere of the Great War. The very people who for twenty years had sniggered over their own superiority to war hysteria were the ones who rushed straight back into the mental slum of 1915. All the familiar war-time idiocies, spy-hunting, orthodoxy-sniffing (Sniff, sniff. Are you a good anti-Fascist?), the retailing of incredible atrocity stories, came back into vogue as though the intervening years had never happened. (*CEJL*, 1:517-18)

By 1944 Orwell realized that there had actually been less patriotic hysteria during the Second World War than during the First (*CEJL*, 3:114-17, 385)—again suggesting that it was the Great War that served as the primary model for *Nineteen Eighty-Four*.

Nineteen Eighty-Four offers only one trace of hope for the future: children. Winston Smith sees that in the prole woman, "blown up to monstrous proportions by childbearing," who hangs diapers out to dry in the yard beneath his window:

> The woman down there had no mind, she had only strong arms, a warm heart, and a fertile belly. He wondered how many children she had given birth to. It might easily be fifteen. She had had her momentary flowering, a year, perhaps, of wildrose beauty, and then she had suddenly swollen like a fertilized fruit and grown hard and red and coarse, and then her life had been laundering, scrubbing, darning, cooking, sweeping, polishing, mending, scrubbing, laundering, first for children, then for grandchildren, over thirty unbroken years. At the end of it she was still singing.... Everywhere, all over the world, hundreds or thousands of millions of people just like this...were storing up in their hearts and muscles the power that would one day overturn the world. If there

was hope, it lay in the proles!...You could not doubt it when you looked at that valiant figure in the yard. In the end their awakening would come.... They would stay alive against all the odds, like birds, passing from body to body the vitality which the Party did not share and could not kill.... Out of those mighty loins a race of conscious beings must one day come. (*NEF*, 180-82)

Orwell's childhood nostalgia ultimately resolved itself into an urge to have children—the only adult way one can ever return to childhood. Like D. H. Lawrence (whom he much admired) and Somerset Maugham (whom he read at Eton) (*GO*, 37), he acquired a visceral faith in the saving power of the procreative impulse. It appears as early as *Keep the Aspidistra Flying* (1936), which ends with Gordon Comstock pressing his ear to his wife's belly, listening for the heartbeat of their unborn child—the only upbeat conclusion Orwell ever wrote in a work of fiction. George Bowling's children are little beasts, but all the same they arouse in him "that feeling you read about in the Bible when it says your bowels yearn," and he is convinced that his "sole importance has been to bring these creatures into the world and feed them while they're young" (*CUA*, 9). Orwell disliked "birth control fanatics," as one can gather from *Wigan Pier* (*RWP*, 216) and the fulminations of Gordon Comstock, and he was devastated when he and his first wife failed to conceive children. Even when she needed a hysterectomy to remove tumors, Orwell resisted the operation. It was on his insistence that they adopted a son (her feelings were more mixed), and he threw himself into the thankless yet vital business of feeding, washing, and diapering the baby (*GO*, 174, 262, 327-30, 333-34). His letters are filled with news about the boy's achievements, adventures, messes, and minor catastrophes, all of which Orwell obviously relished. Two years before he died he explained to Julian Symons the fundamental satisfaction involved in raising children. "They're awfully fun in spite of the nuisance," he wrote, "& as they develop one has one's own childhood over again" (*CEJL*, 4:415).

Notes

1. Jacintha Buddicom, *Eric and Us: A Remembrance of George Orwell* (London: Leslie Frewin, 1974), 38, 75-76.
2. Noel Annan, *Our Age: English Intellectuals Between the World Wars—A Group Portrait* (New York: Random House, 1990), 46-48.
3. Cyril Connolly, *The Evening Colonnade* (London: David Bruce & Watson, 1978), 372.
4. George Orwell, "For Ever Eton," *Observer*, 1 August 1948, 3.
5. Buddicom, *Eric and Us*, 21, 25-28, 30-31, 33-38, 82, 100-1, 106-8; Avril Dunn, "My Brother, George Orwell," *Twentieth Century*, March 1961, 256;

T. R. Fyvel, *George Orwell: A Personal Memoir* (New York: Macmillan, 1982), 11-12, 17.

6. "George Orwell," arranged and narrated by Rayner Heppenstal, BBC Third Programme, 2 November 1960.

7. Malcolm Muggeridge, "George Orwell 1903-1950," BBC 2, 20 November 1965.

8. Interview with Jacintha Buddicom, 4 November 1978; Buddicom, *Eric and Us*, 51.

9. Fredric Warburg, *All Authors Are Equal* (London: Hutchinson, 1973), 95.

10. Buddicom, *Eric and Us*, 39.

11. "The Emperor's New Clothes," BBC Eastern Service Purple Network, 18 November 1943; "Little Red Riding Hood," BBC Home Service, 9 July 1946.

12. Orwell, letter to Dwight Macdonald, 3 January 1946, Yale University Library.

13. For example, Julian Symons, "Power and Corruption," *Times Literary Supplement*, 10 June 1949, 143-44.

14. Buddicom, *Eric and Us*, 20, 50-51.

15. Muggeridge, "George Orwell 1903-1950."

16. Buddicom, *Eric and Us*, 11.

17. Tom Hopkinson, "George Orwell—Dark Side Out," *Cornhill*, Summer 1953, 450-70.

18. Buddicom interview.

19. Ibid.

20. Buddicom, *Eric and Us*, 14-15.

21. Kingsley Martin diary, 11-13 February 1922, University of Sussex Library (Sx Ms 11 7/9).

22. Buddicom interview and *Eric and Us*, 38.

23. G. K. Chesterton, *The Victorian Age in Literature* (London: Oxford University Press, 1961), 58.

24. Kingsley Martin diary, 11-13 February 1922.

25. Cyril Connolly, *Enemies of Promise* (London: George Routledge & Sons, 1938), 244-45.

26. In *George Orwell: The Critical Heritage*, ed. Jeffrey Meyers (London: Routledge & Kegan Paul, 1975), 76-79.

27. Buddicom interview.

28. The lecture that Winston Smith endures at the Community Center, "Ingsoc in relation to chess," undoubtedly drives home the same lesson: eventually, revolutions are always checkmated.

29. George Orwell and Reginald Reynolds, eds., *British Pamphleteers*, vol. 1 (London: Allan Wingate, 1948), 9-10.

30. "Charles II," Orwell Archive.

31. Fragment of a scenario and play about Francis Stone, 1927-28?, Orwell Archive.

32. Connolly, *Enemies of Promise*, 211-12.

33. W. J. West, ed., *Orwell: The War Commentaries* (New York: Pantheon, 1985), 168-69.

34. Jeffrey Meyers, "*Nineteen Eighty-Four*: A Novel of the 1940s," in *George Orwell*, ed. Courtney T. Wemyss and Alexej Ugrinsky (New York: Greenwood Press, 1987), 137. The poem is John McCrae's "In Flanders Fields."

The Classical Heritage of
Airstrip One

Arthur M. Eckstein

George Orwell may have been a lifelong socialist and spokesman for the poor and downtrodden, but Eric Arthur Blair received an education that was straightforwardly upper class.[1] It was an education that, by tradition, laid great stress on the Greek and Latin classical authors. First at St. Cyprian's School in Sussex (1911-1916), and then at Eton (1917-1921), young Blair studied the traditional canon of classical literature in the original: Homer, Euripides, Lucretius, Horace. In fact, Blair majored in Classics at Eton, under the noted Hellenistic scholar A. S. F. Gow. And though he took the comparatively less rigorous of two possible Classics majors there, he still studied seven hours of Latin a week, and six hours of Greek.[2]

Undoubtedly, then, the mature George Orwell was fluent in both Greek and Latin, and had a deep knowledge of classical literature—and ancient history, too, for he took a good dose of that at Eton as well (see *UO*, 114). Yet Orwell as an adult mounted a persistent campaign against the influence of Classics in English education and English writing. He went so far as to attack the use of Greek names for plants and flowers instead of good English names: (*CEJL*, 4:131, n. 1), and he could write with delight about the destruction of classical literature during the Middle Ages (*CEJL*, 3:178-79). He commonly voiced two objections to a classical education: it was used by the upper classes to distinguish themselves, in an artificial and invidious way, from the great mass of the British people; and it did not prepare anyone for life in the real world.

Yet in denouncing classical education—*his* education—Orwell was sometimes simply being an "Old Boy" having a good laugh. He liked to thumb his nose at (his fellow) classicists, to say outrageous things about their mutual educational experience: for instance, that the moral exhortations of Marcus Aurelius could be inspiring in the morning, but that a loud alarm clock was probably better (*CEJL*, 4:268). Orwell, as an adult, could therefore be what he had occasionally been at Eton: a mischievous prankster. It was a sort of rebellion; but it was also the sort of rebellion that was *traditional* at Eton. Orwell's jokes about the Classics were an insider's jokes: he could quote the Latin of Horace with pleasure (*CEJL*, 2:7).

Orwell's early exposure to the ancient world may have left other, more profound effects. He was deeply moved by Flaubert's novel *Salammbô*, a novel based on a classical subject and an ancient Greek writer (Polybius); indeed, in its pessimism about human society, *Salammbô* may well be one of the sources of *Nineteen Eighty-Four*. But in contrast to that pessimism, Orwell was also prepared to admit that an education in Classics could produce a truly civilized person. Thus, the Classics master Porteous is the most benign figure in Orwell's gloomy novel *Coming Up for Air* (1939). Porteous's lodgings are an island of civility in a world going barbaric, and he is the only person whom Orwell's hero George Bowling genuinely likes.

But Porteous is a mere relic of a more secure past, who seems to reflect Orwell's criticism of Classics as irrelevant to modern life. Yet there is also good evidence to suggest that Orwell himself was never completely comfortable with this criticism, and that as he grew older, he had serious second thoughts about it, reassessing the value of a classical education. For one thing, at the crucial turning point in his life—the 1927 decision to become a writer—Orwell went to his old Classics tutor Andrew Gow (and only Gow, of all his Eton teachers) for advice; and Orwell's dealings with Gow, to the end of his life, were always respectful. It is also interesting to find that during his last illness, the author of *Nineteen Eighty-Four* was using the scholarly and language skills he had learned at St. Cyprian's and Eton to attempt to read Dante in the original—though, to be sure, with a crib (*CEJL*, 4:501). Further, at that time Orwell reviewed a novel in which, as in *Coming Up for Air*, a Classics master is a major figure: and he found in the fictional Scott-King a figure to admire, not only for his incorruptibility, but also for his toughness. In this review, in fact, we have hints that as he was dying, Orwell was arriving at a far more positive public assessment of the moral value of a classical education in the ugly modern world. The rote learning of nouns and verbs might be scorned, classical pomposity satirized, but the stubborn Stoic virtues of honesty and honor were a different matter.[3]

One final act, it seems to me, shows Orwell coming full circle. The crusader against the public school regime made sure, before he died, that his adopted son Richard was enrolled in the prestigious Westminster School ("they have abandoned their top hats, I hear"). Richard Horatio Blair was to receive a traditional British public school education.[4]

Orwell's ambivalence toward Classics can already be perceived in his career as a student at Eton. He entered Eton as a King's Scholar— a much sought-after scholarship for which a primary qualification was a high level of proficiency in Greek and Latin.[5] The scholarship put him into the Eton College Election, as opposed to one of the various Houses; this meant he belonged to the elite of the elite. Indeed, in the earliest letter in the *Collected Essays*, we find him referring to the denizens of the Houses (the so-called Oppidans) with the contempt typical of a member of the Election (*CEJL*, 1:11). And at Eton he was originally a Classical Specialist: that is, he took the most difficult Classics curriculum. It was the traditional major among the King's Scholars, the royal road to university and, often enough, high government service.[6]

Young Blair, however, preferred participation in the traditional Eton sports and extracurricular reading (and a bit of writing) to heavy studying. The most obscure member of what was otherwise a brilliant Election,[7] Eric in midcareer also abandoned Classics altogether (*UO*, 113; *GO*, 57). For a year he attempted the Science curriculum instead. This is a sure sign of dissatisfaction with the education he had received at St. Cyprian's and was continuing to receive at Eton; we may even wish to see here a search for an educational experience that would fit him better for the modern world. What is equally important, though, is that in the end he went back to Classics. Apparently his lack of aptitude for mathematics, combined with a general unwillingness to work very hard, led to this decision; so too, perhaps, an inability to find a congenial tutor among the Eton scientists (*GO*, 57). In the end, therefore, he came back under the wing of A. S. F. Gow—but not as a Classical Specialist. He now took the easier (though still quite formidable) Classics curriculum called Classical General, which had a larger admixture of History. In this he persevered, but he only graduated at the lower end of his Eton class.[8]

Orwell's Eton career therefore bears all the earmarks of a grudging compromise. It is tempting to link Eric Blair's evident discomfort in his classical studies with the mature Orwell's criticism of Classics-based education. But we should also remember that Orwell did actually finish a rigorous Eton curriculum based on Classics. Ambivalence is not the same as complete rejection.

Orwell later attacked St. Cyprian's, Eton, and classical education in general for propping up a tradition of English aristocratic class prejudice and snobbery. He recalled that after his education at St. Cyprian's he arrived at Eton "an odious little snob," only to spend the next five years "in a lukewarm bath of snobbery" where he received "training...originally intended for a landowning aristocracy."[9] It is important for us to understand precisely the level of English society Orwell was consorting with in the Classics curriculum at Eton: as an upperclassman, he had as his "fag" the aristocratic Anthony Wagner, later Garter King of Arms; and when he wrote a student broadsheet, his co-authors were a Classical Specialist who would become a brother-in-law of a Prime Minister, and the fabulously wealthy Steven Runciman, the future great Byzantine scholar. Orwell knew what he was talking about when he criticized the connection between Classics, the class system, and snobbery.[10]

Orwell's rebellion against all that helps in part to explain his efforts, most notably in the famous essay "Politics and the English Language" (1946), to purge English of all foreign words—especially Greek and Latin words (*CEJL*, 4:127-40). Orwell argued that such words were often used solely because they were pretentious: "Bad writers, and especially scientific, political and sociological writers, are nearly always haunted by the notion that Greek and Latin words are grander than Saxon ones" (*CEJL*, 4:131, n. 1). He worried that words like these were constantly gaining ground against good plain English, and he warned against "the pretentious latinised style" (*CEJL*, 4:134). At one point he even set himself up as a sort of "Latin-and-Greek Police," ferreting out the pompous classicizing words that deserve purging from his parody of Ecclesiastes.[11] He also set as a conscious public goal the reduction of Latin and Greek in the average English sentence, as part of his program "to make pretentiousness unfashionable" (*CEJL*, 4:138).

This is the Orwell we are most familiar with. But his devotion to "the plain style" was not an early development. Into the mid-1930s, Orwell comfortably used Latin phrases and tags, not only in published work but, more significantly, in private correspondence as well. These involved not just clichés like *mutatis mutandis*, or *extra ecclesiae nulla salus*, but independent Latin constructions like *in articulo mortis* and *in partibus infidelium*, and quotations such as *O mihi praeteritos*.[12] This is also the period when Orwell was willing to publish poems paraphrasing Simonides's famous epitaph for the Spartans who died at Thermopylae.[13] And in *Keep the Aspidistra Flying* (1936), Orwell can have Gordon Comstock proclaim at the crucial point in the novel (and without translation): *vicisti, O aspidistra*.[14]

Even more remarkable is Orwell's attitude toward Latin in *The Road to Wigan Pier* (1937). Here, in his analysis of the problem confronting the socialist movement in Britain, and particularly the haughty relationship of socialist intellectuals to the real working class, Orwell for the first time indicates that Latin is a true anachronism (cf. p. 226). Nevertheless, this long essay on the problems of socialism is itself sprinkled with Latin (and French) phrases: it may be no accident that he never sent copies of the book to the workers he stayed with in Wigan. Indeed, Orwell's use of Latin increases in direct proportion to the amount of anger and anxiety he expresses in the essay (first regarding other intellectuals, then regarding the threat posed by fascism).[15]

But Orwell's direct use of Latin (as well as his penchant for imitating Greek poetry) abruptly disappears about 1937—that is, as the focus of his writing becomes more sharply and continuously political. (In this sense, as in so many others, *Wigan Pier* stands at a crossroads in Orwell's development.[16]) By the mid-1940s, English words with obvious classical roots are themselves being kept to a minimum. Even when Orwell wrote to his old tutor A. S. F. Gow, classicizing words—let alone classical quotations—were absent.[17] The impact of the change is clear: reading through the last three volumes of the *Collected Essays*, one could easily get the false impression that their author was monolingual, instead of actually being fluent in Latin, Greek, and French (including Old French).[18] Moreover, we now know that in the late 1940s Orwell was even keeping a long private list of Latin, Greek, and French words and phrases he wanted eliminated from the language, a list which included even words long established as English. Some selections from that list: *agenda, exit, transit, ego, quorum, versus, status, verbatim, gratis, optimum, crux, sub rosa, deus ex machina, kudos, kinesis.*[19]

Thus Orwell's famous "plain style" was first of all a revolution in his own way of writing. He consciously adopted his new style in an effort to confront, as candidly and directly as possible, the bleak realities he perceived in the modern world. It was also a populist and public-spirited prose, designed to be instantly understandable to any intelligent ordinary person. As he said: "In a peaceful age, I might have written ornate books...and might have remained almost unaware of my political loyalties" (*CEJL*, 1:4). But his was not a peaceful age. Looking back in 1946, Orwell traced the new political focus of his writings to the events of 1936 and 1937, especially the Spanish Civil War (*CEJL*, 1:5): just the period, as we have seen, when his classicism suddenly disappeared.

The plain style allowed Orwell to escape the confines of the class system, and to pretend that he was writing as "a plain Englishman"— which, as an Old Etonian Classicist, he certainly was not. Indeed, one may say that the plain style was an integral part of Orwell's romantic, egalitarian, and very personal socialist ideology. His nonclassical style was thus of a piece with the blue proletarian workshirts he wore—or, as some would say, affected.[20]

But Orwell's championing of "good plain Saxon" over Latin and Greek influence in English always contains a lingering note of ambiguity, satire, and even self-satire. At the end of "Politics and the English Language," Orwell in fact warns against taking simplification and declassicizing too far (*CEJL*, 4:138). And in creating Newspeak he would satirize his own anti-classicism. Orwell himself may have been keeping a private list of foreign words and phrases to be liquidated from English, but the inhabitants of Oceania are forbidden to study any foreign language at all (*NEF*, 162). And if Orwell himself was interested in pruning English vocabulary, that was precisely the sinister job he gave Winston Smith's pathetic friend Syme.[21]

The long, subtly hostile—and, above all, scholarly—exposition of the grammar and vocabulary of Newspeak, the appendix which closes *Nineteen Eighty-Four*, is particularly revealing (*NEF*, 246-56). First of all, this close linguistic analysis, replete with declension of verbs and discussion of present and past participles, everywhere betrays the influence of his public school education. The old intense focus on the principles of grammar, on parts of speech, and on good composition, here bears its final fruit. (It might also be stressed that men of Orwell's education learned their grammar and composition through deep immersion in Latin and Greek, *not* English [*GO*, 67; *CEJL*, 3:178].) Moreover, in the typical sentence of Newspeak which Orwell chooses to dissect in the appendix—namely, "Oldthinkers unbellyfeel Ingsoc" (*NEF*, 250-51)—only the "-soc" (from "socialism") has a classical derivation. All the other monster-words are Anglo-Saxon in origin; and the same is true of the monster-word "Newspeak" itself. None of this was accidental. That Orwell intended us to see that his "good plain Saxon" (presented so approvingly elsewhere) dominates throughout totalitarian Newspeak was clear at least to Anthony Burgess. In Burgess's attempt to do what Orwell claimed could not be done—translate the preamble of the American Declaration of Independence into Newspeak—Burgess came up with a paragraph in which only two words (out of 59) have classical roots.[22]

In contrast to "Oldthinkers unbellyfeel Ingsoc," Orwell continues his analysis of Newspeak with a discussion of words that have been purged from the language. In the world of *Nineteen Eighty-Four*, the words that no longer exist include "*honor, justice, morality, internationalism, democracy, science,* and *religion*" (*NEF*, 251; italics Orwell's). As Bernard Avishai says, Orwell considered these words, and the concepts they expressed, crucial to civilization.[23] And every one of these lost words—every one of these horribly lost concepts—has its roots in classical language and culture.[24] So it may also be no accident that, as Sue Lonoff has pointed out, the language of Goldstein's Book is more "Latinate" than either Newspeak or the rest of *Nineteen Eighty-Four*.[25] In other words: Orwell's use of classicizing prose in Goldstein's Book and the appendix to Newspeak—the two most *truthful* parts of *Nineteen Eighty-Four*—suggest that he had concluded that classically-influenced language, far from obscuring meaning, could convey the full meaning of concepts like *democracy* in a way that "plain language" could not.

Side by side with his more serious criticism of Classics as pretentious and snobbish, Orwell in the late 1930s also began to direct occasional jokes and snide remarks against what had been the basis of his education. For example:

> When the Caliph Omar destroyed the libraries of Alexandria he is supposed to have kept the public baths warm for eighteen days with burning manuscripts, and great numbers of tragedies by Euripides and others are said to have perished, quite irrecoverably. I remember that when I read about this as a boy it simply filled me with enthusiastic approval. It was so many less words to look up in the dictionary.[26]

Also note Orwell's 1939 comments about Dickens and his children: "Why did he not have his sons educated according to some plan of his own, instead of sending them to public school to be stuffed with Greek?" (*CEJL*, 1:445). Or on Swift: "more than one would expect in anyone so free from accepted fallacies, he reveres classical antiquity" (*CEJL*, 3:211). Or again, in "Wells, Hitler and the World State" (1941), note Orwell's attack on "dull-witted schoolmasters sniggering over their Latin tags," and "politicians who could quote Horace but had never heard of algebra" (*CEJL*, 2:144).

The contempt here is patent. Yet this last passage may illuminate, as no other, Orwell's ambivalent attitude toward his classical education: for these are remarks that could have been directed against Orwell himself. It had not been so long before that Orwell had earned his living as a schoolmaster, and had been sprinkling his writing with Latin tags.[27] And it was Eric Blair who at Eton had studied his Horace but had not been able to handle mathematics (see above, p. 99).

Indeed, there is pretty fair evidence that Orwell loved Horace. In 1932 we find him reading the *Odes* with great pleasure (*CEJL*, 1:82). And in an essay written ca. 1940 but not published during his lifetime, we find Orwell quoting Horace and commenting: "I say to myself *Vixi puellis nuper idoneus*, and I repeat this over and over for five minutes for the beauty of the word *idoneus*" (*CEJL*, 2:7).

The egalitarian public persona Orwell constructed is hardly congruent with his fondness for intoning Latin.[28] Nor is it especially congruent with his evident pleasure in purchasing a copy of Lemprière's *Classical Dictionary* (i.e., encyclopedia)—which Gordon Comstock also uses in *Keep the Aspidistra Flying* (*CEJL*, 3:60; cf. *KAF*, 114). Indeed, there are many other indications that, like his public school accent, Orwell never quite got rid of this classical learning. Thus, he is consistent, if a little ironic, in his praise of Homer (whom he had read in the original at Eton). In fact, he can lay out in masterful fashion for a friend just which characters in Joyce's *Ulysses* correspond to the characters in Homer (down to Nausicaa), and he can even discuss—and this may also cause some surprise—the meter of Homer and Virgil in comparison to that of Gerard Manley Hopkins.[29] He also reveals in passing that he has read through Herodotus, and respects Aristophanes and Petronius.[30] The latter is *not* so surprising, however, since at age fourteen Eric Blair had written an entire play, in rhyme, in imitation of Aristophanes (*CEJL*, 1:2). From small remarks made in the 1940s, we also learn that Orwell knew Plutarch on Aristides the Just, and Plato's account of Socrates's death (indeed, while a schoolmaster in the early 1930s, Orwell had been very interested in both Plato and Aristotle)—and kept a Latin dictionary.[31] Then, in the late 1940s, as he became more and more ill, the ironic Latin tag *D.V.* ("God Willing") began to appear in Orwell's private correspondence: a typical Eton touch (*CEJL*, 4:448,449). It is evident that he enjoyed making these classical allusions.

Even in the mid-1940s, at the height of his ideological opposition to "classicizing," when Orwell and his wife Eileen O'Shaugnessy adopted a baby boy, they named him Richard Horatio Blair. "Richard" was a longstanding Blair family name (Orwell's father had been Richard Blair), although the name also seems to have stood for Orwell's friend Richard Rees (*CEJL*, 3:185, n. 2). But the classical "Horatio" is startling. Sonia Brownell, Orwell's second wife, says that Horatio was a Blair family name (ibid.); but if so, it was a very obscure one. We know of no Horatio Blair (or even a Blair with Horatio as a middle name) in the history of the Blair family; certainly no one in Eric Blair's immediate lineage, traced back to 1750, had borne that name for centuries (*UO*, 3-12). And even if Horatio was a (very obscure) Blair family name, it still required Orwell's own personal initiative to propose it (both his parents being dead).

The name is most obviously in part a patriotic gesture, a reference to the great military hero Horatio Nelson. This would make sense in the context of the Second World War, and, as is well known, Orwell's assertive English patriotism set him apart from many intellectuals of his generation.[32] The name Horatio, however, points in another direction too: to antiquity, to that other military hero, the Roman Horatio who had defended the bridge. And as it also happens, the Latin poet most often cited by Orwell could claim allegiance (via manumission and name adoption) to the same clan as the Roman military hero: Horace (Q. Horatius Flaccus).

Orwell's early exposure to classical antiquity and its culture may have had a still deeper effect on him, even in the late 1930s to mid-1940s. At Eton, he not only took classical literature, but also a good dose of ancient history (*UO*, 114). In the autumn of 1938, while he was recuperating in Morocco from wounds suffered fighting for the Left in the Spanish Civil War, he read *Salammbô*, by Gustave Flaubert (*CEJL*, 1:370). This is a novel dealing with the so-called Mercenary War of 241-238 B.C., a war fought between Carthage and her own mercenary soldiers originally hired to fight Rome in the First Punic War. Flaubert based his novel on the detailed account of the bloody, no-quarter conflict between Carthage and the Mercenaries written by the great Greek historian Polybius of Megalopolis (second century B.C.). Like Polybius, Flaubert gave a central place in the narrative to the fierce Hamilcar Barca, the father of Hannibal (the fictional Salammbô is Hamilcar's daughter). It is quite striking to find the post-1936 Orwell interested enough in this obscure topic to pick up Flaubert's book. It was a book he knew about, even if he had avoided it earlier (ibid.). This is understandable, for *Salammbô* seems to have been a favorite among students of ancient history in Orwell's youth. When I questioned Sir Ronald Syme about *Salammbô* in March of 1985—a man of Orwell's generation, and the dean of British ancient historians—he was able to quote by heart the opening passage of the novel, in French.[33]

Orwell not only now read *Salammbô*, he was deeply impressed with it. "Simply stunning," he called it at the time; in 1944 he described it as "a great novel," twice saying that it was far better than his friend Arthur Koestler's attempt to imagine antiquity in *The Gladiators*. (We see here how Orwell could be quite confident about his knowledge of ancient culture.[34]) Orwell was impressed most by what he deemed Flaubert's success in accurately depicting a pre-Christian mentality: a mentality Orwell characterized as "utterly merciless," dominated by "stony cruelty" (*CEJL*, 2:236-37). Flaubert's world was a place where the two sides in a war were each worse than the other, more savage, more progressively heartless (in this, Flaubert follows Polybius), and the novel ends with the torture and destruction of the only character at all motivated by love. Critics at the time were greatly upset by the novel's unremitting pessimism: Sainte-Beuve wrote that Flaubert did not show men as they are but as far worse than they are, and that he had chosen always to depict the worst in men in preference to anything

else.[35] But is is clear that in Orwell's bitter mood of 1938—in the aftermath of the destruction of his beloved Anarchists in Spain, slaughtered
by both the Fascists and the Communists—the social pessimism of
Salammbô had an enormous attraction. After all, within a year Orwell
himself would be writing for the very first time of the death of "liberal-Christian culture" and the specter of worldwide totalitarianism
from which there might be no escape (*CEJL*, 1:525-26, from "Inside the
Whale"). Cruel realism is what Orwell says he found most impressive
about *Salammbô*.

   The connection here is more than just a momentary emotional
catharsis in 1938. For Orwell soon came to believe that he was in fact
living in an age when the worst aspects of the ancient world might be
returning. Hence, for instance, his remarks about slavery—which he
repeatedly associated with the world of *Salammbô*.[36] In "Looking Back
on the Spanish War" (1942), after criticizing the naive British as having
been brought up for generations on happy endings, Orwell comments:

> Consider for instance the re-institution of slavery. Who could have
> imagined twenty years ago that slavery would return to Europe?
> Well, slavery has been restored under our own noses. The forced-
> labour camps all over Europe...are simple chattel slavery.... We
> don't grasp its full implications, because...we feel that a régime
> founded on slavery *must* collapse. But it is worth comparing the
> duration of the slave empires of antiquity with that of any mod-
> ern state. Civilisations founded on slavery have lasted for such
> periods as four thousand years. (*CEJL*, 2:259-60)

This was not the only place where Orwell remarked on "the return of
slavery" from antiquity, or expressed concern about the horrid, mil-
lenia-long stability such "slave-based" civilizations might have (see
CEJL, 2:248; 3:198). These ideas reoccur, in fact, in the climactic torture scenes in *Nineteen Eighty-Four*. When Winston doubts that a civilization can be founded on fear, hatred, and cruelty, O'Brien assures
him that it certainly can, for the proletarians and the slaves can never
rise up of their own accord, "not in a thousand years."[37]

   From 1938 onward, Orwell warned repeatedly about the worst of
the ancient past becoming a pattern for the totalitarian future. I think
it is possible that his reading of *Salammbô*, in the wake of his traumatic experience of brutal politics in Spain, planted this idea in his
head. If this is correct, then *Salammbô*, with its nightmarish pessimism,
would also stand as one of the (many) ultimate sources of *Nineteen
Eighty-Four*—and one not previously noticed.[38] But here, my main
point is that Orwell's early exposure to ancient history at Eton, as part
of his Classics curriculum, helps explain why he picked up a book

like *Salammbô* in the first place. As Orwell himself said in 1942, "One effect of the ghastly history of the past twenty years has been to make a great deal of ancient literature seem much more modern."[39]

That statement brings into focus—and stands in great contrast to—Orwell's earlier assertion that classical education does not prepare people for the horrors of the modern age. Orwell was now beginning to find ancient pessimism about the human condition (for instance, the pessimism of Horace) quite relevant. The ancient Stoic virtues associated with that pessimism, as defended (for instance) by Marcus Aurelius, were taught as part of the public school education Orwell had received (*GO*, 62). In the end, he may have thought they counted for something.

Orwell's ambivalent criticism of classical education is incarnated very well in the character of the Classics master Porteous, in the novel *Coming Up for Air* (1939). Porteous, a man lost in his books, secluded amid his Greek and Latin and pipesmoke in his cozy apartment, is impervious to the most lethal threat to world civilization:

> Hitler? This German person? My dear fellow! I *don't* think of him...I see no reason for paying any attention to him. A mere adventurer. These people come and go. Ephemeral, purely ephemeral. (*CUA*, 185)

George Bowling is amazed at that attitude. He comes to the conclusion that Porteous is "a ghost," that his mind stopped working sometime around 1905, and that people like him cannot defend themselves against the horror that is coming, for they cannot see it when it is right under their noses (*CUA*, 188). It is typical of Porteous that he has never read a modern book, and does not even own a radio. He is "wonderfully learned," but he "just says the same things and thinks the same thoughts over and over again. There are a lot of people like that. Dead minds, stopped inside" (*CUA*, 182-83, 188).

The image of people still living in the Edwardian era—a peaceful and secure era now long gone—is a consistent one in Orwell's writing after 1936; and classical education is an integral part of that image.[40] It is therefore not surprising that some critics believe Porteous was meant to be primarily a negative figure.[41]

But in fact the issue is complicated. Orwell's image of the Edwardian era is a heavily nostalgic one; and to reverse Patrick Reilly's formulation, every minus of Porteous has a plus to it. Porteous is above all a decent man, tellingly contrasted with the hate-mongering speaker at the Left Book Club meeting. Bowling fears that the latter represents the real future:

> The world we're going down into, the kind of hate-world, slogan-world. The coloured shirts, the barbed wire, the rubber truncheons. The secret cells where the electric light burns night and day.... (*CUA*, 176)

Compared to this, Porteous comes as something of a relief. Nor is he, despite his otherworldliness, meant to be seen as completely "unmanly": note the old leather armchairs, the whisky-and-sodas, the pipe.[42] And if Porteous is encapsulated in the past, this is attractive to Bowling, who throughout the novel has been lost in his *own* fond memories of pre-1914:

> The classy Oxford feeling of nothing mattering except books and poetry and Greek statues, and nothing worth mentioning having happened since the Goths sacked Rome—sometimes that's a comfort too.... When I'm fed up with business and home life it's often done me a lot of good to go have a talk with Porteous. (*CUA*, 182, 184)

Porteous is not a comfort on this particular night, of course, for Bowling fears that men like Porteous, trusting in what they call "the eternal verities" and therefore not taking modern politics seriously, will soon allow "Culture" to be destroyed (*CUA*, 186). Nevertheless, it is clear enough that Porteous *is* often a solace. Bowling genuinely likes the Classics master (of what other character in this gloomy novel can that be said?); he shares Porteous's sentiment that the modern world ought never to have happened; he enjoys listening to Porteous read poetry; he does not find him much of a snob (*CUA*, 182-84, 187-89). The portrait is not unsympathetic.

And that makes sense. Bowling, the practical man who longs for the past but tries to confront the modern world, is obviously an Orwell *alter ego* (*CEJL*, 4:422). But we should remember also that Orwell himself had been a master at a public school just five or six years before he wrote *Coming Up for Air* (and that he would continue to try to be a poet). The tall, thin Porteous, the poetic retired schoolmaster, is thus in fact another "Blair-that-might-have-been."[43]

The Porteous that was Orwell's *alter ego* naturally brings to the fore A. S. F. Gow, Orwell's Classics tutor at Eton. Given Orwell's divided (and often hostile) attitude toward classical education, it comes as something of a surprise to learn that this relationship lasted Orwell's entire life. Andrew Gow knew St. Cyprian's School and its graduates well.[44] At Eton, Gow not only taught young Eric Blair his Homer, but also invited him into a small creative-writing circle. Some witnesses claim that Gow saw potential in Blair that no one else did—though

Gow himself later denied this (*UO*, 107-8; *GO*, 63). At any rate, in 1922 Gow told the Blair family that Eric was unlikely to do well enough in scholarship examinations to get the financial aid he needed to attend Oxford or Cambridge; the Classics master's role in Eric's eventual decision to go into the Indian Imperial Police—the young man's chosen, and perhaps preferred, alternative to university—is less clear.[45] What is highly significant is that in late 1927, when Blair was considering resigning from the Indian Police in order to become a free-lance writer, he went to stay with Gow (now a Fellow of Trinity College, Cambridge) and asked for his advice. As Crick says, this is a sure sign that Blair felt "respect and affection" for Gow: he consulted no other of his Eton teachers. Gow was not greatly enthusiastic about the decision, warning Blair of the practical problems (especially financial ones) he would face—a warning Orwell later acknowledged to have been valid. But neither was Gow adamantly opposed ("I said he might as well have a try"), and the conversations at Cambridge were evidently of some importance in confirming Blair in his decision (*GO*, 105; *CEJL*, 4:147).

There ensued a gap of more than twenty years during which the two men did not meet (Orwell later said that in 1927 they were already moving into different worlds). Nevertheless, a few letters did pass between them.[46] One of those letters is in Orwell's *Collected Essays*: it brings Gow up to date on Orwell's activities since before the Second World War, and what is noticeable about this letter is its respectful—even deferential—tone.[47] Finally, as Orwell lay dying in University College Hospital in January 1950, Gow was one of the last people to see him. According to Orwell's sister Avril Dunn, Orwell was in fact embarrassed during the visit because of his young son Richard's "farmyard" (Saxon!) language: he feared it was unsuitable for the distinguished classical scholar's ears (*GO*, 403). For his part, we know that Andrew Gow took an intense private interest in the preservation of Orwell's literary reputation.[48]

It is possible to discern here a very long-term relationship of mutual affection and respect. Respect for an individual classicist does not, of course, necessarily equate to respect for Classics in general. Yet an interesting picture emerges when we combine the interpretation of the fictional classicist Porteous offered above, with Orwell's evident affection and respect for A. S. F. Gow.[49]

And a year or so before Orwell's last meeting with Gow, Orwell wrote a review (February 1949) which suggests that he was indeed coming around to a more favorable general opinion of classicists and classical education. In Evelyn Waugh's *Scott-King's Modern Europe*, Orwell had an excellent opportunity to engage once more in an attack upon classical education as useless in the modern world. The balding, middle-aged Scott-King, senior Classics master at Grantchester, a respectable (if not very important) public school, is "a praiser of the past and a lover of exact scholarship." He is invited by the tyrannical government of "Neutralia" to partake in a scholarly conference on a seventeenth-century Latin poet. For most of the book, Scott-King is an unwitting pawn of the vicious Neutralian state, which is only interested in the indirect endorsement the assemblage of scholars can confer on it. In the end, he barely escapes Neutralia with his life, under the most humiliating circumstances—and totally naked. Back at Grantchester, the headmaster informs him that Classics is increasingly out of favor and suggests that he combine it with something more up-to-date and practical. Scott-King's humiliation is now complete—except that he stubbornly refuses to follow the headmaster's suggestion.

In short, Scott-King is a Porteous who is forced to confront "that German person." But the Orwell of 1949 is not the Orwell of *Coming Up for Air*. He is more sure of the superiority of Porteous's and Scott-King's "eternal verities" over "modernity."

First of all, it is clear that Orwell admires Scott-King's sheer refusal to compromise his principles. He quotes, with evident relish, Scott-King's climactic retort to the headmaster who urges him to begin teaching something more modern and practical:

> "Parents are not interested in producing the 'complete man' any more. They want to qualify their boys for jobs in the modern world. You can hardly blame them, can you?"
> "Oh yes," said Scott-King, "I can and do."[50]

Orwell respected toughness, and Scott-King can be tough.

But second, there is Orwell's attitude toward the *content* of Scott-King's principles: his love of the culture of the classical past. To Scott-King, the modern world is so insane and so unlikely to survive that it is an act of self-corruption to understand it or attempt to come to terms with it. Orwell vividly explains:

> In the chaos that is shortly coming, a few moral principles that one can cling to, and perhaps even a few half-remembered odes of Horace or choruses of Euripides, will be more useful than what is now called "Enlightenment."[51]

It should be stressed that these are Orwell's words, not Scott-King's. It is therefore striking to find Horace once more receiving a positive evaluation.[52] Moreover, Orwell now is not as dismissive of Scott-King as Bowling was of Porteous's attitude here:

> There is something to be said for this view.... One can accept Scott-King's estimate of the modern world, and perhaps even agree with him that a classical education is the best prophylactic against insanity.[53]

"A classical education is the best prophylactic against insanity." That is an absolutely astounding comment to come from Orwell's pen. It marks a significant shift: the first directly positive statement on the enduring value of a classical education in all of Orwell's work.

A shift, of course, is not a revolution. Orwell takes Scott-King—and his creator Evelyn Waugh—sharply to task for their ignorance of modern dictatorship. He does not see how intentional ignorance is, or ever can be, an advantage. He blames Waugh's perfunctory research for creating a politically incoherent Neutralia, presented as a dictatorship of the Right while possessing all the characteristics of a dictatorship of the Left. (Orwell makes it clear that he would have preferred Neutralia to have been presented straightforwardly as a communist state.) While agreeing now with Scott-King that a deep classical education can protect one against modern insanity, he still feels the schoolmaster could fight the modern world more effectively if he would occasionally read a sixpenny pamphlet on Marxism.[54] Nevertheless, if Orwell is impatient with Scott-King here, it is because he is largely on Scott-King's side—as Bowling was on Porteous's side, and perhaps more so.

Orwell's review of *Scott-King's Modern Europe* was one of the last essays he ever published. We cannot know if his attitude toward classical education would have undergone a further shift. But we have already noted that Orwell in the end intended his son Richard to have a traditional British public school education: indeed, much money was put aside for the task (*CEJL*, 4:503, cf. 505; *GO*, 404). And there is one further, tantalizing fact to add. One of Orwell's projects, never completed, was a long essay on George Gissing, whom Orwell considered one of the great British novelists of the nineteenth century (*CEJL*, 4:506). Yet Gissing was also a classical scholar, and in a preliminary study, Orwell could write (in summer 1948) in the following way about Gissing's confrontation with the modern, industrializing world:

> Gissing was a bookish, perhaps over-civilised man, in love with classical antiquity, who found himself trapped in a cold, smoky Protestant country.... Gissing did not, at least consciously, even want to be the kind of writer he was. His ideal, a rather melancholy one, was to have a moderate private income and live in a small comfortable house in the country, preferably unmarried, where he could wallow in books, especially the Greek and Latin classics.... As it was, he spent his life in what appeared to him to be hackwork. (*CEJL*, 4:429-30, 435)

This description is not without a certain sad sympathy for Gissing's desire to withdraw from industrial England into classicism. The image, of course, is that of Porteous in his study.

At the least, then, Orwell's new work on Gissing would have forced him once more to contemplate Porteous, to contemplate the role of Classics and classical education in modern life. We have seen that Orwell's opinions here were always complex. More importantly, those opinions were constantly being revised throughout his life according to his different experiences. We can therefore be sure that the re-evaluation of Classics detectable in his review of *Scott-King's Modern Europe* would not have been Orwell's last word on the subject.[55]

Notes

1. Orwell's "socialism" was of a very particular and personal kind, and his political development in fact followed a pessimistic trajectory: see my "George Orwell's Second Thoughts on Capitalism," below (Chapter 11).
2. See *GO*, 55. On Orwell's curriculum at Eton, see also *UO*, 107-15.
3. See George Orwell, "Mr. Waugh Pays a Visit to Perilous Neutralia," a review of *Scott-King's Modern Europe*, by Evelyn Waugh, *New York Times Book Review*, 20 February 1949, 1, 25 (not in *CEJL*).
4. *CEJL*, 4:503, cf. 505. See also *GO*, 404 (financial arrangements).
5. For a detailed (and hostile) discussion of young Eric Blair's preparations for the language examinations, see *CEJL*, 4:336-38 ("Such, Such Were the Joys").
6. Orwell's concentration in Classics: *UO*, 113-15; *GO*, 55, 57, 67 (Greek and Latin). Note also *GO*, 59 (Orwell was taught French by Aldous Huxley, then a temporary Eton master famous for his emphasis on correct word usage). Of Orwell's Eton Election of fourteen boys, eleven went on to Oxford or Cambridge, while two joined family businesses. See Martin Green, "Orwell as an Old Etonian," *Modern Fiction Studies* 21 (1975): 4.
7. "Who on earth would have thought that Blair would have turned into Orwell?"—Kenneth Johnstone, a classmate, in 1976 (*GO*, 60). See also Green, "Orwell as Etonian," 3.
8. Orwell placed 117th out of a list of 140 graduates; only one member of his Election placed lower. See *UO*, 114.
9. Orwell on Classics and class prejudice: See *CEJL*, 1:460-84 ("Boys' Weeklies"); *CEJL*, 4:335-41 ("Such, Such Were the Joys"). The connection is already made, briefly, in *The Road to Wigan Pier* (1937), 169. On St. Cyprian's, Eton, and snobbery, see George Orwell, "For Ever Eton," *Observer*, 1 August 1948, from which the quotations in the text are taken (not in *CEJL*).
10. (Sir) Anthony Wagner: *GO*, 74. On the *Eton Election Times*, which Orwell edited with (Sir) Roger Mynors, later Corpus Christi Professor of Latin Languages and Literature at Oxford, and brother-in-law of Sir Alec Douglas-Home, and to which (Sir) Steven Runciman also contributed: see Denys King-Farlow, "Eton Days with George Orwell,"" in *Orwell*

Remembered, ed. Audrey Coppard and Bernard Crick (New York: Facts on File Publications, 1984), 55.

11. *CEJL*, 4:133-34 (he found 19 classicizing words out of a total of 38 in the parody).

12. See *CEJL*, 1:34, 80, 96, 102, 138, 236-37.

13. *CEJL*, 1:145 (note the beginning of stanza five) and 166 (the obituary for John Flory in *Burmese Days*, cut by the publisher: note the beginning of stanza three).

14. *KAF*, 240 ("You have won, O aspidistra"). The aspidistra is shaped "like Agamemnon's sword," 21.

15. Latin phrases in *RWP*: *obiter dicta, advocatus diaboli, et hoc genus, mutatis mutandis, in vacuo, in saecula saeculorum, contra mundum, pace, vide* (three times). These phrases are concentrated especially in pp. 205-12 and 244-47, where Orwell is most agitated.

16. After *RWP*, there is a six-year gap in Orwell's use of Latin (none, for instance, in *Homage to Catalonia*); then one small exception appears in 1942 (*CEJL*, 2:251), and another in 1943 (2:323).

17. *CEJL*, 4:146-48. The most "elevated" word in this letter is "apropos." "Ghastly" is an upper-class Etonian adjective. But this is balanced by the vigorous English of "hack work," "rubbish," "racket," and "it was a bad job Bobby Longden getting killed."

18. See the perceptive comments of Hugh Kenner, "The Politics of the Plain Style," in *Reflections on America, 1984*, ed. Robert Mulvihill (Athens, Ga., and London: University of Georgia Press, 1986), 63.

19. The purge list is in an unpublished notebook in the Orwell Archive, University College, London. On this list, see Richard W. Bailey, "George Orwell and the English Language," in *The Future of Nineteen Eighty-Four*, ed. Ejner J. Jensen (Ann Arbor: University of Michigan Press, 1984), 35, and 44 n. 15.

20. The blue proletarian workshirts: see the comments of T. R. Fyvel, *George Orwell: A Personal Memoir* (New York: Macmillan, 1982), 99. On "the plain style" as conscious artifice, see especially Kenner, "Politics," 58-65.

21. *NEF*, 45-46 (Syme: "It's a beautiful thing, the destruction of words...").

22. Anthony Burgess, *1985* (Boston: Little, Brown, 1978), 41 (the two words are "disease" and "parents"). By contrast, the original text by Thomas Jefferson, quoted by Orwell in *NEF*, 256, contains 23 words of classical derivation, including crucial concepts such as *equality, liberty,* and *consent*. That Newspeak is overwhelmingly Anglo-Saxon is noted by Bailey, "Orwell and Language", 34, though only in passing.

23. Bernard Avishai, "Orwell and the English Language," in *1984 Revisited,*, ed. Irving Howe (New York: Harper & Row, 1983), 58.

24. Six words are Latin in origin, one ("democracy") is Greek. It is now clear that one of Orwell's satirical targets in the appendix on Newspeak was C. K. Ogden's simplified "Basic English"—although Orwell had in fact been very interested in "Basic" during his stint at the BBC in the early 1940s. On this, see William J. West, *Orwell: The War Broadcasts* (London: Duckworth/BBC, 1985), 8, 47-48, 62-64.

25. See Sue Lonoff's essay (above Chapter 3).

26. *CEJL*, 3:178. This passage, incidentally, confirms the picture of the young Eric Blair struggling through the classical canon line by line. That is: it is a typical insider's joke.

27. Orwell worked for some eighteen months, in 1932-1933, as a headmaster of a small school in the suburbs of London (see *UO*, 299-300; *GO*, 138). He moved on to a larger and more prestigious prep school in the autumn of 1933, but was taken ill and had to quit; that was the last of his teaching career (*GO*, 153-54). On classicism in his writing in this period, see above, pp. 100-01.

28. Orwell goes on in this essay to remark his "ignorance" of Latin (ibid.)— but since he had studied Latin intensively from the age of eight until he was eighteen, including Horace at Eton, I see no reason to take this seriously. No one who is actually ignorant of Latin goes around quoting Horace! Perhaps his additional comment here reflects a certain continuing embarrassment at his actual classical learning. Note also *CEJL*, 2:274, a reference to "Horace's famous ode '*Eheu fugaces*'." Famous to whom?

29. Praise of Homer: *CEJL*, 3:259; 4:505. Homer compared with Joyce: *CEJL*, 1:127 (a letter to Brenda Salkeld). Homeric and Virgilian meter compared with Hopkins: *CEJL*, 2:132.

30. Herodotus: *CEJL*, 3:167; Aristophanes: *CEJL*, 3:260; Petronius: *CEJL*, 4:258.

31. Aristides the Just: *CEJL*, 4:439; Plato and Aristotle: *CEJL*, 3:267, cf. 1:129; the Latin dictionary: *CEJL*, 4:256.

32. The idea that "Horatio" stands for Horatio Nelson the admiral was suggested to me by Professor James S. Cockburn. Note that as a child, Eric Blair was a great naval enthusiast: see *CEJL*, 1:538 ("My Country Right or Left"), and *GO*, 11.

33. Interview with Sir Ronald Syme, Dumbarton Oaks Center for Byzantine Studies, Washington, D.C., March 1985.

34. *CEJL*, 3:198, 236-37. For other self-confident analyses of classical society, see also 3:65 (suggesting a reading of Thucydides), and "Will Freedom Die with Capitalism?" *Left News*, April 1941, 1683 (suggesting a reading of Plutarch's life of Tiberius Sempronius Gracchus) (not in *CEJL*).

35. C. A. Sainte-Beuve, "*Salammbô*," *La Constitutionelle* (Paris), 22 December 1862.16

36. For the association (though the Mercenary War was not, strictly speaking, a slave revolt), see *CEJL*, 3:198, 236-37.

37. A stable civilization founded on fear, hatred, and cruelty: *NEF*, 221-22. "Not in a thousand years or a million": 216. (The whole torture scene looks like a satire on the Socratic method of teaching which Orwell would have found described in his reading of Plato.)

38. That there is a profound connection between the two books is suggested by the fact that they evoked very similar hostile reactions in some critics: like Orwell, Flaubert was accused of having fallen victim to "the mysticism of cruelty." That famous phrase, of course, is Isaac Deutscher's: "*1984*: The Mysticism of Cruelty," in *Russia in Transition* (London, 1957), reprinted in *Orwell's Nineteen Eighty-Four: Text, Sources, Criticism*, ed. Irving Howe (New York: Harcourt Brace Jovanovich, 1963): 196-203. But compare the remarks of Sainte-Beuve on *Salammbô* (above, p.105-06 and n.36).

39. *CEJL*, 2:206 ("The Discovery of Europe"). It is not likely that Orwell was drawn to *Salammbô* because of a preexisting and intense interest in Flaubert: though Orwell considered Flaubert one of his twelve favorite authors (*CEJL*, 2:24), this judgment was probably based almost solely on *Salammbô* itself. Thus there is no evidence that Orwell ever read Flaubert's masterpiece *Madame Bovary* (cf. *GO*, 137-38)—if he did read it, he never made any intellectual use of it—and his references to *Bouvard et Pécuchet* came to less than five words all told (*CEJL*, 1:456; 2:163). The contrast with the repeated discussion of *Salammbô* is obvious. It is possible that Orwell took *Salammbô* to Morocco partly because the setting of the novel is ancient North Africa—although Carthage is 1000 miles northeast of Marrakech, where Orwell and his wife stayed.

40. See *CEJL*, 2:171; 4:430; also 1:471-79 ("Boys' Weeklies": "the clock has stopped at 1910"); 2:68-72, and 98 ("The Lion and the Unicorn"); and 4:335-38 ("Such, Such Were the Joys").

41. See most recently Patrick Reilly, *George Orwell: The Age's Adversary* (London: Macmillian, 1986), 222-23; and Joseph Browne, "The Times of Their Lives: George Orwell's *Coming Up for Air*," in *Critical Essays on George Orwell*, ed. Bernard Oldsey and Joseph Browne (Boston: Little, Brown, 1986), 158.

42. *CUA*, 182. On Orwell's "masculine ideology," see Daphne Patai, *The Orwell Mystique* (Amherst: University of Massachusetts Press, 1984), passim (to be used with caution, however, despite an excellent basic insight). Orwell does have Bowling describe Porteous as telling smutty jokes in a "rather old-maidish" way, though Bowling also says that dirty stories are a common ground between them (*CUA*, 184). Orwell was, in this respect, not much different from Porteous: see, for instance, the strange scene described by Susan Watson, "Canonbury Square and Jura," in *Orwell Remembered* (above, n. 10), 219.

43. Amid other similarities, note that the classicist Porteous wears Orwell's own old "disgraceful" Harris tweed jacket: *CUA*, 181; cf. Anthony Powell, "A Memoir by Anthony Powell," in *Orwell Remembered* (above, n. 10), 238.

44. See Gow's 1967 letter to Sonia Orwell, quoted in *GO*, 31. This raises the possibility that Gow was in fact instrumental in getting the young Classics scholar Eric Blair admitted to Eton from St. Cyprian's in the first place.

45. Eric met personally with Gow to discuss this decision (*UO*, 143). Gow later denied having recommended the Imperial Police as an alternative to university (*GO*, 73). It is possible that he acquiesced in something young Blair wished to do anyway (*UO*, 218).

46. *UO*, 219. Gow enjoyed keeping up with all his old students: see *Times* (London), 15 January 1979 (Gow obituary).

47. *CEJL*, 4:146-48. Note especially the postscript: "You couldn't be expected to read all the books your ex-pupils have produced, but I wonder whether you saw my last book but one, *Animal Farm*? If not I'd be happy to send you a copy. It is very short and might amuse you."

48. See Gow's 1967 letter to Sonia Orwell, quoted in *GO*, 31. This letter reveals an altogether warmer feeling for Orwell than Gow ever publicly admitted. (On Gow's reticence here, see also next note.)

49. Gow was famous for being the driest and most exacting of classical schol-
    ars, both in print and in lecture; yet he also seems to have been a kind
    man toward his students. See King-Farlow (above, n. 10), 57; acknowl-
    edged directly by Orwell in *CEJL*, 1:225, and indirectly in "For Ever Eton"
    (above, n. 9). It is uncertain whether Orwell was aware of yet another
    side of Gow: he was a machine-gun instructor at Eton early in the First
    World War, and in the mid-1930s (at the age of 50) learned to fly an air-
    plane in order to be better able to evaluate candidates for the RAF (*Times*,
    15 January 1979: Gow obituary). For some reason, Gow in public always
    played down his relationship with Blair/Orwell, from the times at Eton
    right to the last meeting, which Gow presented as an accident: surely false,
    as Crick shows (*GO*, 403). A new Gow mystery has recently come to light:
    Brian Sewell, a close friend of the Soviet spy Anthony Blunt, has accused
    Gow of having recruited Blunt for Soviet intelligence in the first place, this
    on the basis of an alleged conversation with the aged Gow himself, ca.
    1977. See Barrie Penrose and Simon Freeman, *Conspiracy of Silence: The
    Secret Life of Anthony Blunt* (London: Grafton Books, 1986), 479-81. It is
    true that Gow and Blunt were close friends (Blunt felt that the *Times* obit-
    uary gave insufficient attention to Gow's kindliness: see his letter to the
    Times of 22 January 1979). But the trustworthiness of the spy story is com-
    pletely uncertain: why should the normally taciturn Gow have revealed
    his deepest secret to Sewell, a man he barely knew? (On the other hand,
    why should Sewell have made this spectacular accusation against a
    respectable but hardly famous Classics don who was now long dead?) See
    the comments of Penrose and Freeman, 480-81.
50. Orwell, "Mr. Waugh Visits Perilous Neutralia" (above, n. 3), 25.
51. Ibid.
52. The reference in this passage to the possible moral and aesthetic value of
    Euripides also puts into perspective Orwell's joke at Euripides' expense
    (quoted above, p. 103) at *CEJL*, 3:178.
53. "Perilous Neutralia," 25.
54. Ibid.
55. Note that in his last months, Orwell was reading Dante (in the original):
    CEJL, 4:501 (see above, p. 98). Given the presence in the *Divine Comedy*
    of so many figures from antiquity and classical literature (not least Virgil),
    one wonders what impact this project of Orwell's might eventually have
    had on his own writing. He would have been thinking about these ancient
    people (or the fourteenth-century version of them) quite a lot.

"That Frightful Torrent of Trash": Crime/Detective Fiction and *Nineteen Eighty-Four*

W. Russel Gray

Nineteen Eighty-Four cogently demonstrates that popularity need not be the kiss of death to a novel's literary prospects. With a bow to the Russian formalist critics, Ken Worpole identified the *modus vivendi* in such works: "Many important achievements in literature arise through the 'canonization' of inferior (sub-literary) genres'…. Dostoyevsky's novels were in essence crime novels."[1]

The coexistence of "low" and "high" elements in a distinguished novel invites the distinction Mark Rose makes between individual texts and the idea of genres. Though concepts of genres provide an "environment" or "matrix" that facilitates the composition of texts, individual texts need not fall wholly into separate genres. As Rose illustrates, though *The Aeneid* is classifiable as an epic, Sidney's *Arcadia* needs to be received as an epic and a pastoral, and Joyce's *Ulysses* as a "metaphorical extension of the novel into epic." Hence "texts are comparable to language itself; they exist as elements within a continuously changing system of mutually defining terms."[2]

Rarely has a novel as literarily respectable as *Nineteen Eighty-Four* attracted such widespread readership. In the four decades since its publication its popularity has increased exponentially. Its importance was well established by 1970, when Lawrence Malkin could confidently declare that, since World War II, "no political book…fiction or nonfiction…has passed more thoroughly into the English language and the popular consciousness."[3] However, to attain a readership estimated at tens of millions (in sixty-two languages) by the year of its eponymous title,[4]

Nineteen Eighty-Four presumably benefited from factors other than increasing political relevance. One of these, hitherto unacknowledged, was Orwell's close interest in crime fiction as a barometer of changing social and political morality.

In articles published in 1944 in separate languages, Orwell made two significant points about fiction and crime. As in "Raffles and Miss Blandish," he maintained in "Grandeur et Décadence du Roman Policier Anglais" that the crimes in older fiction tended to be petty rather than violent, and the protagonist tended to be a talented, gentlemanly individualist—be he outlaw or detective—rather than a policeman with a powerful organization behind him.[5] It alarmed Orwell that during the 1930s and 1940s the popularity of crime fiction was growing despite an escalation of its violence and a continuing debasement of police figures. At the time when he was making notes for what was to become *Nineteen Eighty-Four*, Orwell was persuaded that crime stories and, if we include his views in "The Decline of the English Murder" (1946), real crimes reflected a decline in taste.

Orwell's growing concern, coupled with his familiarity with crime thrillers and detective stories he did respect ("Good Bad Books"), may have provoked him to speculate via *Nineteen Eighty-Four* upon the shape a crime story of a totalitarian future might take.

Even while disparaging the "literary" value of contemporary crime fiction in 1936, Orwell was well aware of its popularity. In "Bookshop Memories" he remarked that male customers preferred either "novels it is possible to respect" or detective stories. He cited one man who had read four or five of the latter weekly for over a year—plus others from another library—never reading the same one twice. By Orwell's estimate, "that frightful torrent of trash" would amount each year to enough pages to cover nearly three quarters of an acre (*CEJL*, 1:244-45). At this time in Britain alone several hundred such stories were published yearly.[6]

The 1940s brought no abatement. At the entrances to London's underground bomb shelters portable "raid libraries" supplied mystery stories and nothing else—by popular demand.[7] Writing in 1944 of such grim nights, Orwell remarked that the ultraviolence of James Hadley Chase's *No Orchids for Miss Blandish* had helped console his countrymen from the "boredom of being bombed." In Chase's novel Orwell noted eight "full-dress" murders, numerous "casual killings and woundings," an exhumation, the flogging of one lady and the hot-cigarette torture of another, a rubber hose-pipe rape, and a third-degree scene of "unheard of cruelty" (*CEJL*, 3:217-18).

Commenting on public absorption in fictional violence, Orwell referred to a cartoon in which a newsstand customer ignores a display of war headlines only to request a pulp called *Action Stories*. To Orwell that man represented "all the drugged millions to whom the world of gangsters...is more 'real', more 'tough', than such things as wars, revolutions, earthquakes, famines, and pestilences" (*CEJL*, 3:218). In "Raffles/Blandish" Orwell also was intrigued by an ominous shift of sympathies in the adventure stories popular with British and Americans. Formerly heroic figures ("Robin Hood, Popeye the Sailor, Jack the Giant-Killer") were giving way to less admirable protagonists ("Jack the Dwarf-Killer").

If one projected the trend a few more decades, the end result might resemble the fate of Winston Smith in the torture chambers of Miniluv, where Orwell's protagonist is initiated into the power/cruelty mystique adumbrated in "Raffles/Blandish." Particularly striking in this connection is Orwell's reading of the victimized Miss Blandish's suicide in Chase's novel: she had developed such a fondness for her rapist that she was unable to live without him. In *Nineteen Eighty-Four* the power-cruelty bond (or bondage) links Winston and his captor, whose use of a hypodermic recalls the drugging of Miss Blandish. Also, toward *his* violator Winston develops not only dependence but strange affection:

> a blissful, healing warmth spread all through his body. The pain was already half forgotten. He opened his eyes and looked up gratefully at O'Brien. At the sight of the heavy, lined face, so ugly and so intelligent, his heart seemed to turn over. If he could have moved he would have stretched out a hand and laid it on O'Brien's arm. He had never loved him so deeply as at this moment. (*NEF*, 208)

Four years before he would complete *Nineteen Eighty-Four*, Orwell stated in "Raffles/Blandish" that the highspots in power/cruelty thrillers were likely to be scenes of cruelty. The truncheon-flogging of gangster Eddie Schultz, cited by Orwell in 1944, would be paralleled by Winston's beatings by the truncheon-wielding Thought Police. In 1944 Orwell also noted that the hero of Chase's *He Won't Need It Now* stamped on someone's face, crushed the mouth, and ground his heel into it (*CEJL*, 3:218). Similarly, policeman O'Brien plucks a tuft of the emaciated Winston's hair, then wrenches out a loose tooth and tosses it across the cell. "If you want a picture of the future," he tells Winston, "imagine a boot stamping on a human face— forever" (*NEF*, 220).[8] Both Chase and Orwell suggest that the absence of normal love causes or is the result of the perverting influence of power. Chase's impotent Slim Grisson favors killing with a knife: "Slim stood over him while he died, watching and feeling the same odd ecstasy run through him which a killing always gave him."[9] Orwell's

O'Brien joyously predicts the abolition of the orgasm, apparently offering in its place the intoxication of "victory, the sensation of trampling on an enemy who is helpless" (*NEF*, 220).

Given the extent and tone of Orwell's reaction to *No Orchids for Miss Blandish*, similarities between Chase's novel and *Nineteen Eighty-Four* are all the more remarkable. For example, both novelists achieve a subtly dehumanizing effect by incompletely naming most of their characters. We know many of the *No Orchids* cast only by first, last, or nicknames. Furthermore, though Chase provides no Big Brother, there is a fearful Big Mother: Ma Grisson makes the gang's plans and decisions and can still fire a Thompson gun with five bullets in her body. Also, the *No Orchids* police, like O'Brien, have Irish surnames. Finally, private eye Dan Fenner, an accomplished briber and intimidator, has physical features (underlined below) that remind one of O'Brien's "large, burly...thick neck[ed]...prizefighter's physique":

> Fenner was a massively built man...with an attractively ugly face and a pugnacious jaw of a man who likes to get his own way and generally does.[10]

Orwell did not believe that popular crime/detective thrillers had to be distasteful. A year after "Raffles/Blandish" he praised what he called "good" bad books, inviting his readers to practice a form of doublethink to understand the terms of his well-considered oxymoron:

> ...the kind of book that has no literary pretensions but remains readable when more serious productions have perished. Obviously outstanding books in this line are *Raffles* and the Sherlock Holmes stories, which have kept their place when innumerable "problem novels," "human documents" and "terrible indictments" of this or that have fallen into deserved oblivion. (*CEJL*, 4:19)

Even as Eric Blair at Eton, Orwell was familiar with the Holmes formula. One of his putative contributions to a hand-written set of pages lent for reading at a penny was "a laboured parody of Sherlock Holmes with Lestrade as the villain" ("The Adventure of the Lost Meat Card," *GO*, 55-56). Also popular during Eric Blair's school days was Arthur B. Reeve's Craig Kennedy, whose pseudoscientific methods and devices made *The Silent Bullet* (1912; British title *The Black Hand*) one of the early science fiction detective tales. Reeve's mysteries were the first by an American to reach a wide readership in Great Britain.[11] One of Eric Blair's *College Days* stories is a parodic homage: the sleuth in "The Millionaire's Pearl" is none other than Craig Kennedy. In an interesting anticipation of the science fiction gadgetry of *Nineteen Eighty-Four*, Blair's Kennedy uses (in the cause of justice) an apparatus that measures footprints, a galvanic Ouija board by which the detective narrows the field of suspects, and an electronic sensor planted in a room to record the time of entry of an intruder.[12] In another school-days manuscript, Blair tried his hand at a "locked room" mystery. In "The Vernon Murders" the least likely suspect turns out to be the disguised chief of a trio of murderers. The villain is an innocent and harmless-appearing chap like Charrington in *Nineteen Eighty-Four*, and, like him, a practitioner of covert surveillance: he adeptly uses a mirror to read a will in a nearby room.[13]

Orwell's comments on Raffles (he was especially delighted that Raffles' creator was the brother-in-law of Sir Arthur Conan Doyle) reflect an admiration for only outlawry done in a stylish or gentlemanly way—in the commission of relatively petty crimes. Certainly the crime in *Nineteen Eighty-Four* is the pettiest of offenses—thought. Also, Orwell's novel, like Hornung's *Raffles*, limelights not the police but a figure who, though likeable, is a criminal by his society's standards. Like Hornung, Orwell would exploit "the theme of the 'double life,' of respectability covering crime" (*CEJL*, 3:123). Furthermore, Winston Smith's maladjustment stems from the admirable vulnerability Orwell attributed to Raffles—no moral code *per se*, but "the nervous system...of a gentleman" (*CEJL*, 3:224). For, in intuiting the unfairness of the Party's treatment of the putative traitors Jones, Aaronson, and Rutherford, Smith functions as a kind of honorable schoolboy at odds with the system.

Another of Orwell's deservingly popular authors was Edgar Allan Poe; *Tales of Mystery and Imagination* was on a list of "Best Books" that he compiled for Brenda Salkeld. However, in reading *Nineteen Eighty-Four* as a totalitarian police thriller, we are more likely to be reminded of a Poe horror tale than a tale of ratiocination. From the Spanish Inquisition to electroshock, some things have not changed. Poe's tied-down victim of an ideological "truth squad" is menaced by rats. But the horrors of "The Pit and the Pendulum" are eclipsed in Room 101. Although both Poe's and Orwell's rats are chilling symbols of infirmity and death as well as creeping, gnawing menaces, the Poe rats, in loosening the confining bandage which the narrator has rubbed with meat fragments, are ironic agents of deliverance from the pendulum, whereas Orwell's rats so frighten Winston that he delivers himself, through betrayal of Julia, to his tormentor.

Among other works Orwell praised in "Good Bad Books" were thrillers (notably Guy Boothby's *Dr. Nikola*) and crime novels such as Ernest Raymond's *We, the Accused*. In the latter Orwell saw evidence that popular writers could rise above the usual level of performance by identifying with their characters, feeling with them, and inviting sympathy in a way "cleverer" writers would find difficult to accomplish (*CEJL*, 4:20-21).

Dr. Nikola, the sinister villain of five Boothby novels, may have been a model of the powerful archvillain personified by Big Brother. The hypnotic doctor is an "unscrupulous mastermind" who "pays well for assistance when he requires it" but demands "absolute loyalty." At the outset of one adventure he tells three hirelings, "I demand from you your whole and entire labour.... While you are serving me you are mine body and soul."[14]

Nikola's eyes, like those of the Big Brother poster, are his most remarkable feature. The narrator of Boothby's tales, an adventurer named Wilfrid Bruce, remarks, "When he is watching you he seems to be looking through the back of your head into the wall behind, and when he speaks you've just got to pay attention, whether you want to or not."[15] Nikola exercises his charismatic gaze on both friend and foe, explaining at one point to Bruce how his powers of hypnosis make a subject will what the doctor wants. We are reminded of the Big Brother posters, "so contrived that the eyes follow you about when you move" (*NEF*, 5).

Nikola also impresses his British companion with omnipotence and omniscience that rival Big Brother's. For example, having endangered his life by infiltrating a meeting of conspirators in Shanghai and again in Tibet, Nikola rises and speaks so effectively that he is able to manipulate the cabals of his enemies from the inside. The doctor's omniscience is similarly impressive. Unaccountably, he discloses close knowledge of his associate's background and movements, as if Bruce is the subject of an incredibly unobtrusive spying apparatus. Indeed, those who know him accordingly fear him and dare not refuse to act as his agents. The few who betray him have their minds taken over; through his hypnotic power he paralyzes their will. Nikola's craving for power exceeds that of most villains—he seeks to master death as well as life, and escapes with the appropriate manuscripts and chemicals. In this connection we recall Orwell's O'Brien telling the weakening Winston that the death of the individual is not death because he can merge himself into the Party and "then he is all-powerful and immortal," for "The Party is immortal" (*NEF*, 218, 222). Finally, despite his sinister and overtly criminal activities, Nikola commands a strange loyalty from the gentlemanly British narrator, as ultimately Big Brother does from Winston.

Ernest Raymond's *We, the Accused* was based on the celebrated Dr. Crippen case of 1910—the sensational kind of crime Orwell lamented the passing of in "The Decline of the English Murder." When Crippen poisoned his wife and fled across the Atlantic with his mistress, Orwell was seven and no doubt aware of the widely publicized murder case. Crippen was caught by means of a wireless message—the latest in Edwardian high technology (and forerunner of the telescreen)—sent to England by a suspicious ship captain. It was a story that "no novelist would dare to make up," Orwell wrote—a story of doomed and forbidden love with characterization and plot affinities to *Nineteen Eighty-Four* (*CEJL*, 4:99).

We, the Accused would have been an excellent title for the love story of Winston and Julia. In Raymond's novel the strangely named Paul A. Presset (P.A.P.) is a married, middle-class professional not entirely happy with his job and very unhappy in a loveless marriage. Like Winston Smith he has a liaison with a lady who works in the same building. As in *Nineteen Eighty-Four* the plot is advanced by the protagonist's surreptitious writing and its discovery by an authority figure: his love letter to Myra is found and read by his wealthy wife. Like Winston and Julia, Paul and Myra meet clandestinely in London and in sylvan settings. Like Julia, Presset uses walking-club knowledge of the country to establish locales for sexual rendezvous. Winston's and Julia's memorable love scene after hearing a singing thrush is paralleled by Paul and Myra's lovemaking after hearing the wild, defiant cry of a young pheasant. Toward the end of Raymond's novel, Myra hears a single thrush in the empty October evening as Paul's hanging looms closer. Winston once thought of murdering his wife ("the human talking-machine"), but Presset actually does. Afterwards, he exercises something like Orwell's doublethink by reminding himself to be cautious of attracting suspicion, yet half believing that the arsenic may not have been the cause of Elinor's death.

Both *Nineteen Eighty-Four* and *We, the Accused* open in London on a fatalistic note. Orwell begins with the bad-luck omen of a clock striking thirteen in the military time mode. Raymond opens with an ominously military personification of daybreak:

> DAYLIGHT, coming on duty with gradual step, took over London from the night. As a regiment relieves another, secretly and in a great quiet, the daylight crossed the highways and the side-streets, dropping its platoons at their posts of duty.

Three hundred and fifty-seven pages later, as fate closes in on the fleeing lovers, the motif recurs. The sound of the cyclist who is speeding to report sighting them resembles machine-gun fire; similarly, Orwell's novel ends with the suggestion that Smith is about to be executed.

Like Orwell's novel, *We, the Accused* has an implacable detective whose underlings are adept in surveillance, pursuit, and domination of suspects.[16] Boltro's restless manhunt closes in on Presset: hours after his flight from close surveillance, he notes in an evening edition that a complete description has been issued by Scotland Yard "to every police station in the kingdom," observation is being kept at main line terminals, ports and docks, all outgoing ships are being searched, and inquiries are under way at "shipping offices, railway stations, and hotels."[17] Paul is surprised by the quickness of his arrest; two officers in plainclothes swoop down from the high ground and three more close in across the grass. The come-along device with which Boltro incapacitates Paul is a figure-eight set of steel wrist grips; by twisting his end of the figure-eight, Boltro can cause his prisoner to fall backward or on his face—rather complete control. Later, when he is strip-searched in prison, Presset feels humiliation akin to that of Winston. He stands before his warders "a naked, unpropertied, disinherited body...painfully conscious of unshapely limbs, protuberant bones, white flaccid skin.... They ran their fingers in his every fold and cranny, and in his mouth and through his hair."[18]

As he indicated in "Raffles/Blandish," Orwell was well aware of the totalitarian style of law enforcement—particularly in Edgar Wallace's police thrillers. In his prime, Wallace was so popular and prolific that he may have written every fourth book being sold in England.[19] A 1936 letter to Geoffrey Gorer reflected Orwell's interest in the Wallace phenomenon:

> I have often thought it would be very interesting to study the conventions etc. of books from an anthropological point of view.... It would be interesting and I believe valuable to work out the underlying beliefs and general imaginative background of a writer like Edgar Wallace (CEJL, 1:222).

Orwell noted that Wallace was one of the first crime writers to break away from the private detective hero. His central investigator was an organizational man, an effective part of a large, powerful apparatus (like Boltro in We, the Accused). The nickname of one such Wallace figure has a phonetic ring of omnipotence ("Sooper").

Typically the Wallace detective beats his quarry at his own game— be it cunning, intimidation, or unexpected violence. Triumphs come not through ratiocination, clues, intelligence, or deduction, but because of rather melodramatic coincidence or uncanny police foreknowledge. Here is Orwell's 1944 epitome of a Wallace organizational detective:

> A Scotland Yard detective is the most powerful kind of being...the criminal [is] an outlaw against whom anything is permissible....

> [Wallace's] policemen behave much more brutally than British
> police do in real life—they hit people without provocation, fire
> revolvers past their ears to terrify them and so on—and some of
> the stories exhibit a fearful intellectual sadism. (*CEJL*, 3:221)

Wallace's Mr. J. G. Reeder of the Public Prosecutor's office especially attracted Orwell's attention. As with O'Brien of *Nineteen Eighty-
Four*, his Christian name is missing, unknown, or irrelevant. In "The
Treasure Hunt," the apparently mild-mannered Reeder sets a thief to
catch a murderer: like O'Brien, Reeder is an entrapment expert. He
also intimidates an underworld caller by firing his silenced pistol past
the cheek of his departing visitor. Later, to provide himself with an
excuse to question and ponder the facial reactions of a socialite suspect, Reeder composes and delivers an anonymous accusatory letter.
(Here we are reminded of O'Brien's use of Goldstein's heretical "Book"
to entrap thought criminals.)

In *Terror Keep*, Reeder confesses to the curse of having a criminal
mind and also wears a pince-nez through which he never looks (one
thinks of O'Brien's folksy bits of business with his spectacles). A rubber truncheon is one of his favorite weapons, and he knows the psychological effect of a sudden, uncalled for show of force. Needing
information from a criminal, Reeder, from his seat, "stretched out a
long arm, gripped the man by the collar and jerked him savagely
across the desk." The cause of this intimidating show of force?
"Something in the shifty slant of his eyes."[20] *Facecrime?* one wonders.

Aside from what resemble homages to or assimilations from particular thrillers and crime fiction, Orwell echoed many of their genre conventions in *Nineteen Eighty-Four*. To some extent that novel's textual
tension derives from Orwell's use of such popularly familiar elements
in the context of an ideological horror story. Readily apparent are such
hard-boiled crime story staples as the melodramatic plot, decaying
urban setting, intrigue-enmeshed anti-hero, mysterious and tempting
female, and false-friend villain.[21]

Nineteen Eighty-Four's plot closely follows the hard-boiled formula.
A basically decent protagonist (Winston) proves willing to resort to violence to oppose evil. In O'Brien's apartment Winston agrees to commit murder, do acts of sabotage that kill innocent people, distribute
drugs, disseminate venereal disease—in short, do anything to demor-
alize the Party. Like the typical hard-boiled protagonist, Winston does
not trust the police, lives and works in a shabby setting, is somewhat
down on his luck, and is separated from his wife. Also, Winston meets
a beautiful woman, suspects her of being allied with his foe, takes a
risk, and eventually discovers the truth about her. Toward the end of

the adventure he falls into the hands of a sadistic enemy he had trusted.[22]

As in hard-boiled yarns, *Nineteen Eighty-Four*'s city reflects "empty modernity, corruption, and death."[23] True to the formula, a central character is introduced in a seedy setting. The dusty, drab, run-down milieu of the detective's office with its resident bottle of rye or bourbon has its counterparts in Victory Mansions, where the hallways stink of boiled cabbage and old rag mats, the elevator is out of order, the plumbing is stopped up, and Winston seeks solace in a bottle (of Victory Gin).

Another formula parallel is *Nineteen Eighty-Four*'s anti-heroic protagonist who, by his society's code, has crossed the line into outlawry. This character often is "an ordinary man" (who could be more ordinary than a Smith?) whose commonness is "a mask for uncommon qualities" (this Smith has a heroic first name).[24] He becomes involved in a search or quest that leads him to define his own moral position; for Winston, belief in unchanging truth. Winston's acts of unauthorized investigation are another manifestation of anti-heroic behavior. Orwell well knew when he wrote *Nineteen Eighty-Four* that simply being a "private" investigator is an outlaw act in a totalitarian society. He had examples from recent history. At the start of World War II, Italy outlawed popular English detective novelists Agatha Christie and Edgar Wallace; in Germany, all imported detective works were ordered withdrawn from bookshops.[25] Other formula characters interacting with Winston are Julia, the initially mysterious beauty with whom association compromises and eventually betrays the anti-hero, and O'Brien— the power-obsessed false-confidant.

Another crime/detective element in *Nineteen Eighty-Four* was invented by one of Orwell's favorite detective story authors. In the last year of his life (and the year of *Nineteen Eighty-Four*'s appearance) Orwell wrote to Jacintha Buddicom, "Do you remember our passion for R. Austin Freeman? I have never really lost it, and I think I must have read his entire works except some of the very last ones."[26] Like the aforementioned Arthur B. Reeve, Freeman created a 'scientific' detective (Dr. John Thorndyke) who was popular during Eric Blair's youth. Freeman also devised the now-familiar "inverted" mystery, in which the "whodunit" element is eliminated because the reader witnesses the crime early on. Thus, the suspense arises not from the reader's unveiling of the perpetrator, but from whether and how he will be unmasked by the investigator. Viewers of television's *Columbo* see the device in every episode. As a mystery, *Nineteen Eighty-Four* would so qualify: early on the reader knows the identity of the criminal (Winston) and has witnessed his crime (thought).

* * * * *

In "Raffles/Blandish," Orwell the popular culture commentator sensed an "interconnection between sadism, masochism, success worship, power worship, nationalism, and totalitarianism...a huge subject whose edges have barely been scratched" (*CEJL*, 3:222). Orwell's 1944 description of Chase's gangsters and dehumanized "bad" good guys could well be an abstract for the novel he would set four decades later:

> ...a day-dream appropriate to a totalitarian age...a distilled version of the modern political scene, in which such things as...torture to obtain confessions, secret prisons, executions without trial, floggings with rubber truncheons,...systematic falsification of records and statistics, treachery, bribery and quislingism are normal and morally neutral, even admirable when they are done in a large and bold way. (*CEJL*, 3:223)

In *Nineteen Eighty-Four* Orwell would do more than scratch the edges of this grand subject, and his cutting edge would be the relationship between a society and its popular fiction.

To the literary establishment, Orwell the journalist might indeed have resembled a renegade Winston Smith—reading and being too much influenced by "unauthorized" (sub-literary) material. Like Winston Smith, curiously examining mementos of a bygone past in an off-limits prole junk shop, Orwell clung to the memories of humanistic reading experiences he missed in contemporary crime fiction. In the totalitarian thriller he would write, the gentlemanly Holmes or Raffles would be as out of place as Raymond Chandler's Philip Marlowe was when Robert Altman transplanted him to the southern California of the 1970s in a revisionist film version of *The Long Goodbye*.

The one-dimensional characterizations in *Nineteen Eighty-Four* are defensible as reflections of the dehumanization of the individual in a police state. They are the stuff of melodrama—as are the rats in Room 101, quasi-scientific surveillance and brainwashing apparatus, archvillainy, forbidden love, sadistic and/or duplicitous police, and a host of other popular conventions. These echoes of Orwell's reading of Poe, Boothby, Raymond, Wallace, Chase, and the increasingly hard-boiled crime stories of his day might have been to some only unusable jetsam, but the author of *Nineteen Eighty-Four* recycled his "torrent of trash" into a cautionary tale—an imagined totalitarian thriller in which the collapse of human dignity would preclude tragedy, and melodrama would become the state of the literary art; and dehumanization, the art of the state.

Notes

1. Ken Worpole, "The American Connection: The Masculine Style in Popular Fiction," *New Left Review* 139 (May-June 1983): 84.

2. Mark Rose, *Alien Encounters: An Anatomy of Science Fiction* (Cambridge: Harvard University Press, 1981), 17.
3. Lawrence Malkin, "Halfway to 1984," *Horizon* 12 (Spring 1970): 33.
4. Paul Gray, Anne Hopkins, and John Saar, "That Year Is Almost Here," *Time*, 28 November 1983, 46.
5. Patrick Parrinder, "George Orwell and the Detective Story," in *Dimensions of Detective Fiction*, ed. Larry N. Landrum, Pat Browne, and Ray B. Browne (Bowling Green: Popular Press, 1976), 64-65.
6. Julian Symons, *The Detective Story in Britain* (London: Longmans, Green and Co., 1969), 7.
7. Howard Haycraft, Introduction in *A Treasury of Great Mysteries*, ed. Howard Haycraft and John Beecroft (New York: Simon and Schuster, 1957), 5.
8. Jeffrey Meyers, *A Reader's Guide to George Orwell* (Totowa, N.J.: Littlefield, Adams, 1977), 148-49. Jeffrey Meyers called this image *Nineteen Eighty-Four*'s "most famous and frequently quoted symbol...an image of merciless sadism that Orwell could never exorcise from his mind." Meyers traces manifestations of its symbolic connection between "brutality, power worship, nationalism, and totalitarianism" from Orwell's reading of a phrase in Book 4 of *Gulliver's Travels* and an image in Jack London's *The Iron Heel* to a reference by George Bowling in *Coming Up for Air*, an image of power in *The Lion and the Unicorn*; a reference to himself in a 1943 letter ("an orange that's been trodden on by a very dirty boot"); and a 1944 article on General de Gaulle in the *Manchester Evening News*.
9. James Hadley Chase, *No Orchids for Miss Blandish* (Dallas, Pa.: Penguin Offset Paperbacks, 1980), 38.
10. Ibid., 78.
11. Chris Steinbrunner and Otto Penzler, eds., *Encyclopedia of Mystery and Detection* (New York: McGraw Hill, 1976), 231, 340.
12. Orwell Archive, University College London Library.
13. Ibid.
14. Quoted by Steinbrunner and Penzler, 40.
15. Guy Boothby, *Dr. Nikola* (1896; reprint, London: Ward, Lock & Co., n.d.), 14.
16. The cover illustration of the Penguin edition is dominated by a head-on view of the bowlered, mustachioed detective Boltro, whose eyes seem to be directed to all angles and whose bowlered head contains an inset of Paul and Myra.
17. Ernest Raymond, *We, the Accused* (Dallas, Pa.: Penguin, 1983), 286-87.
18. Ibid. 393-94.
19. H. R. F. Keating, *Whodunit? A Guide to Crime, Suspense, and Spy Fiction* (New York: Van Nostrand, 1982), 241.
20. Edgar Wallace, *Terror Keep* (New York: Doubleday, Page, 1927), 206.
21. John Cawelti identifies these elements and discusses them in detail in his "Hard-Boiled Detective Story" chapter in *Adventure, Mystery and Romance* (Chicago: University of Chicago Press, 1976), 139-61.
22. For this summary I am indebted to a paper presented by Dr. Judith B. Kerman at the convention of the American Popular Culture Associations in Toronto on 1 April 1984 ("Private Eye in Dystopia: A Semiotic and Political

Comparison of the Film *Blade Runner* and the Book *Do Androids Dream of Electric Sheep?"*).

23. Cawelti, *Adventure, Mystery and Romance*, 141.
24. Ibid., 145.
25. Howard Haycraft, *Murder for Pleasure: The Life and Times of the Detective Story* (New York: Biblo and Tannen, 1974), 312.
26. Letter to Jacintha Buddicom, 15 February 1949, Orwell Archive.

The Invisible Sources of
Nineteen Eighty-Four

Jonathan Rose

Ever since "1984" became a modern synonym for "hell," readers have wondered why Orwell settled on that particular title. It is often assumed that he simply reversed the last two digits of 1948, the year he completed the book. Some academics have pointed out that the date 1984 also figures importantly in two earlier dystopian novels: G. K. Chesterton's *The Napoleon of Notting Hill* (1904) and Jack London's *The Iron Heel* (1907).[1] It has even been suggested that the number may have some cabalistic significance.[2]

These speculations were ended (or should have been ended) by the publication of the facsimile manuscript of *Nineteen Eighty-Four*, which reveals that Orwell first considered, and then crossed out, 1980 and 1982 (*Ms*, 23). After all, the date was completely arbitrary.

All the same, the title of *Nineteen Eighty-Four* may be more revealing than anyone has imagined. The scholars who closely scrutinize the numeral 1984 look right past its real significance, which lies in the simple fact that Orwell chose a *date* for a title. It was not his first working title, which was "The Last Man in Europe"; he only decided for *Nineteen Eighty-Four* when the manuscript was being completed. Both titles are crucial textual clues that lead us on to several possible literary sources of *Nineteen Eighty-Four*. Specifically, there were a great many earlier futuristic stories published in Britain with titles that were either dates or some variation on "The Last Man." Some of these books, or other books by the same authors, are remarkably similar to *Nineteen Eighty-Four*. It is quite probable that Orwell appropriated from them not only the titles, but also many of the themes, characters, and devices of his own novel.

If these stories can be counted among the many sources of *Nineteen Eighty-Four*, they provide some remarkable insights into Orwell's intentions and methods of composition. Most of them, however, are invisible sources, in the sense that Orwell never mentioned them in his writings. There is plenty of soft evidence that he had actually read them—he had personal connections with their authors, and *Nineteen Eighty-Four* is full of striking textual echoes. But we are dealing here with probabilities, not certainties. In fact, one of the points of this paper is to show just how tricky the business of tracking down literary influences can be.

"The Last Man in Europe" had several precursors, the best-known being Mary Shelley's *The Last Man* (1826), which describes the extinction of humanity by plague. There was also Jean Baptiste Cousin de Grainville's *The Last Man* (1806), Delaval North's *The Last Man in London* (1887), and two books by Olaf Stapledon, *Last and First Men* (1930) and *Last Men in London* (1932). None of these fantasies in any way resembles *Nineteen Eighty-Four*, but Olaf Stapledon bears further investigation. He and Orwell moved in the same left-wing intellectual circles: they both contributed to the *Adelphi, New Statesman*, and *Tribune*. Their lives intersected at at least one point: in 1942 Orwell coedited Stapledon's political tract *Beyond the "Isms"* for Secker and Warburg (*GO*, 273).

That same year—one year before Orwell began to sketch out "The Last Man in Europe"—Stapledon published another book, *Darkness and the Light*. This was an ambitious "future history" along the lines of his earlier *Last and First Men*. And here the scent becomes unmistakable: though it is much clumsier as a work of fiction, *Darkness and the Light* startlingly resembles *Nineteen Eighty-Four*.

Stapledon, like Orwell, was a democratic socialist who feared that "a great planned state, controlled without insight into true community, must turn to tyranny. And, armed with science for oppression and propaganda, it must inevitably destroy the humanity of its citizens." Under the pressure of war, Stapledon warned, the world would slide into totalitarianism:

> For national safety men's actions were increasingly controlled by the state, their minds increasingly moulded to the formal pattern that the state required of them. All men were disciplined and standardized. Every one had an official place and task in the huge common work of defence and attack. Any one who protested or was lukewarm must be destroyed. The state was always in danger, and every nerve was constantly at strain. And because each

state carefully sowed treason among the citizens of the other states, no man could trust his neighbour. Husbands and wives suspected one another. Children proudly informed against their parents. Under the strain even of peace-time life all minds were damaged. Lunacy spread like a plague. The most sane, though in their own view their judgment was unwarped, were in fact fear-tortured neurotics.[3]

That last sentence could serve as a perfect description of Winston Smith, and the whole paragraph reads like O'Brien's harangues ("No one dares trust a wife or a child or a friend any longer" [*NEF*, 220]). Stapledon speculated that, after a series of catastrophic wars, the world would be dominated by two empires (rather than Orwell's three). Russia and China would struggle for world domination while conducting bloody purges at home. Each superpower would have its own version of the Inner Party, Big Brother, and Ingsoc:

> In each of them a minority held effective power over the whole society, and in each a single individual was at once the instrument and the wielder of that power. Each dictatorship imposed upon its subjects a strict discipline and a stereotyped ideology which, in spite of its much-emphasized idiosyncrasies, was in one respect at least identical with the ideology of its opponent; for both insisted on the absolute subordination of the individual to the state. (*DL*, 20)

There, in its essentials, is Goldstein's book. "Collectively, the Party owns everything in Oceania," Orwell wrote, "with the result, foreseen and intended beforehand, that economic inequality has been made permanent" (*NEF*, 170). But Stapledon had described the same kind of oligarchical collectivism some years earlier:

> What had started as a devoted revolutionary corps had developed as a bureaucracy which in effect owned the whole wealth of the empire. Common ownership theoretically existed, but in effect it was confined to the Party, which thus became a sort of fabulously wealthy monastic order. (*DL*, 21)

Stapledon predicted that in China—the country that inspires O'Brien's most sadistic form of punishment—enemies of the state would be "tortured with all the cunning of medical and psychological science" (*DL*, 35). Stapledon never used the phrases "Freedom is Slavery" or "Ignorance is Strength," but he put those concepts into the mouth of a "young official Chinese psychologist," who argued that

> under the divine state the supreme virtue was obedience. For the state in its wisdom would decide what was the right function of every one. As for the right to education, there was no such thing.

> In its place must be set the right and duty of ignorance. Let each
> man know merely whatever was needed for the fulfilling of his
> function. To know more was wicked, and to the truly spiritual
> mind repugnant. Obedience involved also the pious acceptance of
> suffering, one's own and one's neighbour's. But indeed suffering
> was not only to be reluctantly accepted; it must be welcomed....
> In torture, both victim and agent should experience an ineffable
> illumination. Like the union of love, and in a far more vivid man-
> ner, the union of victim and torturer was a creative synthesis in
> which a new and splendid reality was brought into being.... The
> torturer knew well that ecstasy. The victim, if he was spiritually
> disciplined beforehand, should experience an even more
> exquisite, excruciating joy. (*DL,* 38-40)

That sums up exactly the relationship between O'Brien and
Winston. Where Stapledon's Chinese oligarchs "preach sacrifice, self-
immolation, enlightenment in suffering" (*DL,* 39), Orwell's Eastasian
oligarchs call it "Death-worship" or the "Obliteration of the Self" (*NEF,*
162). Where O'Brien ridicules "the stupid hedonistic Utopias that the
old reformers imagined" (*NEF,* 220), the Chinese psychologist demands
not a "milk-sop liberal-socialist Utopia...but the fulfillment of the
potentialities of the existing order" (*DL,* 40). The psychologist calls this
self-contradictory ideology "the synthetic faith"—which literally trans-
lates into Newspeak as "doublethink." It is promoted, as Orwell also
predicted, by a cadre of intellectual workers, "paid servants of the government, engaged on propaganda.... These were concerned chiefly to
put a good complexion on the regime, and to praise the fundamental
principles of the synthetic faith, in particular the virtues of acquies-
cence and obedience, and the ecstasy of cruelty" (*DL,* 64). The result
is a society plagued by "neurotic jealousy and fear," driven by "the joy
of persecution," in which "the infliction of pain on a fellow mortal
could afford a crazy satisfaction" (*DL,* 66).

In Stapledon's nightmare state "the mechanization of propaganda
had been developed to an extent hitherto unknown." Each citizen outside the ruling class has implanted in his skull a device that permits
the police to read his thoughts and transmit propaganda directly to the
brain (*DL,* 66-67). This is cheap Buck Rogers stuff, too incredible to
be really frightening. Orwell made the same concept more plausible
and (hence) much more terrifying with his telescreen, which was
based on technology that already existed in 1948. Still, Orwell does
seem to be shadowing Stapledon very closely here. The top scientific
priority of the Inner Party is to learn "how to discover, against his will,
what another human being is thinking" (*NEF,* 159), and they may have
already succeeded: O'Brien certainly has a diabolic way of knowing
what is inside Winston's head. In *Darkness and the Light,* as in

Nineteen Eighty-Four, it is the children who embrace this kind of mind control most enthusiastically. They easily master the technique that Orwell called *crimestop*: "Dangerous thoughts, even of the mildest type, were for them unthinkable" (*DL*, 68).

Stapledon also anticipated the formula "War is Peace." Realizing that peace may lead to social unrest, his Chinese psychologist urges "the world-wide ruling class to tighten its grip on the people by means of a world war" (*DL*, 41):

> The leaders of the two ruling classes therefore secretly conferred with one another and agreed to institute a world-wide war between the two empires. They agreed also on the rules of this lethal game.... Each side was to refrain from blotting out the other's main centres of population, while seeming to attempt to do so. On the other hand, whenever there was any awkward social disturbance in any locality in one of the empires, the government of the other, if requested by its rival, was to launch a violent air attack on the infected area. (*DL*, 54)

That is precisely Julia's explanation of the rocket bombs that fall on London (*NEF*, 127). Well before Orwell, Stapledon argued that perpetual sham warfare could be a means of deliberately depressing living standards and thus preserving economic inequality: "On the plea of military necessity legislation to protect labour was repealed, hours were lengthened, wages reduced, food adulterated, and rationed in such a way as to leave the rich the chance of buying substitutes which the poor could not afford" (*DL*, 55). Ultimately, the war produces such squalor that cities are overrun by ferocious rats: "They began by devouring the babies whenever they were left for a while unguarded. Sleeping adults were also attacked" (*DL*, 90). Compare O'Brien: "In some streets a woman dare not leave her baby alone in the house, even for five minutes. The rats are certain to attack it.... They also attack sick or dying people" (*NEF*, 234-35).

This is not to suggest that *Nineteen Eighty-Four* is a plagiarism, or that Olaf Stapledon deserves any of the literary glory we have accorded George Orwell. *Darkness and the Light* does contain many of the salient concepts later worked out in *Nineteen Eighty-Four*, but otherwise it is a remarkably incompetent book. Stapledon's story is characterless in every sense of the term—devoid of artistry, description, color, or individualized portraits. Orwell had the kind of genius that can construct a classic novel by borrowing and refashioning elements of ephemeral literature. He had been reading dystopian tales since boyhood, always noting what worked and what didn't—the sort of technical criticism one would expect from someone on the lookout for reusable ideas. As he wrote in 1944, when he discovered Evgeny Zamyatin's *We*, "I am interested in that kind of book, and even keep making notes for one myself that may get written sooner or later" (*CEJL*, 3:95). He cannibalized the best bits of Zamyatin, H. G. Wells, James Burnham, and any number of other authors. If he did the same with Stapledon, he put an original spin on everything he borrowed. For example, to Stapledon "Darkness and the Light" meant only the obvious—evil and good, oppression and freedom. It took an Orwell to realize that "the place where there is no darkness" might be an interrogation cell in a secret police headquarters.

Then again, *Darkness and the Light* consists largely of hazy sketches of futuristic armies clashing in "violent warfare," as if there were some other kind of warfare. Stapledon's vague narrative is so dismally unconvincing that the reader cannot really envision the armageddon chronicled in *Darkness and the Light*. In fact, it all sounds like the war bulletins periodically trumpeted over the telescreen; and it is just possible that Orwell found here the perfect style for reporting an unreal war.

That, granted, is speculation; but it is clear that Orwell appropriated and recast elements of at least one of two books by Alfred Noyes, *The Last Man* (1940) and *The Edge of the Abyss* (1942). The latter, which Orwell reviewed in 1944, proclaimed that in the twentieth century "the totalitarian State...has become the Master, and more than the Master, a blood-stained Idol, a false god." Like Orwell, Noyes condemned the Soviet purge trials, profoundly distrusted bureaucratic elites, and warned that "the 'democracies' are in danger of being forced into totalitarianism to fight totalitarianism."[4] He noted that a mythic leader could be manufactured from nothing by propaganda experts: "Such is the power of suggestion through the modern means of 'publicity,' whereby the giant or figure is 'built up,' paragraph by paragraph, out of straws and inanities, the colour of his ties, the food he eats, and the size of his boots. The inside of his head is very seldom examined" (*EA*, 20-21). Noyes condemned the historical amnesia that, after June 1941, blotted out the fact of Russia's earlier aggression against Finland: "I cannot help possessing a memory.... The State has no memory" (*EA*, 26-27). He also exposed the kind of doublethink that had transformed Stalin, recently Hitler's crony, into Britain's trusted ally:

> We are told that Government X is a government of criminals, murderers, and utterly untrustworthy liars who will say anything and do anything to obtain their ends. Unforeseen circumstances then bring us into co-operation with this government; but, before we lend this government of utterly untrustworthy criminals our full co-operation we naively ask their liar-in-chief to make us a pretty little nursery promise that he will not cease to co-operate with us

before we have achieved our own highly moral and Christian ends. We explain that we are co-operating reluctantly because he is a murderer and a liar, whose first principle is to break his word whenever he finds it convenient; and we then, like infants in pinafores, ask him please to give us his "promise," to which we attach precisely the value which we openly say it does not and cannot possess. (*EA*, 4-5)

Noyes and Orwell both argued that modern intellectuals had dangerously subverted belief in the existence of objective truth and absolute morality. "For more than half a century," wrote Noyes, "in the literature of the pseudo-intellectuals and neo-pagans all over the world, the sapping and mining has been carried on, with a curiously malicious ardour of concentration, confusing all the lines of right and wrong, and all the loyalties of mankind" (*EA*, 15-16). Again like Orwell, Noyes was convinced that "the great mass of the people in the English-speaking world have never lost their sense of certain values which the arbiters of our intellectual fashions have tried for so long to sneer out of existence; and it is here, among the plain people, the 'constituents,' who have been temporarily rendered almost helpless by the bureaucratic machinery, that the hope, the only hope, of the world now abides" (*EA*, 4).

For Noyes, the "plain people" were middle-class, whereas Orwell placed his hope in the proles. But just a few months after he reviewed *The Edge of the Abyss*, Orwell would make the same point in "Raffles and Miss Blandish": "The common people, on the whole, are still living in the world of absolute good and evil from which the intellectuals have long since escaped" (*CEJL*, 3:223). That essay, which sketched out the gangster ideology later embodied in *Nineteen Eighty-Four*, closely echoed Noyes's warning that in "the pseudo-modern and pseudo-intellectual world...'brutality' is mistaken for strength; and, indeed, the word 'brutal' is one of their favourite adjectives of praise" (*EA*, 38-39).

The most horrifying illustration of that blatant sadism, according to Noyes, followed the torpedoing of HMS *City of Benares*. On 17 September 1940, at the height of the Blitz, the *Benares* was transporting one hundred evacuee children from Britain when it was sunk in the North Atlantic by a German U-Boat. Most of the children perished. Before they realized what they had hit, the Germans treated the sinking as a matter for public boasting. When the truth was made known, Joseph Goebbels coldly accused the British of using the incident to score propaganda points.[5] For Noyes, that Nazi response was the real atrocity:

The German wireless immediately exulted in the known fact that no deed now, however horrible, could evoke the natural reactions, even in the most generous hearts. It would merely make, as they said, "a good tear-jerking story."... They knew what they were doing. The effect of that wicked sentence was calculated by expert psychologists. It was a deliberate assault on the human soul. They knew how well the ground had been prepared by the brutal cynicisms of modern writing all over the world. They knew that they could appeal to the new toughness created by our intellectual fashions. They knew that their doings had intimidated the natural reactions of what used to be called "righteous anger," now so thoroughly "out of date" and ridiculous. (*EA*, 35-36, 39-40)

Here, very probably, is the source of one of the most ghastly scenes in *Nineteen Eighty-Four*—the war film that, to the cheers of the audience, gloats over the bombing and strafing of a refugee ship. From Noyes's treatment of the *Benares* incident, Orwell seems to have derived two terrible insights: that in modern warfare atrocities "are looked upon as normal, and, when they are committed by one's own side and not by the enemy, meritorious" (*NEF*, 153); and that the objective of this brutality "was to convince you that mere impulses, mere feelings, were of no account" (*NEF*, 136).

Many of these same themes—wartime massacres of civilians, the destruction of moral absolutes by a corrupt intelligentsia, democracies becoming totalitarian to fight totalitarianism—had been developed earlier by Noyes in *The Last Man*, a novel in which the human race is all but wiped out by a fantastic superweapon.[6] The holocaust is engineered by a Machiavellian villain named Mardok. Like O'Brien, he worships power ("If I have the power, I have the right") to the point where he believes he can achieve a kind of immortality.[7] Unlike O'Brien, Mardok envisions a future world free of sexual inhibitions, but their monologues on this subject read like negative images of each other:

> *The Last Man*: Religion would be abolished.... [Sexuality] would be controlled by the race to come, and turned on at their pleasure, exactly as they turned on the electric light. There would be no more broken hearts, for all those sentimental entanglements which used to be described as "affections" would be destroyed like so much poison-ivy.[8]

> *Nineteen Eighty-Four*: In our world there will be no emotions except fear, rage, triumph, and self-abasement. Everything else we shall destroy—everything.... The sex instinct will be eradicated. Procreation will be an annual formality like the renewal of a ration card. We shall abolish the orgasm. (*NEF*, 220)

The Last Man and *Nineteen Eighty-Four* have the same triangular plot: the hero, alone in a nightmarish world, manages to find a sympathetic young woman, enjoys a brief idyll with her, and then is persecuted for it by a diabolical sadist. Mardok is driven by sexual jealousy; and O'Brien may well have the same motive, however sternly he tries to repress it. As Julia says, the Inner Party bosses can't stand the thought that anyone else might sleep with her, "but there's plenty that *would* if they got half a chance. They're not so holy as they make out" (*NEF*, 104).

There is no direct evidence that Orwell read *The Last Man*, except for its resemblances to "The Last Man in Europe." He did, however, acknowledge that *The Edge of the Abyss* had made some telling points about the decline of "common decency,"

> the growing acquiescence of ordinary people in the doctrines of expediency, the callousness of public opinion in the face of the most atrocious crimes and sufferings, and the black-out memory which allows blood-stained murderers to turn into public benefactors overnight if "military necessity" demands it. Quite new, too, is the doubt cast by the various totalitarian systems on the very existence of objective truth, and the consequent large-scale falsification of history. Mr. Noyes is quite right to cry out against all this, and he...is also within his rights in saying that the intelligentsia are more infected by totalitarian ideas than the common people, and are partly to blame for the mess we are in now. But his diagnosis of the reasons for this is very shallow, and his suggested remedies are doubtful, even from the point of view of practicability.

As a Roman Catholic convert, Noyes had argued that civilization could only be saved by a return to Christian morality. Orwell objected that three-quarters of mankind was not Christian, and that even in the Christian world religious faith was irreversibly declining. "The real problem of our time," he concluded, "is to restore the sense of absolute right and wrong when the belief that it used to rest on—that is, the belief in personal immortality—has been destroyed" (*CEJL*, 3:99-100).

All the same, *The Edge of the Abyss* had clearly made an impression on Orwell. In the months following that review, he repeatedly returned to the subject of Alfred Noyes in his journalism (*CEJL*, 3:36, 144, 159-60, 172, 265). "Incoherent and, in places, silly though it is," Orwell concluded, "this book raises a real problem and will set its readers thinking, even if their thinking only starts to be useful at about the place where Mr. Noyes leaves off" (*CEJL*, 3:100-1).

That is exactly the place where *Nineteen Eighty-Four* picks up. *The Last Man* concludes on a note of divine grace, with the survival of a small Catholic community in Assisi. Orwell, who was quite hostile to the Catholic Church,[9] inevitably rejected such a sunny ending. He argued that, far from being a bulwark against totalitarianism, the Vatican had appeased or supported Fascism. The Jesuitical overtones of O'Brien's speeches may have been intended as a direct repudiation of Noyes on that point. In fact, given that Noyes traced the beginnings of Western moral decline to Copernicus and Darwin (*EA*, 73), O'Brien's denial of heliocentrism and evolution just might be a satiric shot aimed directly at *The Edge of the Abyss*.

In a similar way, Orwell took off from a dystopia created by another Christian apologist whom he once grouped with Noyes: C. S. Lewis (*CEJL*, 3:263-65). Among the many sources of *Nineteen Eighty-Four*, one that is usually overlooked is Lewis's *That Hideous Strength* (1945). Orwell's review of that book makes the resonances pretty clear:

> A company of mad scientists—or, perhaps, they are not mad, but have merely destroyed in themselves all human feeling, all notion of good and evil—are plotting to conquer Britain, then the whole planet, and then other planets, until they have brought the universe under their control. All superfluous life is to be wiped out, all natural forces tamed, the common people are to be used as slaves and vivisection subjects by the ruling caste of scientists, who even see their way to conferring immortal life upon themselves. Man, in short, is to storm the heavens and overthrow the gods, or even to become a god himself.

It is not difficult to see the Orwellian parallels in Lewis's "N.I.C.E. (National Institute of Co-ordinated Experiments), with its world-wide ramifications, its private army, its secret torture chambers, and its inner ring of adepts ruled over by a mysterious personage known as The Head." Writing only a few days after the bombing of Hiroshima, Orwell saw "nothing outrageously improbable in such a conspiracy.... It sounds all too topical. Plenty of people in our age do entertain the monstrous dreams of power that Mr. Lewis attributes to his characters, and we are within sight of the time when such dreams will be realisable." Orwell found the book "as exciting as any detective story.... For in essence it is a crime story"—which incidentally supports Russel Gray's argument that *Nineteen Eighty-Four* was built around the framework of a detective novel. (And to reinforce a point made earlier in this chapter, *That Hideous Strength* may have also directed Orwell to another literary model: in the preface Lewis acknowledged a great debt to the writings of Olaf Stapledon.)

But if Orwell saw much to emulate in Lewis and Noyes, he uncompromisingly rejected their religious orthodoxy. He would have cut out all the Christianity and mysticism from *That Hideous Strength*,

not only because they offend the average reader's sense of probability but also because in effect they decide the issue in advance.
When one is told that God and the Devil are in conflict one always
knows which side is going to win. The whole drama of the struggle against evil lies in the fact that one does not have supernatu-
ral aid.[10]

That is why Winston Smith explicitly repudiates any belief in God
(*NEF*, 222). The awful tension of *Nineteen Eighty-Four* would have
been dispelled by the suggestion that human decency would ultimately
triumph. Any dissident who takes up the struggle against totalitarianism does so knowing that he may achieve nothing but his own vapor-
ization. The reader of *Nineteen Eighty-Four* cannot taste that existential
uncertainty unless God is erased from the text.

In selecting the title of *Nineteen Eighty-Four*, Orwell followed a
convention established by a succession of rubbishy dystopian tales.
These included Frederick Carrell's *2010* (1914), which postulated a
future of racial wars; the Earl of Halsbury's novel *1944* (1926), in
which a Russian dictator launches an invasion of Western Europe; and
Hamish Blair's *1957* (1930), which described a repeat of the Sepoy
Mutiny. In 1915 the immensely popular author Edgar Wallace wrote
"1925": The Story of a Fatal Peace, in which he predicted that
Germany, after suffering defeat in the Great War, would later launch
a second war of revenge.

There is no reason to think that Orwell knew of any of these books.
In fact, in only one case can we be certain that he ever read a novel
with a date for a title: Robin Maugham's *The 1946 Ms.* (1943), which
depicts Britain under a military dictatorship. Orwell admired that story
(*CEJL*, 3:55-56), and it might have suggested one literary device used
in *Nineteen Eighty-Four*: like Winston Smith, Maugham's narrator tries
to send a message to future generations by keeping a diary, though
he knows it may never be read by anyone.[11]

Another possible root of *Nineteen Eighty-Four* is *1938: A Pre-view
of Next Year's News*, which Malcolm Muggeridge and Hugh Kingsmill
published late in 1937. Orwell and Muggeridge first made contact
around that time, when they exchanged appreciative letters about
Orwell's article "Spilling the Spanish Beans."[12] *Nineteen Thirty-Eight* is
a whimsical spoof of popular newspapers; in tone, it is poles apart
from *Nineteen Eighty-Four*. But quite remarkably, Muggeridge and
Kingsmill did predict the Nazi-Soviet Pact two years before the fact.
The Great Purge Trials were also satirized in *1938*, where Stalin has
Lenin and Marx posthumously condemned as Trotskyite deviationists.
Most interesting of all, another purge victim mentioned in the book
happens to be named Goldstein.[13]

There are more arresting parallels in the anonymous *1920: Dips into the Near Future*. That story first appeared as a series of articles in the *Nation* in late 1917, and was published in booklet form early the following year. The title echoes not only *Nineteen Eighty-Four* but also "A Peep into the Future," Eric Blair's first essay in dystopian fiction, which was written by June 1918.

Nineteen Twenty is a satire on totalitarianism—in this case, the state controls and repression imposed during the First World War—and it describes an England that is essentially the equivalent of Airstrip One. The nation is locked in a vicious, pointless, and endless war, in which "the one war aim was the continuance of the war."[14] Bombs continually rain down on London, and food shortages are so severe that the elderly are herded into state crematoriums. Like the audience at the war flick in *Nineteen Eighty-Four*, the British people exult over the bombing of German children, glad to be done with "the period of humanitarian humbug, when patriots still pretended to distinguish between big and little Huns, male and female Huns, innocent and guilty Huns. Now, thank heaven! we recognise only two sorts of Huns—live Huns and dead Huns" (*1920*, 16). Women are urged to breed for the State, but separation is permitted (as it is in the case of Winston and Katharine Smith) if the marriage has "not yielded the proper quota required to meet the estimated future needs of the military authority for the maintenance of our fighting forces" (*1920*, 52-53).

There is a tyrannical Big Sister in *1920*—and her name is Dora. In actuality, DORA was the sardonic acronym applied by the British public to the Defense of the Realm Act, the First World War emergency legislation that empowered the government to resort to practically any measure deemed necessary to the war effort, including the suppression of antiwar agitation. In *1920*, everyone knows that Dora can tap their telephones, read their mail, and cut their rations. Dora also enforces a blanket ban on "enemy associations," a phrase so vague that it can encompass any kind of thoughtcrime. "The conspicuous merit of the term depends on its not meaning anything *exactly*," one official explains:

> It is one of Dora's master-strokes in semi-legal linguistics. You see, it can cover everything, from the possession of a German dictionary to plotting to deliver the Woolwich Arsenal to the enemy. And the best of it is that it isn't an offence against the law, no charge can be brought, and so no evidence is required, no legal trial follows, no cross-examination or other defence, and, above all, no publicity. (*1920*, 36-37)

That is scarcely an exaggeration of the state of civil liberties in Britain in 1917; and it is all very like Oceania, where there are no laws, no indictments, no trials, no publicity, and no rights. In *1920* this repression is justified on the grounds that Slavery is Freedom:

> There is just as much liberty as ever—only it is concentrated at the top.... That is our Dora launching her Controls, her Prohibitions, and her Permits. And in her service there is perfect freedom. (*1920*, 47)

Nineteen Twenty also has an O'Brien, an Oxford philosophy don turned war bureaucrat. In a schoolmasterish way, he explains "the relativity and adaptability of knowledge...the simple notion that truth is a raw material, infinitely malleable and adaptable to the purposes of the State" (*1920*, 26-27). This ideology is based on the philosophy of Pragmatism: like Ingsoc, it holds "that the actual world of experience was a sort of jelly on which a man stamped his own meaning and personal purposes, and that the truth of any statement depended on whether it worked." As the philosopher argues:

> Truth is what works. But works for what? The one weak spot in pre-war Pragmatism was its failure to give a really convincing answer to that question. With a sudden flash of illumination, war, the intensest of all human purposes, brought the needed answer. Truth is what helps to win the war. (*1920*, 22-24)

This intellectual apparatchik supervises his own Minitrue—a "Psychological Laboratory for the Preparation of War-Truth." One department concocts bogus statistics, another invents patriotic myths. Doublethinking with alacrity, the philosopher explains that even a wholly fabricated "myth cannot possibly be false; because, you see, 'it works.' Indeed it is supremely true" (*1920*, 24, 29-30).

Historians in *1920* have likewise "shed their early scruples about 'objective facts' and 'absolute reality.'" Anticipating Winston Smith's profession, they have formed a "Joint Committee for Historical Reconstruction," producing monographs on "How Blucher Lost Us Waterloo." The narrator is assured that "there is plenty of work to be done for our schools and colleges in re-writing history in the *entente* spirit, so as to delete the fabulous French wars, and to put in its true light such episodes as that of Joan of Arc." German books are taken from the Bodleian Library and burned, and any German cultural figure who cannot be libelled simply becomes a nonperson, as in a scholarly paper on "Seven Proofs of the Non-existence of Immanuel Kant" (*1920*, 31-34).

That satiric arrow was clearly aimed at the "Oxford Pamphlets on the War," in which distinguished academics grossly distorted history in

the interests of fighting the Kaiser. Many British intellectuals white-
washed Soviet tyranny during the 1930s and 1940s, but there was a
precedent for that kind of deception in the First World War, when historians at Cambridge and the University of London described their
Russian ally as a true democracy and a protector of smaller national-
ities.[15] My earlier essay argued that the seeds of *Nineteen Eighty-Four*
were planted during the First World War, and that theory would be
greatly bolstered if it could be confirmed that Eric Blair read *1920* in
1918. He would have found in that pamphlet a completely realized
dystopia based on the "Conscription of Mind," a program designed

> to drill the whole intellectual and spiritual forces of the nation into
> complete harmony with the supreme purpose of a State at war....
> Of course, in an informal sort of way, a good deal had already
> been done in our schools, universities, and churches to bring them
> into line with the purposes of a patriotic culture and a genuinely
> British Christianity. (*1920*, 24-26)

As a product of St. Cyprian's and Eton, an author of flag-waving
schoolboy poems and an OTC member, Eric Blair could not have failed
to appreciate that last sentence—assuming, of course, that he read it.
However tempting it may be to leap to that conclusion, this caveat
needs reemphasis: except for textual similarities, which are extraordinary but might still be coincidental, there is no proof that Orwell read
1920 or most of the other stories discussed here.

The dangers of relying on that kind of circumstantial evidence are
illustrated by the anonymous pamphlet *One Thousand Eight Hundred
and Twenty Nine*, which on the surface appears to be another likely
model for *Nineteen Eighty-Four*. Published in 1819, this tract warned
that, within a decade, the Roman Church would subdue England and
bring back the Inquisition. Protestants would be tortured, heretics
would be burned, and complete intellectual submission to Rome
would be reimposed. The Church would demand of the faithful a kind
of doublethink: "The indispensable purpose of Catholic Ascendancy
authorized every good Catholic, either to speak falsehood, in the spirit
of truth, or truth in the spirit of falsehood."[16] Some passages of *One
Thousand Eight Hundred and Twenty Nine* do sound suspiciously
Orwellian:

> Time makes no alteration in our Church—*Nullum tempus occurrit
> ecclesiae*—Centuries past, and centuries to come, have with her
> unvarying identity. She neither *was*, nor *will be*:—her friends know
> her, and her enemies feel her, one eternal *IS*.[17]

Compare *Nineteen Eighty-Four.*

> Who controls the present controls the future: who controls the present controls the past....We, the Party, control the past, do we not?....Reality exists...only in the mind of the Party, which is collective and immortal. (*NEF*, 204-5).
> The Party lives forever, in an eternal present. (*Ms*, 333)

"We trample them [Protestants] to the dust," gloats the triumphalist of *One Thousand Eight Hundred and Twenty Nine.* "The end justifieth the means."[18] O'Brien dismisses the Inquisition as an amateurish affair, but he uses the same kind of language: "Power is not a means, it is an end.... Always, at every moment, there will be the thrill of victory, the sensation of trampling on an enemy who is helpless" (*NEF*, 217, 220).

But had Orwell actually read this book? He did have a number of anti-Catholic tracts in his huge collection of pamphlets, and he edited (with Reginald Reynolds) an anthology of *British Pamphleteers*—but *One Thousand Eight Hundred and Twenty Nine* is not to be found in either of them. It seems safest to conclude that *Nineteen Eighty-Four* draws on a long tradition of English anti-Catholic literature. *One Thousand Eight Hundred and Twenty Nine* resembles Orwell's novel because it belongs to that same tradition, but not necessarily because Orwell had any knowledge of it.

One could say the same about many of the futuristic tales that seem to anticipate *Nineteen Eighty-Four.* Like any other literary genre, dystopian fiction offers a pool of traditional motifs, cliches, and conventions that authors may borrow from. O'Brien is just such a convention: the machiavel who, just before the story reaches its climax, reveals how the whole dirty system works. He has his counterparts in *The Iron Heel* and *Brave New World*, as well as in *The Last Man* and *1920.* Orwell could have appropriated him from one of the sources listed here, or from one of the books discussed by William Steinhoff in *George Orwell and the Origins of 1984*, or from one of the roughly two hundred dystopian stories published in Britain between 1903 and 1945.[19] It is more probable that O'Brien, along with many of the other elements that went into *Nineteen Eighty-Four*, was borrowed from several sources. Literary derivation is usually not a matter of one book "influencing" another, like two billiard balls clicking together, but a process of collective reinforcement over a lifetime of reading. In the course of his wide reading in dystopian literature, Orwell would have encountered certain storytelling conventions over and over again, and those are the devices he would have most likely absorbed and reused in his own work. That is why, even though *Nineteen Eighty-Four* uncannily resembles *Darkness and the Light* and *The Last Man*, it does not necessarily follow that Orwell read the latter two books: it is possible that he and Stapledon and Noyes were simply drawing on the same body of literary conventions. And of course it would hardly be surprising if these three authors, who all lived and wrote in the age of the great dictators, responded similarly—but quite independently—to the horrors around them.

Ultimately, this case depends on a large body of mutually reinforcing but inconclusive evidence. If you were to take the political ideology laid out in *Darkness and the Light*, and the machinery of totalitarian controls described in *1920*, and the plot and characters of *The Last Man*; and if you then welded these three structural elements together, you would arrive at the complete basic framework of *Nineteen Eighty-Four*. Given that, one is tempted to declare the case solved, but in the end we are left with what must be, for the literary detective, the most frustrating of all conclusions: a solution that hangs together perfectly, but cannot be absolutely proven.

Notes

1. Courtney T. Wemyss and Alexej Ugrinsky, eds., *George Orwell* (New York: Greenwood Press, 1987), 5, 173.
2. John Rodden, *The Politics of Literary Reputation: The Making and Claiming of "St. George" Orwell* (New York: Oxford University Press, 1989), 260-62.
3. Olaf Stapledon, *Darkness and the Light* (London: Methuen, 1942), 6. Hereafter cited in text as *DL*.
4. Alfred Noyes, *The Edge of the Abyss* (London: John Murray, 1944), 3. Hereafter cited in text as *EA*.
5. Ralph Barker, *Children of the Benares* (London: Methuen, 1987), 22-25, 118-20.
6. Alfred Noyes, *The Last Man* (London: John Murray, 1940), 6, 141, 144, 203.
7. Ibid., 238.
8. Ibid., 131-32.
9. William Steinhoff, *George Orwell and the Origins of 1984* (Ann Arbor: University of Michigan Press, 1975), 67-71, 184-85, illustrates the depth of Orwell's anti-Catholicism. James Connors, in an unpublished paper, shows that this antipathy to the Catholic Church was fundamental to Orwell's anti-authoritarian turn of mind.
10. George Orwell, review of *That Hideous Strength*, by C. S. Lewis, *Manchester Evening News*, 16 August 1945, 2.
11. Robin Maugham, *The 1946 Ms.* (London: War Facts Press, 1943), 3.
12. Malcolm Muggeridge, "A Knight of the Woeful Countenance," in *The World of George Orwell*, ed. Miriam Gross (London: Weidenfeld and Nicolson, 1971), 166.

13. Hugh Kingsmill and Malcolm Muggeridge, *1938: A Pre-view of Next Year's News* (London: Eyre & Spottiswoode, 1937), 41, 76, 126, 143, 145, 150.

14. Lucian, *1920: Dips into the Near Future* (London: Headley Bros., 1918), 85. Hereafter cited in text as *1920*.

15. Stuart Wallace, *War and the Image of Germany: British Academics 1914-1918* (Edinburgh: John Donald, 1988), chap. 3.

16. Anonymous, *One Thousand Eight Hundred and Twenty Nine* (London: J. J. Stockdale, 1819), 27-28.

17. Ibid., 31-34.

18. Ibid., 27-28.

19. As compiled by I. F. Clarke in *Tale of the Future*, 3d ed. (London: Library Association, 1978).

George Orwell
and the
Tory-Radical Tradition

William E. Laskowski, Jr.

And it struck me that an idea *is very like a tune...that it goes through the ages remaining the same in itself but getting into such very different company.*

—Orwell in a letter to Brenda Salkeld (*CEJL*, 1:137)

Nineteen eighty-four, that numerically eponymous year, provided a number of critics with the opportunity to attempt to place George Orwell along a political axis. It also tempted some of them to score fresh blows against Orwell's "apostate" socialism. But such simplistic ideological litmus tests generally fail to apprehend that Orwell's thinking grew out of a substantial literary-political tradition that began with Jonathan Swift, evolved through William Cobbett and William Hazlitt, and flowered in the hybrid figure of "Chesterbelloc," who was read quite avidly by the young Eric Blair. Ignorance or misperception of this tradition leads to the misplacement of Orwell from and on both ends of the spectrum (q.v., Raymond Williams and Norman Podhoretz). The few critics who refer to this tradition give it a fairly cursory mention. George Woodcock, for instance, in *The Crystal Spirit*, claims that Orwell "was the last of a nineteenth-century tradition of individualist radicals which bred such men as Hazlitt, Cobbett, and Dickens."[1] In the same vein, Bernard Crick explains Orwell's patriotism in terms "of his rather old-fashioned radicalism that links his 'Tory anarchist' or individualist phase to his final socialist period.... dust from Cobbett's *Rural Rides* seems never far from his nostrils" (*GO*, xvii).

The best brief analysis of Orwell's precursors in this Tory-Radical tradition was by Lionel Trilling in his 1952 introduction to *Homage to Catalonia*. After showing Orwell's affinities with G. K. Chesterton, Trilling examines in detail the close connections that can be drawn out between Orwell and William Cobbett and William Hazlitt. He notes the

possible relationship between Cobbett's *Grammar* and Orwell's invention of Newspeak since "both had a love affair with the English language." (It might have slipped Trilling's mind that Hazlitt also wrote a
Grammar.) And he finds Orwell's resemblance to Hazlitt of "a more
intimate temperamental kind" in that Hazlitt's "unshakable opinions
never kept him from giving credit when it was deserved by a writer of
the opposite persuasion" (*HC*, xii–xiii). While Trilling does not use the
label "Tory-Radical," it nevertheless seems fairly clear that he is referring to this tradition.

The difficulty in defining the Tory-Radical tradition can be seen in
the variety of terms for it: Woodcock's "individualist radical," Crick's
"'Tory anarchist' or individualist." Orwell himself used the phrase "Tory
anarchist" to describe his own philosophy and that of Jonathan Swift.
The term "Tory-Radical" is often applied to the "Young England" party
of Benjamin Disraeli (a writer whom Orwell refers to rarely, but with
an understanding of Disraeli's idiosyncratic politics).[2] Alice Chandler
uses this label almost as a synonym for Orwell's "Tory anarchist" when
she remarks in her detailed study of nineteenth-century medievalism,
A Dream of Order: "This ambivalence toward the poor makes the com-
pound epithet Tory-Radical an apt one for the writers here considered."[3] She similarly calls Cobbett's definition of freedom ("full and
quiet enjoyment of your property") "Tory and medievalistic, for all his
radicalism."[4] In this sense, "Tory" does not *necessarily* imply an absolutely conservative political inclination, as Chandler hints later when
she points out "the Tory-Radical, medievalist belief in the alliance
between rich and poor."[5] This brand of "Toryism" is very close to that
"Young England" movement of the 1840s, led by Disraeli and fed by
the works of Southey and, surprisingly often (as Chandler shows), by
the works of Cobbett. Whatever its previous incarnations or usages,
Tory-Radicalism in the authors studied here can be defined as an ideological division between a deep concern for the protection of the individual, and a concomitant yet often conflicting desire to improve the
total well-being of the group. This definition of "toryism" is based on
Hazlitt's, who acutely defined its deeper essence as an excessive concern for the individual.[6]

The first of Tory-Radicalism's major implications is a deep cherish-
ing of the past, "an older and simpler time," as Trilling puts it. The past
gives the individual his meaning; it is what separates him from all other
individuals. It makes the writer unique, and provides a connective
thread by which the individual can give meaning to further events and
experiences. It is the chief criterion of comparative evaluation, not only
for the individual but for society. The past as it is embodied in the
nation presents itself in the land, the love for which, says Trilling,

"served to give [Orwell's] radicalism a conservative—a conserving—cast" (*HC*, xii). Yet, as Orwell pointed out to those who might be called the "Tory-Anglicans" and "Tory-Etruscans" of his own time such as Eliot and Lawrence, the main danger for Tory-Radicals is searching for a chimerical utopia in the past which must be replicated in a future ideal society—whether it be classical Europe for Swift, England before the Reformation for Cobbett, or the Lake Country before the early Romantic poets turned Tory for Hazlitt. But whatever its implicit danger, memory remains one of the most important imaginative capacities for the Tory-Radicals.

Tory-Radicals are likewise fascinated by the prospect of the Just Society—a community in which the needs of individuals are met while their rights as individuals are honored. Tory-Radicals always view their times as governed by tyranny, whether by a political party or a commercial class or a social group. Liberty is their key political concept. How such a program of political liberty meshes with the world of *realpolitik*, both foreign and domestic, is a subject they seldom specifically address. Their hatred of one kind of tyranny often seems to some a desire for another form of it. But a hatred of empire, a distrust of war, a mistrust of organized political parties, and an uneasy perception of the many ways in which revolution and democracy can be perverted, are all corollaries of the Tory-Radicals' love of freedom. How to reconcile this freedom with the demands of the group is the question which the Tory-Radicals never quite solve, or if they do invent a complete scenario of such an attempt (the fourth part of *Gulliver's Travels*, for instance), it is hard to tell whether the resulting utopia is consciously or inadvertently portrayed as soulless and inhuman. As Hugh Kenner puts it, "The masters of the Plain Style demonstrate...how futile is anyone's hope to subdue humanity to an austere ideal."[7]

An equally important but often overlooked component of the Tory-Radicals' program is economic. While disdainful of money in particular and capitalism (both nascent and mature) in general, they place the ultimate economic value on productive labor, work which results in something tangible and useful. War obviously does not meet this criterion. When Orwell speaks about his feelings for "the surface of the earth" and the enjoyment he derives from "solid objects" (*CEJL*, 1:6), it is this love of productive work he is referring to. Thus the Tory-Radicals have a special fondness for the working class that is entrusted with such labor, but also sometimes become exasperated with its obtuseness in not realizing what is in its best interests, as the Tory-Radicals define them. People must be well-fed, clothed, and housed, to be really free. Moreover, the single most important aspect of the Tory-Radicals' economic program is a constant drive toward self-sufficiency. They mistrust the present system (Cobbett was said to have coined the term "Establishment" to describe that system), and mistrust those who propose to lead the workers in establishing a new order, which would then take the form of an old tyranny. Since major systemic economic revisions are beyond their visions or capacities, Tory-Radicals insist on the economic independence and sufficiency of the individual, which is delicately built up into larger self-sufficient aggregates: first the family, then the class, then the nation, and finally the world. As long as the lines of power radiate outward from the individual to the group, then freedom can be preserved. Once the direction of power implodes on the individual from the mass, once control is usurped by the group, then liberty is abandoned.

The last major component of the Tory-Radicals' *Weltanschauung* concerns language. On the most basic level, they advocate plain, simple, direct, easily understandable language—"prose like a window pane," in Orwell's famous simile. Its purpose is to communicate with as great a number of people as clearly as possible. Language as ornament or decoration is anathema. Once words cease to represent things and can be considered (in whatever light) as things in themselves, they lose their meaning. The possibility of not being understood over time as well as throughout space is abhorrent to the Tory-Radicals. They denounce the process of linguistic change as "corrupt" or "decaying." By using concrete language, individuals can communicate truthfully with other individuals. But there is a group aspect to language that the Tory-Radicals can neither ignore nor forget. For individuals to communicate about themselves as members of a group, abstractions are also necessary. Although they are the most easily corruptible parts of a language, too often used for hiding, evading, lying, avoiding, and escaping, abstractions are absolutely necessary for individual freedom within the group.

Hence Tory-Radicals confront the problem of literary form. V. S. Naipaul, writing about a couple of the Tory-Radicals dealt with here (Cobbett and Hazlitt) and another not yet sufficiently studied (Richard Jefferies), claims they "would have had their gifts diluted or corrupted by the novel form as it existed in their time"; they "found their own forms."[8] The implication is that writers such as Swift, Cobbett, and Hazlitt rejected the novel perhaps because it was, at the same time, too paradigmatic and not paradigmatic enough. If the protagonist of a novel is to carry any meaning as a member of a group, he must be considered as standing for something else—Gulliver as fallen humanity, Boxer as the working class. And if a character is written as a paradigm, then his representation will not be fluid enough novelistically. The protagonist cannot function as an individual; when he attempts to, he becomes the author's facile mouthpiece, as so many of Orwell's early protagonists are. But if the protagonist is worked out as an individual, given novelistic independence (Forster's "roundness"), then he loses group meaning. Such characters cannot be taken as representative of anything but themselves. One of the main criticisms against the greatest English novelist of Cobbett's and Hazlitt's lifetime was that a reader of hers would not know that the Napoleonic Wars were going on while her characters agonized over love matches and marital settlements. Of course, it is precisely this quality of giving individuality to her characters that makes Jane Austen so great a novelist. As Roger Sale points out, critics who find her too "narrow" because she overlooks important sociological or historical events "are in fact responding to her variousness, which demands from her readers an absorption in this time and that place that makes generalization difficult."[9] And Tory-Radicals cannot help but generalize—as Sale remarks, Cobbett "excels...at passionate bursts of generalization from observation"; "he *must* generalize"[10] (emphasis added). The direction again is, as it were, from the individual to the group. Tory-Radicals are weakest when they move from generalization to the particular; Orwell has often been castigated (rightly) for his blanket observations that usually begin with a variation of "Every thinking person usually feels at one time or another that...." These are weak precisely because they are *not* observations. The self that produces the novel, as Naipaul approvingly quotes from Proust, is "'the innermost self which one can only recover by putting aside the world and the self that frequents the world.'"[11] And it is in the world and in that self that the Tory-Radicals are most firmly grounded—"the surface of the earth."

If Tory-Radicals approach the novel at all, it is only in the sense that the fable can be considered a novel. As Kenner claims, "If the fiction speaks political truths, then, it does so by allegory."[12] And here those who *do* choose the novel triumph—with *Gulliver's Travels,* and with *Animal Farm* and *Nineteen Eighty-Four* (which are successful as fables to the same degree that Orwell's early novels are weak as works of fiction). Tory-Radicals seek out prose forms that allow individual expression of group problems: the investigatory pilgrimage (*Rural Rides, The Road to Wigan Pier*); the personally informed history (Swift on Queen Anne's reign, *Homage to Catalonia*); the pamphlet, the newspaper article, the polemic; and most successfully, the periodic essay. While these are the most ephemeral of forms, they allow the greatest range for the individual expression of group concerns, as in Orwell's opening sentence of *The Lion and the Unicorn*: "As I write, highly civilized human beings are flying overhead, trying to kill me" (*CEJL*, 2:56). The sense of outrage erupts as much from the object of the action ("kill *me*") as from the action itself ("civilised beings" killing). Granted, the ultimate personal affront that war represents can just as easily and perhaps more forcefully be portrayed in fiction, but is Prince Andrei Bolkonsky's death affecting because it is Andrei dying as a unique human being, or as all human beings must die? Why does the emotive power of this scene seem inversely proportional in effect to the theorizing of Part Two of *War and Peace?* To lecture upon history with the effectiveness and memorability of a novel, yet in a form that preserves the framework of historicity, requires another kind of speaker—perhaps an Orwell drawing a bead on a fascist whose pants are down, and then refusing to fire.

This study, then, concentrates on some of the principal thematic relationships of three early Tory-Radicals—Jonathan Swift, William Hazlitt,[13] and William Cobbett—to George Orwell. It traces (to use Orwell's simile to Salkeld) the various "tunes" that these writers played, the modulations and variations they underwent, and how they were recapitulated and transformed by Orwell: the love of the past, the necessity of major political change, the need for economic self-sufficiency, the politics of language. All these writers felt themselves isolated, set upon at various points in their careers by groups of enemies—Swift by the Whigs, Hazlitt by the Tory press, Cobbett by the government (the only one whose "paranoia" resulted from a prison sentence), Orwell by the pro-Soviet Left (chiefly represented by Kingsley Martin and Victor Gollancz). Each writer saw himself as *contra plures unum*—against the many, one—which is one reason, perhaps, why the psychological emphasis in much of their writing is upon what is defined here as the tory rather than the radical. Thus critics, particularly of their politics, have overlooked their concerns for the group while focusing on their lamentations over the individual. This study seeks to explain this conflict, and to restore that balance: to revise the criticisms from the Left like those of Raymond Williams, and the misappropriations from the Right, like those of Norman Podhoretz. Its purpose is to demonstrate and account for the duality of emphasis in the work of all four writers—to spell out, in other words, their common intellectual heritage; and at the same time, by mediating between the partisan criticism and the partisan praise, to achieve a properly balanced view of George Orwell.

I: The Past as Touchstone

Many critics find the credibility of Orwell's radicalism vitiated by its backward perspective; a conservative at the simplest level of meaning, after all, is one who, like Winston Smith, drinks a toast to the past.

Orwell himself drew a distinction between conservatism and patriotism in *The Lion and the Unicorn*: "It is actually the opposite of Conservatism, since it is a devotion to something that is always changing and yet is felt to be mystically the same. It is the bridge between the future and the past" (*CEJL*, 2:103). Yet at other times he came down unashamedly in defense of the past, particularly his personal past: "A human being cannot continue developing indefinitely, and...a writer, in particular, is throwing away his heritage if he repudiates the experience of his early life.... one is likelier to make a good book by sticking to one's early-acquired vision than by a futile effort to 'keep up'" (*CEJL*, 4:445-46). He advocated this stance more unabashedly in "Why I Write": "I am not able, and I do not want, completely to abandon the world-view that I acquired in childhood" (*CEJL*, 1:6).

Swift likewise championed the Ancients against the Moderns in *The Battle of the Books* and *A Tale of a Tub*, and he upheld the glory of Roman politicians and the English yeoman as models for the degenerate Parliament and peasantry of his own age. Nevertheless, he at times (1708) was capable of a conflicting insight when ruminating on his own personal past:

> I have observed from my self and others...that Men are never more mistaken, than when they reflect upon past things, and from what they retain in their Memory, compare them with the Present. Because, when we reflect on what is past, our Memoryes lead us onely to the pleasant side, but in present things our Minds are chiefly taken up with reflecting on what we dislike in our Condition. So I formerly used to envy my own Happiness when I was a Schoolboy, the delicious Holidays, the Saterday afternoon, and the charming Custards in a blind Alley; I never considered the Confinement ten hours a day, to nouns and Verbs, the Terror of the Rod, the bloddy Noses, and broken Shins.[14]

Somewhere in Swift's mind remains his own "Glass of Nature" (to use a phrase of the narrator of *A Tale of a Tub*) which can realistically count hours and summon up injuries, as Orwell does so exhaustively in his remembrances of his schooldays, "Such, Such Were the Joys." Yet in later (1729) brooding upon his own condition, Swift could zero in on a seemingly trivial incident, detecting almost symbolic resonances. "I never wake without finding life a more insignificant thing than the day before:...but my greatest misery is recollecting the scene of twenty years, and then all of a sudden dropping into the present. I remember when I was a little boy, I felt a great fish at the end of my line which I drew up almost on the ground, but it dropt in, and the disappointment vexeth me to this very day, and I believe it was the type of all my future disappointments."[15] As in George Bowling's flashback of the uncaught carp in *Coming Up for Air*, the fish is a symbol for unfulfilled ambitions. Personal memory becomes a curse for those who can unmask the past through the "glass" of remembrance; the personal past is not necessarily golden, and sometimes bitter.

Yet to live only for and in the present moment is more self-deceiving to the Tory-Radicals. Orwell held that many people in his age felt "that nostalgic feelings about the past are inherently vicious. One ought, apparently, to live in a continuous present, a minute-to-minute cancellation of memory, and if one thinks of the past at all it should be merely in order to thank God that we are so much better than we used to be" (*CEJL*, 4:445). Swift has the narrator of *A Tale of a Tub* make a similarly modish statement. "But I here think fit to lay hold on that great and honourable Privilege, of being the *Last Writer*. I claim an absolute Authority in Right, as the *freshest Modern*, which gives me a Despotic Power over all Authors before me" (*PW*, 1:81).[16] Such a reliance on the present leads to the infamous definition of happiness as "*a perpetual Possession of being well deceived*," because

> the Debate meerly lies between *Things past*, and *Things conceived*; and so the Question is only this, Whether Things that have Place in the *Imagination*, may not as properly be said to *Exist*, as those that are seated in the *Memory*; which may be justly held in the Affirmative, and very much to the Advantage of the former, since This is acknowledged to be the *Womb* of Things, and the other allowed to be no more than the *Grave*. (*PW*, 1:108)

Since there is no verifiable distinction that can be made between remembered events and imagined events, the past is infinitely malleable, and of no intrinsic objective worth. The narrator exposes by irony Swift's own contrary position. Thus, in *Nineteen Eighty-Four* the last man in Europe, Winston Smith, is led by the "last author" in Europe, O'Brien—a true Modern—to what *The Tale*'s narrator calls "the Serene Peaceful State, of being a Fool among Knaves" (*PW*, 1:110): an accurate description of the political life in Oceania.

The integrity of the personal past is pursued even more rigorously by Hazlitt. However, while Swift defended the past against the advocates of the present, Hazlitt contested with the partisans of the future: "I conceive that the past is as real and substantial a part of our being, that it is as much a *bona fide*, undeniable consideration in the estimate of human life, as the future can possibly be" (*CW*, 8:22).[17] Also like Swift, Hazlitt bases his argument on the internal integrity of the human personality. "Nay, the [future] is even more imaginary, a more fantastic creature of the brain than the [past],...for the future, on which we lay so much stress, may never come to pass at all, that is, may never be embodied into actual existence in the whole course of events, whereas the past has certainly existed once, has received the stamp of truth, and left an image of itself behind" (*CW*, 8:22-23). Just as reading helps forge his own sense of personal identity, Hazlitt claims that "it is the past that gives me most delight and most assurance of reality" (*CW*, 8:24). This reality, for Hazlitt, almost has an objective existence, and it is with things that he crowds his past: "The past is alive and stirring with objects, bright or solemn, and of unfading interest. What is it in fact that we recur to oftenest? What subjects do we think or talk of? Not the ignorant future, but the well-stored past" (*CW*, 8:25). I remember; therefore I am. In *Nineteen Eighty-Four*, Orwell will come to the conclusion that the past is not merely the "most assurance of reality" but its *only* assurance. Hazlitt would agree with O'Brien that he who controls the store of the past controls the ignorant future.

As much as Tory-Radicals rely on history, they distrust historians. In Part III of *Gulliver's Travels*, Gulliver finds that when he summons the shades of the past, the commentators on great writers keep quite clear of their subjects, "because they had so horribly misrepresented the Meaning of those Authors to Posterity" (*PW*, 11:181). Gulliver later "was chiefly disgusted with modern History. For having strictly examined all the Persons of greatest Name in the Courts of Princes for an Hundred Years past, I found how the World had been misled by prostitute Writers" (*PW*, 11:183). Cobbett, uncovering what he feels to be the truth behind the Protestant "Reformation," claims: "The far greater part of those books, which are called '*Histories of England*,' are little better than romances" (*HPR*, 38).[18] Orwell quotes two such "romances" in his fiction. In *A Clergyman's Daughter*, Dorothy Hare finds only one available history text to teach, "a horrid little book called *The Hundred Page History of Britain*" (*CD*, 229). Dated 1888, its ignorant glorification of the past is mirrored in the child's history book Winston Smith reads in *Nineteen Eighty-Four*, in which the past is ludicrously evil, an anti-Eden. When he tries to summon up the shades of history in books to find out the truth about the past, Winston fails; he has no touchstone, since his own education has been corrupted.

If history books cannot be trusted, is it possible to learn from oral tradition and personal memory what the past was like? Swift has Gulliver encounter the Struldbruggs, who Gulliver characteristically hopes will help humanity by "Warning and Instruction" to "prevent that continual Degeneracy of human Nature, so justly complained of in all Ages" (*PW*, 11:194). The reality is, of course, the opposite. Their personal memories are of no avail: "They have no Remembrance of any thing but what they learned and observed in their Youth and

middle Age, and even that is very imperfect: And for the Truth or
Particulars of any Fact, it is safer to depend on common traditions than
upon their best Recollections. The least miserable among them, appear
to be those who turn to Dotage, and entirely lose their Memories"
(*PW*, 11:196). Winston tries to get at personal historical truth from the
old prole in the pub, and the result is just as ironically futile. The past
only exists as far as it impinges upon the contours of one's own emotional being, which is often not political. "They remembered a million
useless things,...all the relevant facts were outside the range of their
vision. They were like the ant, which can see small objects but not
large ones" (*NEF*, 79). Winston tries to explain this process to Julia
with words that recall Swift's warnings and Hazlitt's boasts. "Do you
realize that the past, starting from yesterday, has been actually abolished? If it survives anywhere, it's in a few solid objects with no words
attached to them, like that lump of glass there.... Nothing exists except
an endless present in which the Party is always right.... The only evidence is inside my own mind, and I don't know with any certainty
that any other human being shares my memories" (*NEF*, 128). Thus,
the tramp Bozo's words to the narrator of *Down and Out*, "'You just
got to say to yourself, "I'm a free man in *here*"—he tapped his fore-
head—'and you're all right'" (*DOPL*, 165), for him an assertion of freedom, has become in Oceania a sentence of isolation.

If the memory and history are fallible, then what is left? As Hazlitt
and Winston suggest, the past must be read in things, and for some
Tory-Radicals, the past could be read in the landscape and buildings
of England. In his *Rural Rides*, Cobbett was continually deciphering
what he beheld in order to interpret the history of England. Like
George Bowling in *Coming Up for Air*, Cobbett finds that gentrifica-
tion has caused the loss of boyhood play spots: "The ancient *fish-
ponds*, at Netley Abbey, [are] 'reclaimed,' as they call it. What a *loss*,
what a *national loss*, there has been in this way.... You can see the
marks of old fish-ponds in thousands and thousands of places. I have
noticed, I dare say, *five hundred*, since I left home" (*RR*, 508).
However, Cobbett more often noticed the despoiled, abandoned, and
underpopulated churches throughout the English countryside. "This
[Hambledon] must have once been a considerable place; for here is a
church pretty nearly as large as that at Farnham in Surrey, which is
quite sufficient for a *large town*. The means of living has been drawn
away from these villages, and people follow the means" (*RR*, 125).
Cobbett also reads the land itself: "In ancient times, part of that which
is now *downs* and *woods* was *corn-land*, as we know from the *marks
of the plough*" (*RR*, 437).[19] All these changes show how the present
society in England has degenerated from the standards of the past,

when (according to Cobbett) the Catholic Church provided for the poor, and England was a more populous and happier place.

These same images keep linking the Tory-Radicals together in their treatments of the past. The novel of Orwell's perhaps most concerned with the dichotomy of the past and present, *Coming Up for Air*, presents the Edwardian Thames valley as a rural Eden. That paradise, Lower Binfield, as remembered by Bowling, is very much like Swift's beloved Laracor when he wrote to Stella:

> Oh, that we were at Laracor this fine day! the willows begin to peep, and the quicks to bud. My dream's out: I was a-dreamed last night that I eat ripe cherries.—And now they begin to catch the pikes, and will shortly the trouts (pox on these ministers), and I would fain know whether the floods were ever so high as to get over the holly bank or the river walk; if so, then all my pikes are gone; but I hope not.... And then my canal, and trouts, and whether the bottom be fine and clear?[20]

When the posters about King Zog send Bowling mentally back to Lower Binfield, his first memory, significantly, is of a church. When he returns in reality to Lower Binfield, this church is the only place that is unchanged; except, like Cobbett on so many of his rides, Bowling remarks upon the absence of people in the building: "For almost the first time since I got back to Lower Binfield I didn't have the ghostly feeling, or rather I had it in a different form. Because nothing had changed. Nothing, except all the people were gone" (*CUA*, 225). And as Cobbett too had noted, Orwell comments that most students of his day "never wondered who built the English churches or what Fid. Def. on a penny stands for" (*CD*, 240).

In *Nineteen Eighty-Four*, Orwell uses churches even more intently as a symbol of the past. Like the coral paperweight and the taste of wine for Winston, Charrington's "half-remembered rhymes...belonged to the vanished, romantic past, the olden time as he liked to call it in his secret thoughts" (*NEF*, 141). These "half-remembered rhymes," which Winston is continually trying to "read," are about a certain type of famous London building: "All the London churches were in it—all the principal ones, that is" (*NEF*, 83). The steel engraving in Winston's room, which also reminds him of the past, is of St. Clement's Dane Church. Although they were both fundamentally areligious, Cobbett and Orwell saw the great and traditional past of England represented, indeed proven by—its *churches*.

Orwell's nostalgia for the past is recaptured in a poem that might well have been forgotten with the rest of his verse if he had not curiously reprinted it in "Why I Write":

A happy vicar I might have been
Two hundred years ago,
To preach upon eternal doom
And watch my walnuts grow;

But born, alas, in an evil time,
I missed that pleasant haven....

And later still the times were good,
We were so easy to please,
We rocked our troubled thoughts to sleep
On the bosoms of the trees.

All ignorant we dared to own
The joys we now dissemble;
The greenfinch on the apple bough
Could make my enemies tremble.

But girls' bellies and apricots,
Roach in a shaded stream,
Horses, ducks in flight at dawn,
All these are a dream.

It is forbidden to dream again;
We maim our joys or hide them;
Horses are made of chromium steel
And little fat men shall ride them....

I dreamed I dwelt in marble halls,
And woke to find it true;
I wasn't born for an age like this;
Was Smith? Was Jones? Were you? (*CEJL*, 1:4-5)

The second and last stanzas reveal that in spite of his criticism of T. S. Eliot's assessment of modern culture (*CEJL*, 4:455-57), Orwell too felt that his age was "an evil time." The first stanza's "Two hundred years ago" put Orwell within the lifetime of his favorite literary clergyman, Jonathan Swift, similarly exiled to an unwished-for world of politics, dreaming of rural fruit and fish. Indeed, Swift's poem about an envisioned country retreat, his imitation of the sixth satire of the second book of Horace, is clearly one source for "A Happy Vicar":

I often wish'd, that I had clear
For Life, six hundred Pounds a Year,
A handsome House to lodge a Friend,
A River at my Garden's End,
A Terras Walk, and half a Rood
Of Land set out to plant a Wood.

Thus in a Sea of Folly tost,
My choicest Hours of Life are lost:
Yet always wishing to retreat;
Oh, could I see my Country Seat!
There leaning near a gentle Brook,
Sleep, or peruse some ancient Book;
And there in sweet Oblivion drown
Those Cares that haunt the Court and Town.[21]

The early Tory-Radicals were, however, confident, despite some misgivings, that the objective truth of the past would survive into the future, and they used similar phrases to express their hopes. In the *Examiner* Swift was troubled about the Whigs' twenty-year rule: "I have been perplexed what to do with that Maxim...That *Truth will at last prevail.*" Yet he held that, because of his efforts, truth, "however sometimes late," would in the end win out (*PW*, 3:12, 13). Cobbett believed that Protestant propaganda would eventually be defeated by his truth-telling. "But TRUTH is immortal; and though she may be silenced for a while, there always, at last, comes something to cause her to claim her due and to triumph over falsehood" (*HPR*, 144). For Orwell, the prospect was bleaker. "One has only to think of the sinister possibilities of the radio, state-controlled education and so forth, to realise that 'the truth is great and will prevail' is a prayer rather than an axiom" (*CEJL*, 1:376).[22]

II: The Politics of Common Sense

As their label implies, Tory-Radicals are difficult to pin down politically. One critic of Swift, for instance, at one point called him "consistently a champion of liberty"; just three years later, he claimed Swift "was by no means the unequivocal champion of 'liberty' that some of his modern admirers would like him to have been."[23] Hazlitt remarks of Cobbett, "The Reformers read him when he was a Tory, and the

Tories read him now that he is a Reformer" (*CW*, 8:52). And Orwell called himself, at various stages, a Tory anarchist, a "Jacobite in exile" (*RWP*, 138), and a democratic Socialist. A more revealing admission, perhaps, is Orwell's assertion that "the thinking person" is "by intellect usually left-wing but by temperament often right-wing" (*RWP*, 211). Does this mean Orwell was a tory at heart, but a radical in his thinking? This ambivalence is what he seems to be referring to in "Why I Write" when he admits his "job is to reconcile my ingrained likes and dislikes with the essentially public, *non-individual* activities that this age forces on us" (*CEJL*, 1:6; emphasis added).

It becomes obvious that the party labels of their times meant little to the Tory-Radicals. Although Swift engaged in fierce partisan polemics when he was seeking favor, in the more dispassionate political analysis of *Gulliver's Travels* he makes his ideal monarch, the King of Brobdingnag, inquire ironically of Gulliver whether he "were a *Whig* or a *Tory*" (after "an hearty Fit of laughing") (*PW*, 11:91). Hazlitt held that "the distinction between Whig and Tory is merely nominal: neither have their country one bit at heart" (*CW*, 19:261). Cobbett thought that in Parliament "the 'gentlemen *opposite*' are opposite only as to mere *local position*. They sit on the opposite side of the house: that's all" (*RR*, 210). Orwell came to a similar conclusion about parliamentarians during the Second World War: "Except from the places they sit in (the Opposition always sits on the Speaker's left), you can't tell one party from another" (*CEJL*, 3:77). So what do Tory-Radicals base their politics upon?

Their key watchwords are liberty and freedom. Those critics who have held that Swift indeed was a champion of liberty base it on statements like that of the Drapier: "And I ever thought it the most uncontrolled and universally agreed Maxim, that *Freedom consists in a People being Governed by Laws made with their own Consent; and Slavery in the Contrary*" (*PW*, 10:86-87). Hazlitt reduced his political credo to one principle: "This is the only politics I know.... The question with me is, whether I and mankind are born slaves or free. That is the one thing necessary to know and to make good.... Secure this point and all is safe: lose this, and all is lost" (*CW*, 7:9). Cobbett believed that it was not merely poor economic conditions that deprived the English of their liberty: "a slave, a real slave, every man is, who has no share in making the laws which he is compelled to obey" (*AYM*, 324). And what Orwell found most appealing in Spain was that while the Communists stressed "centralism and efficiency," the Anarchists emphasized "liberty and equality" (*HC*, 61). Thus the question becomes for the Tory-Radicals: how do people lose their liberty?

Much of the time it was through war, both internal and external, and Tory-Radicals are fundamentally opposed to armies and the political use made of them. Thus Gulliver tells his Houyhnhnm master that "the Trade of a *Soldier* is held the most honourable of all others: Because a *Soldier* is a *Yahoo* hired to kill in cold Blood as many of his own Species, who have never offended him, as possibly he can" (*PW*, 11:230-31). The Lilliputian army is treated to an embarrassing view of their new superweapon as they parade through Gulliver's legs and catch unflattering glimpses through his torn trousers. Yet even the most anti-militaristic Tory-Radicals can have unexpectedly positive feelings about the military. The Brobdingnagian freemen militia (Swift's model army) exercise and cause Gulliver to exclaim, "It looked as if ten thousand Flashes of Lightning were darting at the same time from every Quarter of the Sky" (*PW*, 11:122). Cobbett, who felt that the Napoleonic Wars were waged against freedom both on the Continent and in England, could nevertheless fondly recall his military experiences in Nova Scotia with pride. "I always had [exercise] on the ground in such time as that the bayonets glistened in the rising sun, a sight which gave me delight, of which I often think, but which I should in vain endeavour to describe" (*AYM*, 40-41). And Orwell felt similar emotions when he watched a trainful of troops leave for the front in Spain: "The guns on the open trucks making one's heart leap as guns always do, and reviving the pernicious feeling, so difficult to get rid of, that war *is* glorious after all" (*HC*, 192). But more characteristic of the Tory-Radicals' attitude toward war is an image which connects *Gulliver's Travels* with *Nineteen Eighty-Four*. Gulliver boasts to his master about the bravery of English warriors: "I assured him, that I had seen them blow up a Hundred Enemies at once in a Siege, and as many in a Ship; and beheld the dead Bodies drop down in Pieces from the Clouds, to the great Diversion of all the Spectators" (*PW*, 11:231). The spectators are equally delighted when Winston Smith goes to the "flicks." "All war films. One very good one of a ship full of refugees being bombed...then there was a wonderful shot of a childs arm going up up up right up into the air" (*NEF*, 11).

How is it that the body politic, to say nothing of the human body, is assaulted and divided so thoroughly by the enemies of liberty? Swift and Orwell both basically broke society down into three groups. For Swift it was the classic division into monarchy, aristocracy, and commons; on this basis, in the best form of government, control should be divided equally: "The Power in the last Resort, was always meant by Legislators to be held in Ballance among all Three...among every free People" (*PW*, 1:196-97). But this desired balance is soon overthrown, usually by a revolution of the people, which soon reverts to another form of tyranny.

> Again, In all Free States the Evil to be avoided is *Tyranny*, that is to say, the *Summa Imperii*, or unlimitted Power solely in the hands of the *One*, the *Few*, or the *Many*...although most Revolutions of Government in *Greece* and *Rome* began with the Tyranny of the People, yet they generally concluded in that of a single Person. So that a usurping Populace is its own *Dupe*, a meer Underworker, and a Purchaser in Trust for some single Tyrant; whose State and Power they advance to their own Ruin....(*PW*, 1:227)

Similarly, in *Nineteen Eighty-Four* Goldstein divides all societies into the High, Middle, and Low, and the assessment of the cycles of historical change is analogous to Swift's.

> [The High] are then overthrown by the Middle, who enlist the Low on their side by pretending to them that they are fighting for liberty and justice. As soon as they have reached their objective, the Middle thrust the Low back into their old position of servitude, and themselves become the High.... From the point of view of the Low, no historic change has ever meant much more than a change in the name of their masters. (*NEF*, 166-67)

The main difference between Swift's and Orwell's analyses lies in the historical rise of the class which was just beginning to become important in Swift's time: the middle class. Cobbett declared that political reform was impossible "without the middling classes *to take the lead....* Even the Ministers themselves, if they were so disposed (and they must be so disposed at last) could make none of the reforms that are necessary, *without actually being urged on by the middle classes of the community*" (*RR*, 105). Orwell likewise argued in *The Road to Wigan Pier* that the lower section of that class had to be converted. "Obviously the Socialist movement has got to capture the exploited middle class before it is too late; above all...the office-workers, who are so numerous and, if they knew how to combine, so powerful" (*RWP*, 226). If they were not converted, the revolution would be impossible. "When the pinch came nearly all of them would side with their oppressors and against those who ought to be their allies. It is quite easy to imagine a middle class crushed down to the worst depths of poverty and still remaining bitterly anti-working class in sentiment; this being, of course, a ready-made Fascist party" (*RWP*, 226)—or Ingsoc's Inner Party.

Most Tory-Radicals agree, at least, on the right, if not the necessity, of revolution. Swift is the most cautious: "Whenever those evils which usually attend and follow a violent change of government, were not in probability so pernicious as the grievances we suffer under a present power, then the publick good will justify such a Revolution" (*PW*, 9:31). Hazlitt argued that revolutions did not occur frequently enough. "As a general rule, it might be laid down, that for every instance of national resistance to tyranny, there ought to have been hundreds, and that all those which have been attempted ought to have succeeded" (*CW*, 7:278). Cobbett preached incessantly of the imminence and necessity of apocalyptic change, if there were no general reform. "What injustice! What unnatural changes! Such things cannot be, without producing *convulsion in the end*!" (*RR*, 117). The apocalypse, when it comes, will be annihilating: "What a mass of materials for producing that general and *dreadful convulsion* that must, first or last, come and blow this funding and jobbing and enslaving and starving system to atoms!" (*RR*, 279). During the Second World War, Orwell similarly saw the Blitz as a sign of hope: "On the day in September when the Germans broke through and set the docks on fire, I think few people can have watched those enormous fires without feeling that this was the end of an epoch. One seemed to feel that the immense changes through which our society has got to pass were going to happen there and then" (*CEJL*, 2:54-55). Yet that longed-for apocalypse never brought the revolution.

Why do revolutions so often fail? Tory-Radicals sometimes blame it on the inner docility of the people. Swift asserted that unprincipled leaders so quickly found followers because "man is so apt to *imitate*, so much of the nature of Sheep,...that whoever is so bold as to give the first *great Leap over the Heads of those about him* (though he be the worst of the Flock), shall be quickly followed by the rest" (*PW*, 1:232-33). Orwell became similarly disgusted with the radicals he met in the North of England. "I suppose these people represented a fair cross-section of a more revolutionary element in Wigan. If so, God help us. Exactly the same sheeplike crowd...that you see everywhere else" (*CEJL*, 1:181), rather like the sheep in *Animal Farm*. Hazlitt used an animal simile reminiscent of *Animal Farm* to describe the French Revolutions of 1789 and 1830: "If a herd of overloaded asses were to turn against their drivers and demand their liberty and better usage, these could not be more astonished than the Bourbons when the French people turned against them and demanded their rights" (*CW*, 19:330-31).

More often, though, Tory-Radicals blame the failure of the revolution on unscrupulous manipulation. Hazlitt declared that liberty was weak because it relied on the hopes of many, while "power then is fixed and immoveable, for this reason, because it is lodged in an individual who is driven to madness by the undisputed possession, or apprehended loss of it; his self-will is the key-stone that supports the tottering arch of corruption" (*CW*, 7:19). Cobbett found a microcosm of his society in the conventional schools of his day (as some have suggested Orwell projected from his experiences in "Such, Such Were the Joys"): "The master is, in some sort, their enemy; he is their overlooker; he is a spy upon them; his authority is maintained by his absolute law of punishment; the parent commits them to that power; to be taught is to be held in restraint" (*AYM*, 292). Swift's Drapier anticipates Room 101 when he ironically protests, "For those who have used *Power* to cramp *Liberty*, have gone so far as to resent even the *Liberty* of *Complaining*; although a Man upon the Rack, was never known to be refused the Liberty of *roaring* as loud as he thought fit" (*PW*, 10:63). Hazlitt denounces princes in similar terms: 'It is not enough that they have secured the whole power of the state in their hands...a word uttered against it is torture to their ears.... Till all distinctions of right and wrong, liberty and slavery, happiness and misery, are looked upon as matters of indifference, or as saucy, insolent pretensions" (*CW*, 7:264). O'Brien boasts that the Inner Party has completely erased all such distinctions through doublethink: "It is intolerable to us that an erroneous thought should exist anywhere in the world, however secret and powerless it may be" (*NEF*, 210).

According to the Tory-Radicals, there is only one defense against this form of mind control: common sense. The King of Brobdingnag in *Gulliver's Travels* reduced the art of government "within very *narrow bounds*; to common sense and Reason" (*PW*, 11:119). Hazlitt, who agrees that "Swift's Toryism did not...deprive him of his common sense" (*CW*, 19:157), complains that "exclusive" patriotism (similar to Orwell's definition of Nationalism) "*excludes* even the shadow of a pretension to common sense, justice, and humanity" (*CW*, 7:50). He claims that "a man...who disdains the use of common sense...is like a person who should deprive himself of the use of his eyesight, in order that he might be able to grope his way better in the dark" (*CW*, 1:124-25). Cobbett, like the political writer Tom Paine whose bones he returned to England, also appeals to that capacity in his readers. "Common sense tells us that there are some things which no man can reasonably call his property" (*RR*, 471). "Put these questions calmly to yourself; common sense will dictate the answers" (*AYM*, 57). Why is this amorphous aptitude so important to these Tory-Radicals?

To understand this concept, toryism must be further defined. Hazlitt identified the root of toryism in its emphasis on the individual versus the mass:

> Every thing is in Tory politics referred to the aggrandisement of the individual...the part is always greater than the whole; for the imagination embodies one, or a few individual objects, but it has no means of doing justice to a million, whose interests or rights can only be expressed by a general principle, for which the imagination has no language; and, therefore, in this language (the language of poets and romance-writers, not of philosophers or historians), the million is always sacrificed to the individual. This is the very essence of Toryism. (*CW*, 19:291).

(In this sense, Newspeak is a tory language because all its vocabulary is literal; the tory, says Hazlitt, "has not even the capacity of conceiving an abstract proposition" [*CW*, 19:288].) While Hazlitt in this radical mood is protesting against "the aggrandisement of the individual," in other moods he himself expresses "tory" tendencies in terms that bring to mind one of the three great slogans of Ingsoc, and Winston Smith's futile protest against them:

> I deny that liberty and slavery are convertible terms.... It needs no sagacity to know that two and two make four; but to persist in maintaining this obvious position, if all the fashion, authority, hypocrisy, and venality of mankind were arrayed against it, would require a considerable effort of personal courage, and would soon leave a man in a very formidable minority. (*CW*, 7:7)

Winston wonders, "Perhaps a lunatic was simply a minority of one" (*NEF*, 68). If all are "arrayed against" him, then the lover of liberty must regard himself as an individual, and in declaring himself to be one, Hazlitt obliquely refers to one of Swift's most famous sarcasms:

> I pretend to be master of my own mind.... Within that little circle I would fain be an absolute monarch. I do not profess the spirit of martyrdom.... I do not wish to be flayed alive for affirming that two and two make four, or any other intricate proposition...but if I do not prefer the independence of my mind to that of my body, I at least prefer it to every thing else. (*CW*, 17:22)

Thus common sense, that ability to say that 2 + 2 = 4, is the means to establish and maintain the independence of the individual. When Orwell defines what common sense means to Swift, he is defining it in this same sense that Hazlitt employs: "Acceptance of the obvious and contempt for quibbles and abstractions" (*CEJL*, 4:211).

Of course, in the face of Hitler's rise to power, Orwell sometimes lost faith in "the idea that common sense always wins in the end.... It is

quite possible that we are descending into an age in which two and
two will make five when the Leader says so" (*CEJL*, 1:375-76).[24] Other
Tory-Radicals have succumbed to the same sort of disappointment
when faced with the revolution betrayed or aborted. "Instead of patriots and friends of freedom, I see nothing but the tyrant and the slave,
the people linked with kings to rivet on the chains of despotism and
superstition," Hazlitt protested. "I was taught to think, and I was willing to believe...that liberty was not a name.... Now I would care little
if these words were struck out of the dictionary" (*CW*, 12:135)—which,
of course, is precisely what Newspeak lexicographers do. What is ultimately (and characteristically) ironic about the importance Tory-
Radicals place on common sense is how the practice of a mental
capacity which is by definition common to all can lead its advocates
to a state of isolation and solitude.

III. The Economics of the Self

In a hitherto uncollected review of two long-forgotten political
books, Orwell offhandedly betrays the implicit question that lies
behind Tory-Radical literary and social criticism. "Does this writer, or
does he not, take account of the economic basis of society?" He goes
on to make a connection fundamental to the way Tory-Radicals ana-
lyze society: "If the economic structure of any society is unjust, its
laws and its political system will necessarily perpetuate that injustice."[25] Of course, any political economist or any Marxist would have
said much the same thing. The difference is that Tory-Radicals do not
consider economics an exact science because it involves human
beings, who are never as rational as Utilitarians or dialectical materi-
alists would have them be. "Whatever depends on human will and
opinion (sometimes right and sometimes wrong)," Hazlitt declared, "is
not a science" (*CW*, 19:282). Orwell pointed out that in his century,
the powers of wrong could subvert this "science" for their own ends:
"Economic laws do not operate in the same way as the law of grav-
ity...they can be held up for long periods of time by people who, like
Hitler, believe in their own destiny" (*CEJL*, 2:31).

Thus, Tory-Radicals view their society as organic and intercon-
nected, and for many of them, their analysis centered on the break-
down of English agricultural society in the eighteenth and early
nineteenth centuries. Swift, in his *persona* of M. B. Drapier, warned
that adopting Wood's pence would weaken the framework of Irish
society. "The *Gentlemen of Estates* will all turn off their *Tenants* for
want of Payment.... The *Farmers* must *Rob* or *Beg*, or leave their

Country. The *Shop-keepers* in this and every other Town, must *Break* and *Starve*; For it is the *Landed-man* that maintains the *Merchant*, and *Shopkeeper*, and *Handicrafts-Man*" (*PW*, 10:7-8). Hazlitt once, as Cobbett did so often, questioned a farm worker to ascertain the reasons for rural workers' problems and was told "the inclosing of the commons [was] a hardship on the poor (and no advantage to the rich), by depriving them of the means of keeping a pig, two or three geese or fowls, perhaps even a cow, &c" (*CW*, 19:301). Cobbett, as did Hazlitt, blamed this collapse on the Napoleonic Wars; the landlords' "estates have been taxed to pay the interest of debts contracted with these Stock-Jobbers, and to make wars for the sale of the goods of the Cotton-Lords. This drain upon their estates has collected the people into great masses" (*RR*, 331). Cobbett found in this process a kind of primitive social Darwinism, a law of tooth and fin: "It frequently happens too, that a big gentleman or nobleman, whose estate has been big enough to resist for a long while, and who has swilled up many caplin-gentry, goes down the throat of the loan-dealer with all the caplins in his belly" (*RR*, 313).

Orwell viewed these events of English history from much the same perspective. He observed that Oliver Goldsmith, like Swift, protested against

> the growth of a new moneyed class with no sense of responsibility. Thanks to the expansion of foreign trade and wealth accumulated in the capital, the aristocracy were ceasing to be rustics. England was becoming more and more of an oligarchy, and the life of the countryside was broken up by the enclosure of the common lands and the magnetic pull of London. The peasants were proletarianised, the petty gentry were corrupted. (*CEJL*, 3:271-72)

His history of capitalism later in that century recapitulates Cobbett's view of what had happened to the small landholders earlier:

> The tendency of small businesses to merge together into large ones robbed more and more of the moneyed class of their function and turned them into mere *owners*, their work being done for them by salaried managers and technicians....It explains the decay of country life, due to the keeping-up of a sham feudalism which drives the more spirited workers off the land. (*CEJL*, 2:70)

Most of these workers ended up in the cities, which most Tory-Radicals abhorred. Swift always pined for Laracor while in London. Hazlitt, unlike the others, found city life enjoyable, because it afforded "a visible body-politic, a type and image of that huge Leviathan the

State...we learn to venerate ourselves as men, and to respect the rights of human nature." Country dwellers were, by his definition, tories. "In the country, men are no better than a herd of cattle or scattered deer. They have no idea but of individuals, none of rights or principles— and a king, as the greatest individual, is the highest idea they can form" (*CW*, 12:77). Cobbett, however, called London the "Great Wen," and felt cities bred moral and political disease: "Jails, barracks, factories, do not corrupt by their walls, but by their condensed numbers. Populous cities corrupt from the same cause" (*AYM*, 291-92). He found their source to be the same as Orwell did. The debt drew "*wealth into great masses*. These masses produce a power of *congregating* manufacturers, and of making the many work at them, *for the gain of the few*" (*RR*, 160). Orwell said one of the evils of capitalism was "the piling-up of millions of human beings in hideous ant-heaps of cities,"[26] and quite plainly listed "big towns" as one of his dislikes (*CEJL*, 2:24). However, when Hitler threatened all of England, Orwell overcame his aversion and immersed himself in London.

One of the evils which cities multiply are the poor, and the Tory-Radicals usually reject punitive treatment of the destitute, as Swift does with devastating effect in *A Modest Proposal*. Hazlitt accuses the Utilitarians of leaving out the most important questions in their Poor Law reforms: "It is some difference whether a man has one or two meals a day, whether he has meat for his dinner once a week or not, whether he does or does not lie, coarsely indeed, but warm, whether he is in rags or decently and comfortably clad?" (*CW*, 19:298). When Hazlitt walks the streets of prosperous London and witnesses "a beggar thrust from a door on the plea that there is not another morsel of food to supply the *surplus* population, I know what to think of an age and country that can tolerate such a sophism as one of the first laws of God and nature" (*CW*, 19:285n). When Cobbett in his manuals of advice addresses mainly a middle-class audience, he warns them: "Poverty is not a crime, and though it sometimes arises from faults, it is not, even in that case, to be visited by punishment beyond that which it brings with itself" (*AYM*, 322). Orwell found the root of this attitude to be national. "The English are a conscience-ridden race, with a strong sense of the sinfulness of poverty" (*DOPL*, 202). More directly, Orwell remarks about workers forced to live in caravans during the Depression: "No doubt there are still middle-class people who think that the Lower Orders don't mind that kind of thing and...immediately assume that the people lived there from choice. I never argue nowadays with that kind of person" (*RWP*, 64).

Reformers of the poor usually insisted that the poor had to reform their lives as well, a requirement that the Tory-Radicals denounced.

Hazlitt abjured those who would deny the poor any meager satisfaction to allay their miseries.

> A man who has only got money to buy a loaf will not lay it out in an ice. But may he lay it out in a dram? Yes; because to the wretched it is often more important to forget their future than even to supply their present wants. The extravagance and thoughtlessness of the poor arise, not from their having more than enough to satisfy their immediate necessities, but from their not having enough to ward off impending ones,—in a word, from *desperation*. This is the true answer to Mr. Malthus's politico-theological system of parish ethics, the only real clue to the causes and the cure of pauperism! (*CW*, 7:221).

Orwell likewise defended the working poor against charges that they frittered their few pennies away on nonessentials. "They don't necessarily lower their standards by cutting out luxuries and concentrating on necessities; more often it is the other way about—the more natural way, if you think about it" (*RWP*, 88). Cheap flashy clothes, a few cigarettes, a tip on the horses, all helped make up for the dinginess of life on the dole.

But probably the most noxious recommendation that the reformers made was that the poor should abstain from sex in order to hold down their numbers. Cobbett characteristically declaimed, "Talk as long as Parson Malthus likes about 'moral restraint,' and report as long as the Committees of Parliament please about preventing 'premature and improvident marriages' amongst the labouring classes, the passion that they would restrain, while it is necessary to the existence of mankind, is the greatest of all the compensations of the inevitable cares, troubles, hardships, and sorrows of life" (*AYM*, 92). An early letter of Orwell's complained about an Anglican bishop's pronouncements "about the undesirable multiplication of the lower classes. His latest phrase is 'the social problem class,' meaning all those below a certain income. Really you sometimes can't help thinking these people are doing it on purpose" (*CEJL*, 1:121). An Orwellian catalog of objectionable advocates of socialism usually includes a swipe at "birth-control fanatics" (*RWP*, 216).

Conspicuous consumption at the expense of the poor naturally offended the Tory-Radicals. "We cannot for ourselves approve," objected Hazlitt, "of the privations, of the hunger, cold, or nakedness, to which these poor families are exposed, to keep up the flesh and spirit of the sleek and high-mettled inhabitants of the warm, well-littered stable, even though they were of the breed of Swift's Houyhnhnms!" (*CW*, 7:224). On one of his rides, Cobbett calculates that a "cavalry horse has, I think, *ten pounds of oats* a day and *twenty pounds of hay....* One horseman and his horse cost what would feed *twenty-five* of the distressed creatures" (*RR,* 429). During the Second World War, Orwell makes a similar computation. "There are said to be still 2,000 race-horses in England, each of which will be eating 10-15 lb of grain a day, i.e. these brutes are devouring *every day* the equivalent of the bread ration of a division of troops" (*CEJL,* 2:397).

The bread thus wasted was produced by the Tory-Radicals' favorite laborers: the farmers, who are admirable because they produce a necessity. *The Drapiers's Letters* conclude with Swift's encouragement of agriculture: "Few *Politicians,* with all their Schemes, are half so useful Members of a Commonwealth, as an *honest Farmer,* who, by skilfully draining, fencing, manuring and planting, hath increased the intrinsick Value of a Piece of Land...and thereby done a *perpetual Service* to his Country" (*PW,* 10:141). The King of Brobdingnag makes exactly the same (invidious) comparison, emphasizing the product: "Whoever could make two Ears of Corn, or two Blades of Grass to grow upon a Spot of Ground where only one grew before; would deserve better of Mankind, and do more essential Service to his Country, than the whole race of Politicians put together" (*PW,* 11:119-20). Cobbett's rhapsodies to farmers, "the most able and most moral people that the world ever saw" (*AYM,* 236-37), are well known, as is the fact that they are based on the idyllic recreations of a way of life he originally ran away from. Orwell was also sympathetic to this class; partially this was temperamental: "At a pitch I could be a tolerable road-sweeper or an inefficient gardener or even a tenth-rate farmhand" (*RWP,* 32). Near the end of his life he could make apposite two adjectives describing Hertfordshire that revealed an eye similar to Cobbett's: "a very attractive county in places, very agricultural" (*CEJL,* 4:507). While Cobbett complained that "the labourers retreated to hovels called cottages" (*RR,* 277), Orwell recommended that "the problem of getting people, and especially young, spirited people, to stay on the land would be partly solved if farm labourers had better cottages" (*CEJL,* 3:35).

The congruence between Cobbett and Orwell on many economic subjects, not only agricultural, reveal affinities which shade from the theoretical to the temperamental. Thus Cobbett advocated home-brewed beer over "the poisonous stuff served out to us by common brewers" (*CE,* 16), and Orwell railed at "the filthy chemical by-product that people will pour down their throats under the name of beer" (*RWP,* 204). They both viewed this degradation as the result of the removal of brewing from local hands: "Like all London publicans he was in the claw of the brewer" (*KAF,* 184). Cobbett found tea, because of its tax, preparation time, and lack of nourishment, unspeakably hateful—"slops." Orwell, although he loved tea and detailed an eleven-step process which would assure a proper "cuppa" (recipe-giving being a favorite activity of Cobbett's as well), could evince an equal distaste for the soporific effects of tea. During the Second World War he wrote of the tea shortage: "The endlessly stewing teapot was one of the bases of English life in the era of the dole, and though I miss the tea myself I have no doubt we are better without it" (*CEJL*, 2:232-33).

Both Cobbett and Orwell saw the family, particularly the working-class family, as the most important unit of society. Cobbett declared that the family unit, if truly cohesive, is invulnerable within itself. The well-fed laborer, surrounded by his family, is a touchstone for Cobbett. "A labourer's cottage, on a Sunday; the husband or wife having a baby in arms, looking at two or three older ones playing between the flower-borders going from the wicket to the door, is, according to my taste, the most interesting object that eyes ever beheld; and it is an object to be beheld in no country upon earth but in England" (*AYM*, 109). Or again: "If we suppose the great Creator to condescend to survey his works in detail, what object can be so pleasing to him as that of the labourer, after his return from the toils of a cold winter day, sitting with his wife and children round a cheerful fire, while the wind whistles in the chimney and the rain pelts the roof?" (*CE*, 133). Such scenes are reminiscent of Orwell's notorious depiction of the idyllic working-class family described at the end of part one of *The Road to Wigan Pier*:

> Especially on winter evenings after tea, when the fire glows in the open range and dances on the steel fender, when Father, in shirt-sleeves, sits in the rocking chair at one side of the fire reading the racing finals, and Mother sits on the other with her sewing, and the children are happy with a pennorth of mint humbugs, and the dog lolls roasting himself on the rag mat—it is a good place to be in, provided that you can be not only in it but sufficiently *of* it to be taken for granted. (*RWP*, 117)

Some critics view this scene as almost blasphemous, but neither Orwell nor Cobbett is as nostalgic for a class as they are for a family. In these tableaux, Cobbett casts himself as the father, when his own family, as recent biographers have revealed, was the opposite of the happy brood he boasted about in his voluminous writings. Orwell, in this scene and in a similar one in *Coming Up for Air*, sees himself as the son whose father was not off in India (the "happiness" of the above domestic scene is a matter of "whether Father is in work"—in more ways than one), the son not sent off to prep school because of his family's social ambitions. Like Cobbett, Orwell declared "the family...in the modern world is the sole refuge from the State," but he did not view its future with Cobbett's hope: "All the while the forces of the machine age are slowly destroying the family" (*CEJL*, 4:91). A reflection like this led to the satire of *Nineteen Eighty-Four*, in which the Party seeks to destroy the family unit while replacing it with the larger "family" led by Big Brother, and the illusory family of the revolutionary "Brotherhood."

Cobbett and Orwell both held that the land of England had been unjustly taken away from its people, and they railed against the game laws. "Every man is owner of a part of the deer, the game, and of the money that goes to the keepers" protested Cobbett, "and yet, any man may be *transported*, if he go out by night to catch any part of this game!" (*RR*, 490). Orwell called the overabundant red deer on Jura "an absolute curse" because they were protected; the pheasant for him was "that enemy of England," partially because of "the vicious game laws that it has been responsible for" (*CEJL*, 3:144). Orwell's analysis of the decline of English agricultural life is one that Cobbett would have agreed with. "The enclosures, industrialism, the vast differentiation of wealth, and the cult of the pheasant and the red deer had all combined to drive the mass of English people off the land" (*CEJL*, 3:106).

As deeply as they trust the land, Tory-Radicals mistrust money. Swift argued against the adoption of a spurious form of currency, Wood's pence, in Ireland. Cobbett inveighed against paper money, which not only "could CREATE nothing of any value, it was able to TRANSFER every thing of value" (*RR*, 373). While Swift and Cobbett were mainly concerned with false kinds of money, Orwell gives the impression that *all* forms of money have become inherently specious and corrupt. Gordon Comstock's obsession with money becomes rancorous, and *Keep the Aspidistra Flying* fails as a novel partly because Orwell does not distance himself enough from it. During the Second World War, Orwell (perhaps once again over-anticipating the revolution) went so far as to claim that money was inherently worthless— "We have learned now, however, that money is valueless in itself, and only goods count."[27] And none of Orwell's rhetorical strategies is more like Cobbett's than his continual itemization, tabulating, and toting up of columns of monetary figures: how much he earned at hop-picking, the stoppages a coal-miner was subject to, the rates for the unemployed, how much he spent on books. While Utilitarians and Fabians present and argue from national statistics, the Tory-Radicals look in their own wallets as well.

This fixation on money leads to a preoccupation with the way wealth is accumulated without producing anything, such as Swift's imprecations against the stock-jobbers and money-interest in their manipulations of the markets. Unfortunately, even Hazlitt repeated what had begun in Swift and was to grow into an ugly stream in Cobbett: the involvement of Jews in this sector of the economy. Often in Hazlitt these are only asides, but they show how at times he shared in the rhetoric (and perhaps the spirit) of his age. "The vulgarity of the [*Times*] Editor's style might even receive a romantic tincture from the Hebraism of its pronunciation, and its monotony would be agreeably relieved by the discordant gabble of that disinterested congregation of stock-jobbing Jews and Gentiles" (*CW*, 19:357). "We cannot learn from Moses and the Prophets what Mr. Vansittart and the Jews are about in 'Change-alley'" (7:273). Along with Cobbett, Hazlitt's main objection to the Jews seemed to be that they were not involved in *producing* anything. But, unlike Cobbett, who wrote a more scurrilous than usual pamphlet about the Jews, Hazlitt later came to defend the Jews (perhaps prompted by Cobbett's noxious example). He removed the reference to the *Times* editor, among other things, when he reprinted the above essay in *Political Essays*. In "Emancipation of the Jews," one of his last essays, he writes: "If they are vicious it is we who have made them so. Shut out any class of people from the path to fair fame, and you reduce them to grovel in the pursuit of riches and the means to live.... The Jews barter and sell commodities, instead of raising or manufacturing them. But this is the necessary traditional consequence of their former persecution and pillage by all nations" (*CW*, 19:321). Hazlitt concludes "that we have no superiority to boast of but reason and philosophy, and that it is well to get rid of vulgar prejudices and nominal distinctions as fast as possible" (*CW*, 19:324).

In his earlier works, Orwell's antisemitism appears to be, like Hazlitt's and Cobbett's, mainly economic in its basis. The narrator in *Down and Out* declares about a character, "After knowing him I saw the force of the proverb 'Trust a snake before a Jew and a Jew before a Greek, but don't trust an Armenian'" (*DOPL*, 73). Dorothy Hare learns in London that "men took an offensive interest in you. The Jew on the corner, the owner of Knockout Trousers Ltd., was the worst of all" (*CD*, 164). One of the characters in that novel is known simply as "The Kike."

But in his essay on Dickens, written in 1939, Orwell claims approvingly that "the 'Jew joke,' endemic in English literature until the rise of Hitler, does not appear in his books" (*CEJL*, 1:433). And from around this point on, any form of "Jew joke" or disparagement disappears from Orwell's novels. As with Hazlitt, his radical conviction overcame his tory antisemitism when he became aware of the terrible consequences of that kind of prejudice. He writes of Hitler: "The thought of a world in which...Jews [would be] treated as human beings brings him the same horror and despair as the thought of endless slavery brings to us" (*CEJL*, 2:106). In 1942 he wrote to John Beaven at the *Observer*, emphasizing "the importance of giving prominence not only to the persecution of the Jews but to any proposed relief scheme in order to forestall the Axis claims that this is some sort of Jewish invasion of Palestine and other countries."[28] His most extensive treatment of the subject, "Antisemitism in Britain" (like Hazlitt, he devoted an entire essay to the topic), hints that his fascination with it might have had a personal basis: "Antisemitism should be investigated...by people who know that they are not immune to that kind of emotion" (*CEJL*, 3:341).

IV: Politics vs. Language

Almost any collection of essays on the English language by English literary figures will include some piece by a Tory-Radical, most probably Swift's *A Proposal for Correcting, Improving and Ascertaining the English Tongue*, or Orwell's "Politics and the English Language." Cobbett's *Grammar of the English Language* has always been one of his most popular works, and Hazlitt's *A New and Improved Grammar of the English Tongue* does not altogether deserve its neglect. What needs to be emphasized in studying the Tory-Radicals' treatment of language is how centered it is on the relationship between language and politics. Even the most overtly nonpolitical of them, Hazlitt's *Grammar*, a money-earning piece intended as a textbook for schoolboys, manages to steal in many political lessons.

Swift shows how political history can change language with his analysis of how Latin altered and "decayed." Two of these reasons are similar to the process which, he claims, changed English—the intrusion of outsiders ("foreign Pretenders") which then caused a "great Corruption of Manners, and Introduction of foreign Luxury, with foreign Terms to express it." But two other reasons are more overtly political, and stem from his libertarian sentiments: "the Change of their Government into a Tyranny, which ruined the study of Eloquence; there being no further Use or Encouragement for popular Orators"; and "the slavish Disposition of the Senate and People; by which the Wit and Elegance of the Age were wholly turned into Panegyrick, the most barren of all Subjects" (*PW*, 4:8). A slavish age produces a slavish language. English has been similarly corrupted since its zenith, which Swift locates in the period of the last Tudor and the first two Stuarts. (For Orwell as for Swift, the King James Bible is a model of clear prose.) Since then, Cromwell's followers used "Enthusiastick Jargon," and the Restoration set loose "that Licentiousness" which "infect[ed] our Religion and Morals," then "corrupted our Language." Thus the Court, once a model, has become, and continues to be, "the worst School in *England*" for "Propriety, and Correctness of Speech" (*PW*, 4:10).

Cobbett often gives the impression that *all* official political language of his time is corrupt: "This is House-of-Commons' language. Avoid it as you would avoid all the rest of their doings" (*GEL*, 105). "You constantly hear talk like this amongst those whom the Boroughs make law-makers.... What incomprehensible words! Very becoming in the creatures of corruption, but ridiculous in any other persons of the world" (*GEL*, 108). "It is a very common parliament-house phrase, and therefore, presumably *corrupt*" (*GEL*, 81). He comes close to making Orwell's causal connection between bad language and bad politics. "The bad writing...I do not pretend to look on as the *cause* of the present public calamities, or any part of them; but, it is a proof of a *deficiency in that sort of talent*, which appears to me to be necessary in men intrusted with great affairs. He who writes badly thinks badly" (*GEL*, 145-46). From here it is not far to "Politics and the English Language": "In our time it is broadly true that political writing is bad writing" (*CEJL*, 4:135).

The Tory-Radicals view with anxiety a future that may not understand their writings. Only Hazlitt sees linguistic development as a natural process: "Does not every language change and wear out?" (*CW*, 10:29). Yet he considers the changes that English has undergone to be merely "a sprinkling of *archaisms*" (*CW*, 10:28), and in his *Grammar*, as in his philosophical considerations of time, the future is not even to be considered. "Accurately speaking, the English verb has only two variations expressive of time, namely, the present, and past or imperfect tense" (*CW*, 2:45). For Swift, however, the prospect of change is much more ominous.

Fashionable court English is dangerous for him chiefly because it would be indecipherable to "a Man of Wit, who died Forty Years ago" (*PW*, 2:175). Hooker and Parsons, who both lived a century before him, are good writers because they are still "clear and intelligible" (*PW*, 2:177). One of the reasons that English must be "ascertained" (fixed) is because "the Fame of our Writers is usually confined to these two Islands; and it is hard it should be limited in *Time*, as much as *Place*, by the perpetual Variations of our Speech.... How then shall any Man, who hath A Genius for History, equal to the best of the Antients, be able to undertake such a Work with Spirit and Chearfulness, when he considers, that he will be read with Pleasure but a very few years, and in an Age or two shall hardly be understood without an Interpreter?" (*PW*, 4:14, 18). Thus the Struldbruggs have to undergo a torment particularly frightening to Swift: "The Language of this Country being always upon the Flux, the *Struldbruggs* of one Age do not understand those of another; neither are they able after two Hundred Years to hold any conversation (farther than by a few general Words) with their

Neighbours the Mortals; and thus they lye under the disadvantage of living like Foreigners in their own Country" (*PW*, 11:197).[29]

Cobbett also expresses an unease with the transitory nature of meaning in language when he complains about a diplomatic communication of the Prime Minister: "Fifty years hence no man, who should read it, would be able to ascertain its meaning.... And yet, most momentous transactions, transactions involving the fate of millions of human beings, have been committed to the hands of this man!" (*GEL*, 169). Orwell's fear of the change that time works on language is perhaps greater than Swift's, and similarly linked to politics. He shows this by inventing a language that, ironically, is fixed—Newspeak. A language thus frozen would be immortal, freed from the restraints of history. No longer would the "sprinklings of archaisms" (that favorite phrase of Hazlitt's) be there, like Charrington's junk-shop, to tempt the thought-criminal. While Swift pleaded with Oxford for the possibility to be understood after fifty years, Syme taunts Winston with the irrevocability of Newspeak's divorce from the past: "Has it ever occurred to you, Winston, that by the year 2050, at the very latest, not a single human being will be alive who could understand such a conversation as we are having now?" (*NEF*, 47).

The Classical languages greatly influenced the Tory-Radicals' attitudes toward the English language. Swift seemed the most congenial with them, as when he contrasts the "Example of the *Greeks* and *Romans*" to "the *Gothick* Strain, and a natural Tendency towards relapsing into Barbarity" (*PW*, 2:175). But Hazlitt mistrusted them because they were a means of boosting literary reputations and power: "Among other things, the learned languages are a ready passport to this sort of unmeaning, unanalysed reputation" (*CW*, 8:207). Dr. Johnson's language is artificial and ultimately meaningless, since he uses only "words with the greatest number of syllables, or Latin phrases with merely English terminations. If a fine style depended on this sort of arbitrary pretension, it would be fair to judge of an author's elegance by the measurement of his words, and the substitution of foreign circumlocutions (with no precise associations) for the mother-tongue" (*CW*, 8:243). Cobbett, too, finds writers like Johnson not immune from errors in English because of their Classical education: "A knowledge of the Greek and Latin is not sufficient to prevent men from writing bad English.... With what propriety, then, are the Greek and Latin languages called the '*learned languages*'?" (*GEL*, 71). Those who trumpet the superiority of classical languages over English, besides betraying their ignorance, use it as a means of maintaining their power. Previous writers of grammars have already been taught Latin, and "unwilling to treat with simplicity that, which, if made somewhat of a mystery, would make them appear more *learned* than the mass of the people, they have endeavoured to make our simple language turn and twist itself so as to become as complex in its principles as the Latin language" (*GEL*, 104). Cobbett warned that classical languages could also be used as a smokescreen for political deceptions. Long before "Politics and the English Language," he realized that hiding something behind a classically-derived name can disguise its true function. Riding in the countryside, he notices a strange building, and learns that it is a semaphore. "To call it an *alarm-post* would not have been so convenient; for, people not embued with Scotch *intellect*, might have wondered *why* the devil we should have to pay for *alarm-posts*" after the victories in the Napoleonic Wars. "By calling the thing by an outlandish name, these reflections amongst the unintellectual are obviated" (*RR*, 288). Thus he warned his pupils "to avoid the use of any foreign or uncommon word, if you can express your meaning as fully and clearly by an English word in common use" (*GEL*, 8). This (as well as Hazlitt's strictures against "the substitution of foreign circumlocutions") is directly echoed in Orwell's rule v in "Politics and the English Language": "Never use a foreign phrase...if you can think of an everyday English equivalent" (*CEJL*, 4:139).

Orwell as well recognized the political misuses classical languages could facilitate. "Bad writers, and especially scientific, political and sociological writers, are nearly always haunted by the notion that Latin or Greek words are grander than Saxon ones" (*CEJL*, 4:131). Authors "friendly to totalitarianism," Orwell accuses, have "a strong tendency to drop into Latin when something unpleasant has to be said" (*CEJL*, 4:156-67). An Anglo-Saxon–based vocabulary was more acceptable to him because it was usually the more concrete.

The Tory-Radicals have all been famous, of course, as advocates of the concrete, plain style. For ease of understanding, Swift recommends cultivating that "Simplicity which is the best and truest Ornament of most Things in human Life" (*PW*, 2:177). The authors of the King James Bible produced the supreme monument of the plain style in English, "owing to the *Simplicity* that runs through the Whole." Because of their wide provenance, they "have proved a Kind of Standard for Language, especially to the Common People" (*PW*, 4:15). This quality is reflected in Swift's more famous definition of style, "Proper Words in proper Places" (*PW*, 9:65), which he gives in his *Letter to a Young Gentleman, Lately Entered into Holy Orders*. There he counsels the new clergyman to avoid "*hard Words*," and relates the example of "an Old Person of Quality" who tried out doubtful ones on a chambermaid (as legend has it Swift did with his own servants in reading to them *Gulliver's Travels* in progress). The admirable Brobdingnagians, like Cobbett and Orwell, treasure brevity and simplicity: "Their Stile is clear, masculine, and smooth, but not Florid; for they avoid nothing more than multiplying unnecessary Words, or using various Expressions" (*PW*, 11:121).

Hazlitt called it the "familiar" style. "To write a genuine familiar or truly English style, is to write as any one would speak in common conversation, who had a thorough command and choice of words, or who could discourse with ease, force, and perspicuity, setting aside all pedantic and oratorical flourishes" (*CW*, 8:242). The Johnsonian style is an evasion: "The florid style is the reverse of the familiar. The last is employed as an unvarnished medium to convey ideas; the first is resorted to as a spangled veil to conceal the want of them" (*CW*, 8:246). Orwell would have heartily agreed: a window pane cannot be varnished.

Cobbett, Hazlitt declared, "writes himself plain William Cobbett" (*CW*, 8:53), suggesting that the plain style is both a *dictum* and a *persona* (as Eric Blair wrote himself "plain George Orwell"). Cobbett advises, "Let chambermaids and members of the House of Commons, and learned Doctors, write thus: be you content with plain words which convey your meaning" (*GEL*, 86). He would have agreed with Orwell's rule iii: "If it is possible to cut a word out, always cut it out" (*CEJL*, 4:139). As Cobbett says, "One of the greatest of all faults in writing and in speaking is this; the using of many words to *say little*. In order to guard yourself against this fault, inquire what is the *substance*, or *amount*, of what you have said. Take a long speech of some talking Lord, and put down upon paper what the *amount* of it is. You will mostly find, that the amount is very small" (*GEL*, 143). However, the most important implication of the plain style for Cobbett is that mastery of it confers political power: "Grammar, perfectly understood, enables us, not only to express our meaning fully and clearly, but so to express it as to enable us to defy the ingenuity of man to give our words any other meaning than that which we ourselves intend them to express" (*GEL*, 7-8).

Orwell saw the dilemma of the political writer as a struggle "against vagueness, against obscurity, against the lure of the decorative adjective, against the encroachment of Latin and Greek, and, above all, against the worn-out phrases and dead metaphors with which the language is cluttered up" (*CEJL*, 3:26). The whole thrust of his linguistic reform is, like Hazlitt's, toward concreteness and colloquialness: "But if you habitually say to yourself, 'Could I simplify this? Could I make it more like speech?' you are not likely to...say...'static water' when you mean fire tank" (*CEJL*, 3:138) (or "semaphore" when you mean "alarm-post"). Orwell's first specific guidelines for writing, set down in 1944, stress, like Cobbett's, terse specificity: "There is only the general principle that concrete words are better than abstract ones, and that the shortest way of saying things is always the best" (*CEJL*, 3:26).

In devising guidelines for composition, the Tory-Radicals agree that words should follow thought, not vice versa. Swift advised his young clergyman: "When a Man's Thoughts are clear, the properest words will generally offer themselves first...and his own Judgment will direct him in what Order to place them, so they may be best understood" (*PW*, 9:68). Hazlitt counseled: "You must find the proper words and style to express yourself by fixing your thoughts on the subject you have to write about" (*CW*, 8:243). "*Think* before you write," Cobbett advised. "The *order* of the matter will be, in almost all cases, that of your thoughts.... *Never write about any matter that you do not well understand.* If you clearly understand all about your matter, you will never want thoughts, and thoughts instantly become words" (*GEL*, 65, 141, 143). Orwell's recommendations in "Politics and the English Language" follow these same lines. "What is above all needed is to let the meaning choose the word, and not the other way about. In prose, the worst thing one can do with words is to surrender to them.... Probably it is better to put off using words as long as possible and get one's meaning as clear as one can through pictures or sensations. Afterwards one can choose—not simply *accept*—the phrases that will best cover the meaning" (*CEJL*, 4:138-39).

Tory-Radical theories of writing are all based on this fundamental premise that the thing or the idea precedes the word, that the best language is basically concrete. In *Gulliver's Travels*, the worthy Brobdingnagians have no need for abstract nouns. "And as to Ideas, Entities, Abstractions and Transcendentals, I could never drive the least Conception into their Heads." Consequently, "their Libraries are not very large; for that of the King's, which reckoned the largest, doth not amount to above a thousand Volumes" (*PW*, 11:120). The Houyhnhnms also have a reduced vocabulary; in their case, fewer emotions led to fewer words. "It put me to the Pains of many Circumlocutions to give my Master a right Idea of what I spoke; for their Language doth not about in Variety of Words, because their Wants and Passions are fewer than among us" (*PW*, 11:226). They have *no* libraries: "The Inhabitants have not the least Idea of Books or Literature" (*PW*, 11:219). Yet does Swift unequivocally endorse this incomprehension of abstractions, this paucity of emotions, leaving the creatures "no Word in their Language to express any thing that is *evil*, except what they borrow from the Deformities or ill Qualities of the *Yahoos*" (*PW*, 11:259)? Does he then argue for a return to an exact correspondence between word and thing?

Not entirely, for Swift's most famous linguistic satire occurs in Part III, where the Laputan academicians destroy the signification of all words. Their word frames—the forerunner, as many critics have noted, of the "versificator" in *Nineteen Eighty-Four*—allow "the most ignorant Person at a reasonable Charge, and with a little bodily Labour, [to] write Books in Philosophy, Poetry, Politicks, Law, Mathematicks and Theology, without the least Assistance from Genius or Study" (*PW*, 11:166-68). Like Syme, the Newspeak lexicographer who believed in the beauty of the destruction of words, one projector at the School of Languages proposes "to shorten Discourse by cutting Polysyllables into one, and leaving out Verbs and Participles; because in Reality all things imaginable are but Nouns." His proposal leads quickly to its logical conclusion, the abolition of language: "Since Words are only Names for *Things*, it would be more convenient for all Men to carry about them, such *Things* as were necessary to express the particular Business they are to discourse on." Since these "scientists" are not a ruling body, the proles of their time—"the Vulgar and Illiterate"—threaten revolution if they cannot "speak with their Tongues." "Such constant irreconcilable Enemies to Science are the common People," Gulliver adds with unconscious irony (*PW*, 11:169).

In his essay "On Familiar Style," Hazlitt criticizes overblown, artificially stylized writers such as Dr. Johnson because they have divorced words from the thoughts behind them:

> A thought, a distinction is the rock on which all this brittle cargo of verbiage splits at once. Such writers have merely *verbal* imaginations, that retain nothing but words.... Such persons are in fact besotted with words, and their brains are turned with the glittering, but empty and sterile phantoms of things.... They may be considered as *hieroglyphical* writers. Words affect them in the same way, by the mere sound, that is, by their possible, not by their actual application to the subject at hand.... Objects are not linked to feelings, words to things. (*CW*, 8:246-47)

The same contempt for the use of words as things-in-themselves led Cobbett to deride those who would intimidate others with the knowledge of Latin and Greek: "The learning is in the *mind* and not on the *tongue*: learning consists of *ideas*, and not of the *noise* that is made by the mouth" (*GEL*, 118). He rejects elegant variation, different words for the same thing or idea, for the same reason; it is not merely "useless" but "a great deal worse; for it creates a confusion of ideas in the minds of the reader...it is always a mark of great affection and of false taste, when pains are taken to seek for synonymous words in order to avoid a repetition of sound...the littleness of mind [is] exposed" (*GEL*, 154). Overusing adjectives was wrong for the same reason. "Strength must be found in the *thought*, or, it will never be found in the *words*.

Big-sounding words, without thoughts corresponding, are efforts without effect" (*GEL*, 88). Orwell proceeds from the same basis:

> When you think of a concrete object, you think wordlessly, and then, if you want to describe the thing you have been visualising, you probably hunt about till you find the exact words that seem to fit it. When you think of something abstract you are more inclined to use words from the start, and unless you make a conscious effort to prevent it, the existing dialect will come rushing in and do the job for you, at the expense of blurring or even changing your meaning. (*CEJL*, 4:138)[30]

In his search for an exact match between language and meaning, Orwell makes a point like Gulliver's Master: "The lumpishness of words results in constant falsification.... If words represent meanings as fully and accurately as height multiplied by base represents the area of a parallelogram, at least the *necessity* for lying would never exist" (*CEJL*, 2:6). Houyhnhnms likewise do not know how to lie, "to say the Thing which was not."

Inevitably, however, Tory-Radicals become aware of the need for the abstract as well as the concrete. It is not enough to explain, as Charles Scruggs does, that "while recognizing the need for abstractions, Swift and Orwell were ruthless in attacking them when they concealed or distorted meaning."[31] The answer lies in the Tory-Radical split. The tory—the individualist—in Swift, like the Brobdingnagians, distrusted "Entities and Transcendentals." A tory, according to Hazlitt, "has not even the capacity of conceiving an abstract proposition" (*CW*, 19:288). Therefore, once words have been fixed, time can be conquered, the past recaptured, the writer more than "a tedious Relater of Facts" (*PW*, 4:19). Words are captive to the things they signify. However, Swift was also a radical, and also saw the dangers of such slavishness. To be totally self-sufficient, totally without words, as the Laputan projectors advocate, is not to be free at all; the "Sages" nearly sink "under the Weight of their Packs, like Pedlars." And it is the common people who threaten to "raise a Rebellion" if they lose their "Oldspeak," "the Liberty to speak with their tongues after the Manner of their Forefathers" (*PW*, 11:169). The abstract, the language of the group, is also necessary. The Brobdingnagian beggars are "the most horrible spectacles that ever an *European* eye beheld" (*PW*, 11:96). The word-frames can produce bogus works in "Philosophy, Poetry, Politicks, Law, Mathematicks and Theology"—subjects steeped in abstractions. The superrational Houyhnhnms, who have not the epistemic apparatus to conceive of a lie, can, at each of their quadrennial Grand Assemblies, blandly discuss genocide: "Whether the *Yahoos* should be exterminated from the Face of the Earth" (*PW*, 11:255). Orwell finds that this unanimity between general thought and word reveals "the highest stage of totalitarian organisation" (*CEJL*, 4:216) in Houyhnhnm society.

Thus simplicity, the plain style, is a great virtue to the Tory-Radical writer, but without a proper balance between the concrete and the abstract, real *virtue* is impossible. Orwell's ideas about the relationships between thoughts and words led him to an interest in Basic English, a language touted as a modern version of the Brobdingnagians' or Houyhnhnms'. In 1944 he observed, "In Basic, I am told, you cannot make a meaningless statement without its being apparent that it is meaningless—which is quite enough to explain why so many school-masters, editors, politicians and literary critics object to it" (*CEJL*, 3:210). (Its opponents belong to those professions that also excited the ridicule of Swift, Hazlitt, and Cobbett.) But during this period, Orwell began to distrust a language which lacked the means to *verify* abstract mean-ings. Sometime after 1943, when he first wrote the term "Newspeak" in the outline for "The Last Man in Europe," Orwell invented a lan-guage in which he would parody almost every rule he proposed in "Politics and the English Language." That essay first appeared in 1946; Orwell could have developed both linguistic ideas concurrently. Perhaps the essay and the novel are meant to be taken as cautionary tales of the danger of going to either linguistic extreme: "But if thought corrupts language, language can also corrupt thought" (*CEJL*, 4:137).

V: "Torn Both Ways"

John Rodden, in *The Politics of Literary Reputation*, points out that many studies of Orwell have centered on what commentators call dilemmas or contradictions: "Critics have been pronouncing Orwell a 'paradox' for more than a quarter-century now, and simply walking away." Rodden prefers to term these "tensions."[32] Daphne Patai notes that Orwell is a "writer almost universally acclaimed but one who arouses broad disagreements about what it is we are to admire in him."[33] And there is almost equal disagreement about what is to be most condemned in him, culminating in Raymond Williams's study and the collection *Inside the Myth: Orwell: Views from the Left.*[34] How, then, should Orwell be placed? How can these contradictions (or ten-sions) best be explained without "walking away"?

Tory-Radicals certainly share a fondness for criticizing the most cherished beliefs of their own party. Even Hazlitt had harsh words for democracy, in light of his admiration for Napoleon. In fact, Tory-

Radicals suffer from a kind of philosophical schizophrenia (which often exposes them to charges of actual mental unbalance). For them the individual must be free—politically, economically, and socially; but where does that leave the group's need for equality, and a sense of solidarity? Tory-Radicals are always striving to resolve these tensions, and sometimes the answers come all too easily. Hazlitt declares that liberty and equality are easily coexistent, and uses for his analogy a favorite haunt: "In a theatre, each person has a right to his own seat, by the supposition that he has no right to intrude into anyone else's. They are convertible propositions. Away, then, with the notion that liberty and equality are inconsistent" (*CW*, 19:307). But what if there are not enough seats in the theater? Who gets the tickets? Who is left in the street? Indeed, who decides how to answer these questions?

This is the dilemma Orwell hints at when he claims the "thinking person" (read Orwell) is "by intellect usually left-wing but by temperament often right-wing" (*RWP*, 211). What produces this contradictory temperament in so many English writers—Carlyle, Morris, Chesterton, not to mention those we have been examining? In other words, why does England seem to have produced a branch of radicalism that is, so surprisingly often, tory at its roots? Orwell himself provides a clue in his explanation for the subservience of English publishers toward the Ministry of Information during World War II: "the really well-trained dog is the one that turns his somersault when there is no whip. And that is the state we have reached in this country, thanks to three hundred years of living together without a civil war" (*CEJL*, 3:181). The Civil War produced in England a constitutional monarchy, and as the monarch grew less and less powerful, there was no one figure on which to vent any radical fervor. England began to be controlled by groups, ruling cliques, which were not always as easily identifiable as the favorites around a despot were. Initially it was ministries; thus Swift opposes the Tories, then the Whigs, and all the time carries on a running battle with what proved to be the most powerful group of all, the mercantile capitalist class. He rails against the tyranny of the *few*; it is an oligarchy, not a democracy, that most upsets him. Cobbett sometimes attacked a Castlereagh, a Sidmouth, a Ricardo, but more often he cannot even get a handle on whom to oppose; it is "the Establishment," "the THING," a surprisingly neutral term from this master of invective. More than Cobbett, Hazlitt found himself in opposition to monarchies, yet he spends more thought and space on refuting philosophical systems such as Malthusian economics than he does on some political questions. This helps to explain the predilection of Tory-Radicals for antisemitism. Here is a group that can be identified, separated, and blamed, particularly for economic conditions.

By Orwell's time the system, the THING, had ossified to the point where he could describe it as "a family with the wrong members in control" (*CEJL*, 2:68). The villains, again, are almost nameless—certainly quite faceless, not individuals. Orwell condensed all his characteristic Tory-Radical fears into the system he called "Oligarchical Collectivism": the tyranny of the group over the individual. As O'Brien tells Winston: "The first thing you must realize is that power is collective. The individual only has power in so far as he ceases to be an individual" (*NEF*, 218). Paradoxically, this hegemony of the group produces what Winston calls "the age of solitude," and he dreams of a time "when men are different from one another and do not live alone" (*NEF*, 27).

The Tory-Radicals' dual commitment to community and individuality is often rooted in their sense of exile. Swift was an Englishman when in Ireland, and an Irishman in England. Cobbett was, at various points in his life, a soldier in Canada, an exile in Philadelphia, and a fugitive on Long Island. Hazlitt spent part of his childhood in America, and felt isolated (in the root meaning of the word) when the Napoleonic wars prevented him from traveling to the Continent. Orwell, of course, was born in India, a moneyless "ugly" scholarship boy in school, a policeman in Burma, down and out in Paris, a soldier in Catalonia, and a refugee from civilization on a Hebridean island. Thus the Tory-Radical, while searching for solidarity, never really belongs in his society; not only is he an observer, he is an outsider. Like Swift at Laracor, and Cobbett at Botley, Orwell longed for a stable home base where he could virtually support himself and shut out the rest of the world. His first approach to this was at the Stores at Wallington, and he came closest to it near the end of his life at Jura. From this kind of base he would emerge to study unemployment in the north of England, fight fascists in Spain, and tour war-ravaged Europe—just as Cobbett had ranged over the south of England in *Rural Rides*. (Projects Orwell contemplated but never undertook for health reasons were a book on poverty at the end of the Thirties, a trip to India just before the war, and a journey to the southern United States to examine the plight of the blacks there just before his death.) The contradiction of the pilgrim who had no physical need to leave home is another manifestation of the Tory-Radical tradition: the individual who wants to be independent of the group, but cannot cease from investigating it. This led (to borrow Pritchett's famous phrase) to Orwell's "going native in his own country" when he first returned to England to merge with a group, "the lowest of the low," "to be one of them," to have "been among them and accepted by them" (*RWP*, 148-50).

Finally, we can only understand Orwell's ambivalence toward progress and history by placing him within the Tory-Radical tradition.

Janus-faced, Winston Smith dedicates his diary "to the future or to the past" (*NEF*, 26). In *The Road to Wigan Pier*, the recurring phrase that describes the dilemma of the socialist confronted by the Machine that sums up the inherent contradictions of the Tory-Radical position: "You feel yourself torn both ways" (*RWP*, 83). As Orwell later put the particular problem which the future posed, "All sensitive people are revolted by industrialism and its products," yet poverty cannot be stamped out and workers liberated without *more* industrialization (*CEJL*, 4:411). However much tinned milk, gas-pipe chairs, and the "antiseptic" utopias of H. G. Wells disgusted him, Orwell concluded that the Machine could not be destroyed. The question was how to remain decent while employing it: "It is more useful to try to humanise the collectivist society that is certainly coming than to pretend...that we could revert to a past phase" (*CEJL*, 4:103). Orwell wondered how, in an age dominated by the luxuriousness made possible by the Machine, athletic records could still be regularly broken. He worried that devices invented for the comfort of the group were threatening the well-being of the individual.

As he put it in the next-to-last entry in his diary: "Qy. how to reconcile?" (*CEJL*, 4:515). That question serves as a *summa* for the Tory-Radicals' dilemma. And since the Tory-Radical usually evades rather than reconciles, it was Orwell's final achievement as a writer to invent a name for the ability to hold two conflicting, often mutually exclusive, thoughts simultaneously. That he did not discover any other way of reconciling the rights of the individual and the obligations of the group is perhaps the most significant opportunity lost by the premature death of the last influential Tory-Radical of the twentieth century.

Notes

1. George Woodcock, *The Crystal Spirit: A Study of George Orwell* (Boston: Little, Brown, 1966), 55.
2. Disraeli, according to Orwell, "did think in terms of hereditary privilege, and was able to combine this with very enlightened views on many subjects.... He had an unjustified admiration for the British aristocracy. The society he wished for was a kind of moralised feudalism, a society neither plutocratic nor equalitarian." He appeals, Orwell claims, to the neo-Tories of Orwell's own time because "they want a better world with the same people on top." "Tapping the Wheels," *Observer*, 16 January 1944, 3.
3. Alice Chandler, *A Dream of Order: The Medieval Ideal in Nineteenth Century English Literature* (Lincoln: University of Nebraska Press, 1970), 5.
4. Ibid., 71.
5. Ibid., 161.
6. In this discussion, "tory" shall refer to the word's more general meaning as a synonym for conservative; "Tory" shall refer to the particular party

label. For "Tory-Radical" the upper-case is consistently used, since the thesis is that, however much each individual author is *sui generis*, it is a somewhat consistent philosophy.

7. Hugh Kenner, "The Politics of the Plain Style," in *Mazes* (San Francisco: North Point Press, 1989), 269.

8. V. S. Naipaul, "On Being a Writer," *New York Review of Books*, 23 April 1987, 7.

9. Roger Sale, *Closer to Home: Writers and Places in England, 1780-1830* (Cambridge: Harvard University Press, 1986), 79.

10. Ibid., 75, 80.

11. Naipaul, 7.

12. Kenner, 268.

13. Other than in the implications of Trilling's brief comparison, Hazlitt is not often thought of as a Tory-Radical. One of the goals of this study is to show in how many ways he was, even though in other important respects he does not fit the pattern.

14. *The Correspondence of Jonathan Swift*, ed. Harold Williams, 5 vols. (Oxford: Clarendon Press, 1963-1965), 1:109.

15. Ibid., 3:329.

16. Unless otherwise noted, all quotations of Swift's prose are taken from *The Prose Works of Jonathan Swift*, ed. Harold Davis et al., 14 vols. (Oxford: Blackwell, 1939-1968); hereafter abbreviated as *PW*.

17. All quotations of William Hazlitt are taken from *The Complete Works of William Hazlitt*, ed. P. P. Howe, 21 vols. (1930; reprint, New York: AMS Press, 1967); hereafter abbreviated as *CW*.

18. All quotations from William Cobbett's works are cited in the text using the following abbreviations:

HPR   *A History of the Protestant "Reformation," etc.* (London: Charles Clements, 1824). This edition is unpaginated; numbers in the text refer to paragraphs.

RR   *Rural Rides, etc.*, ed. G. D. H. and M. Cole, 3 vols. (London: Peter Davies, 1930). Since the volumes are continuously paginated no volume numbers are given in the text.

AYM   *Advice to Young Men, etc.* (Oxford: Oxford University Press, 1984).

CE   *Cottage Economy* (London: Douglas Pepler, 1916).

GEL   *A Grammar of the English Language, etc.* (Oxford: Oxford University Press, 1984).

19. George Woodcock says about *Rural Rides* that Cobbett's "tendency to be convinced only by what he actually saw was a positive advantage; it saved him from either utopian or anti-utopian visions. Had he lived in our century he might well have written something like *The Road to Wigan Pier*, he could never have written a *1984*" (Appendix to *Rural Rides* [Harmondsworth: Penguin, 1967], 492). Yet considering Cobbett's belief in the reality and importance of the historical past, in state-sponsored deliberate falsification of the past, in the historical power of words, in the decay of the present, and with his hatred of double-thinking, he would have understood all the major points of Orwell's last work. For Cobbett, the solidarity of the past had to be recaptured by overthrowing the nightmare solitude of the depopulated present.

20. Jonathan Swift, *Journal to Stella*, ed. Harold Williams, 2 vols. (Oxford: Clarendon Press, 1948), 1:220.

21. *The Complete Poems of Jonathan Swift*, 2d ed., ed. Harold Williams, 3 vols. (Oxford: Clarendon Press, 1957), 1:198, 202.

22. Charles Scruggs points out the correspondence of Swift's and Orwell's use of the maxim in "George Orwell and Jonathan Swift: A Literary Relationship," *South Atlantic Quarterly* 76 (1977): 180.

23. F. P. Lock, *The Politics of Gulliver's Travels* (Oxford: Clarendon Press, 1980), 10; F. P. Lock, *Swift's Tory Politics* (Newark: University of Delaware Press, 1983), vii.

24. Steinhoff and Crick have claimed that Orwell's immediate historical source was Eugene Lyons's *Assignment in Utopia* (which Orwell reviewed), in which Stalin's Five-Year Plan was expressed $2 + 2 = 5$ (Crick, annotations to *Nineteen Eighty-Four* [Oxford: Clarendon Press, 1984], 440 n. 55). Steinhoff argues that Orwell was influenced by Chesterton's, Zamyatin's, and Dostoyevsky's use of $2 \times 2 = 4$ as a trope (18, 172-75). The element of a belief obdurately held in the face of all opposition, however, is missing in Steinhoff's influences, as is the correct mathematical sign.

25. Orwell, "Tapping the Wheels," 3.

26. George Orwell, Introduction to *The British Pamphleteers*, ed. Orwell and Reginald Reynolds (London: Allan Wingate, 1948), 9.

27. *George Orwell: The Lost Writings*, ed. W. J. West (New York: Arbor House, 1985), 73.

28. Ibid., 237-38.

29. Swift's proposal to set up an English Academy to regulate language is echoed in Orwell's many informal proposals for linguistic "academies" for various purposes. In "New Words," for instance, he proposes "a society for the invention of new and subtler words" (*CEJL*, 2:7), some of whose duties would be similar to those described by Swift for his academicians.

30. To chart Orwell's attitudes toward adjectives is to chart his development as a political writer. In 1936 he challenged that "if your motto is 'Cut out the adjectives,' why not go a bit further and revert to a system of grunts and squeals, like the animals?" (*CEJL*, 1:227). He cheered at the end of the decade: "The adjective has come back, after its ten years' exile" (*CEJL*, 1:497). In 1940 he complained that the "plain" style of the Thirties with its lack of "unnecessary adjectives" "tend[ed] to emasculate the language altogether" (*CEJL*, 2:43). Yet by 1944, as noted above, he was warning "against the lure of the decorative adjective" (*CEJL*, 3:26). In "Why I Write" (1946), he confessed that when he "lacked a *political* purpose" he was lured into, among other sins, "decorative adjectives" (*CEJL*, 1:7). Sonia Brownell declared that at her first meeting with Orwell he "said one shouldn't use adjectives" (to which C. Day Lewis replied, "What about Shakespeare?"). (Michael Shelden, *Friends of Promise: Cyril Connolly and the World of Horizon* [London: Hamish Hamilton, 1989], 159). Yet in *Nineteen Eighty-Four*, the repellent Syme's job is just such an elimination of adjectives, and "The Principles of Newspeak" affirms that few current English adjectives lasted into Newspeak.

31. Scruggs, 179.

32. Rodden, 39.

33. Daphne Patai, *The Orwell Mystique: A Study in Male Ideology* (Amherst: University of Massachusetts Press, 1984), 3.
34. Raymond Williams, *George Orwell* (New York: Viking, 1971); *Inside the Myth: Orwell: Views from the Left*, ed. Christopher Norris (London: Lawrence and Wishart, 1984).

George Orwell's Second Thoughts on Capitalism

Arthur M. Eckstein

To the end of his life, George Orwell remained a socialist. In "Why I Write" (1946), we find his programmatic statement: "Every line of serious work that I have written since 1936 has been written, directly or indirect, *against* totalitarianism and *for* democratic Socialism, as I understand it" (*CEJL*, 1:5). Orwell had fiercely attacked the attitude of capitalist society toward the poor in *Down and Out in Paris and London* (1933) and in *The Road to Wigan Pier* (1937). He always made a point of wearing the blue shirt of the French working class.[1] And in the last summer of his life (1949), Orwell enrolled his adopted son Richard in the anarchist colony at Whiteway (*CEJL*, 4:507). On *Nineteen Eighty-Four* specifically, Orwell wrote to Francis Henson: "My recent novel is NOT intended as an attack on Socialism or on the British Labour Party (of which I am a supporter)..." (*CEJL*, 4:502 [16 June 1949]).

Yet if Orwell remained in his own mind a man of the Left (indeed, of the far Left), a paradox appears if we survey the references to the capitalist "past" in his last and greatest work. The capitalist "past" of *Nineteen Eighty-Four* is, of course, Orwell's present. And seen from the nightmare world of Ingsoc, the capitalist "past" has much to recommend it—in fact, just about everything to recommend it. Orwell's attitude toward capitalism in *Nineteen Eighty-Four* is so out of kilter with what scholars have normally emphasized as his socialism that it raises the question of whether Orwell's view of capitalism was not more complex than is usually thought (see, e.g., *GO*, 393-99, especially 397-99). This paper will argue that Orwell's view of capitalism was indeed complex, and became more complex over time, as he re-evaluated capitalist society in accordance with his own life experiences.

In *Nineteen Eighty-Four*, the vanished capitalist "past" possesses two outstanding characteristics. First, material life for the average person had been far better in that "past" than it was under Ingsoc. Examples are numerous: the wide availability of real coffee, real sugar, real chocolate, good beer, wine, fruit, solidly-built furniture, elevators that worked.[2] Above all: the wide availability of well-made books and even objects kept for their intrinsic beauty alone (*NEF*, 9 with 80; 81 with 121).

Second, in the "past" there had existed individual freedom: freedom of thought, human rights, even freedom of speech. The total suppression of individual freedom under Ingsoc is, of course, the main theme of *Nineteen Eighty-Four* and needs no detailing. But that such freedom had once existed Orwell is careful to make clear in the novel: we are not dealing here with mere theoretical human possibilities. In the "past," then, it had been usual for people to read books in the cozy privacy of their own homes—without fear of the Thought Police. People had felt free to keep diaries, to record events and thoughts for themselves. Human relationships had existed naturally, without constant state interference—which is why the life of intimacy and honesty lived by Winston Smith and Julia above the junk shop is explicitly called a relic of an earlier age. There had been no imprisonment without trial, no public executions, no torture to extract confessions. In the "past," orators espousing all kinds of political opinions had even had their free public say in Hyde Park.[3]

And from Goldstein's Book, Winston Smith learns that the previous existence of relative plenty and relative individual freedom had not come about by accident. Relative plenty had resulted from the increasing use of industrial machines, which by the early twentieth century had led in turn to wider distribution of goods and very greatly increased standards of living. Relative individual freedom had prevailed because

> the heirs of the French, English, and American revolutions had
> partly believed their own phrases about the rights of man, freedom
> of speech, equality before the law...and had even allowed their con-
> duct to be influenced by them to some extent. (*NEF*, 168)

Capitalism, according to the Party, had meant a world of poverty and slavery (*NEF*, 61-63, 81). Winston Smith's varied historical research—interviews, the collecting of artifacts, and the reading of Goldstein's Book—reveal to him that this is a lie.[4] The capitalist "past" had not been perfect: prosperity and freedom had been only partial (*NEF*, 157). But obviously, the previous capitalist civilization had been beyond measure preferable to the current Ingsoc State. This is surely one reason why Winston, in the famous scene where he and Julia are inducted into the bogus underground movement (*NEF*, 146), chooses to toast not the future but the past.

Since Orwell was a socialist, this basically positive depiction of "past" capitalist society in *Nineteen Eighty-Four* represents a problem. And the problem is compounded by a closer examination of the Henson letter. Orwell explains, as we noted above, that *Nineteen Eighty-Four* is not intended as an attack on socialism; yet in the very next phrase he also says that the novel is intended as "a show-up of the perversions to which a centralised economy is liable" (*CEJL*, 4:502). Indeed, as Goldstein's Book explains to Winston, it is Ingsoc itself which is directly responsible for the conditions of poverty and slavery that afflict his world (*NEF*, 152-64). Thus, a convinced socialist has written a work in which the effects of a centralized, planned economy are socially disastrous and in which capitalist society appears quite attractive—especially (but not solely) by contrast. The latter point is intriguing since, strictly speaking, it is unnecessary to the novel. That is, there was simply no need for Orwell to portray the "past" capitalist world so attractively in order to condemn the brutal totalitarianism of the Ingsoc State. We are dealing here with an ambivalence—even a contradiction—in Orwell's socialism. Basically, Orwell despised capitalism; but especially in his most pessimistic moods, he was willing to concede it a crucial virtue.

In Orwell's earliest forebodings about the destruction of civilization (1933), the engine of destruction would be Huxley's "Fordification": capitalism and consumerism. The populace of the world would be reduced to docile wage-slaves, their lives utterly in the hands of "the bankers" (*CEJL*, 1:121-22). Under the impact of the cataclysmic events of the 1930s, however—the coming of Hitler, the Soviet purge trials, his experience in the Spanish Civil War—a different vision eventually began to impose itself on Orwell. By 1938 he was coming to fear that civilization would be destroyed by the worldwide triumph of state dictatorship (*CEJL*, 1:330).

The first truly detailed exposition of Orwell's dark vision of eventual worldwide totalitarianism occurs in his essay on Henry Miller, "Inside the Whale" (written in the summer and autumn of 1939, published in March 1940). In seeking to explain the political quietism of Miller's writing, Orwell argues that an inevitable historical process is leading to the destruction of "western civilization"—which he defines as *laissez-faire* capitalism plus liberal-Christian culture. What is coming is the centralized state, and the new world war will only hasten its arrival. But the implications of this development have not yet been fully understood, Orwell says, because people have falsely imagined that socialism would most likely be a better sort of liberalism. On the contrary: "Almost certainly we are moving into an age of totalitarian dictatorships," an age in which both freedom of thought and the autonomous individual are going to be stamped out of existence. But this in turn means that "literature, in the form we have known it, must suffer at least a temporary death"—for literature has depended on the existence of the autonomous individual writer. In the present a writer may well choose to aid the coming of the new age, but he cannot contribute to this political process as a writer, "for *as a writer* he is a liberal, and what is happening is the destruction of liberalism." Hence Henry Miller's political quietism. As a writer—as a liberal—the only honest subject left to Miller in this age of violent political change is personal life and sexuality (*CEJL*, 1:525-27).

In this essay Orwell emphasizes that Western literature has depended on individual freedom of thought, and that both Western literature and individual freedom of thought have depended on the existence of a "liberal-Christian culture"—which is disappearing, in favor of the centralized state. No direct link is made as yet between literature and the existence of capitalism as a specific economic system. There are hints in that direction, but only hints: *laissez-faire* capitalism is paired with liberal-Christian culture as an essential element in the definition of "Western civilization"; and the autonomous, honest writer is described as "a hangover from the bourgeois age" (*CEJL*, 1:525). Nor is Orwell against socialism: the centralized state which is now coming may be grim, but it may also be a grim necessity. This is why Orwell allows writers to participate in the struggle to bring about the revolutionary new world (although, he emphasizes, not as writers). And Orwell does not completely abandon hope that this new world might eventually produce its own great literature (of a new sort, it is true). Thus he ends the essay with the assertion that Miller's political quietism demonstrates the impossibility of any major literature "*until* the world has shaken itself into its new shape" (*CEJL*, 1:527; my italics).

Still, this is only a small ray of light in an otherwise very dark landscape. In fact, Orwell's publisher, Victor Gollancz, a man of strong left-wing views, was upset with "Inside the Whale" and wrote Orwell that he was being too pessimistic about the future. Orwell replied (4 January 1940):

> You are perhaps right in thinking I am over-pessimistic. It is quite possible that freedom of thought etc. may survive in an economically totalitarian society. We can't tell until a collectivised economy has been tried out in a western country. (*CEJL*, 1:409)

But at the moment, Orwell continues, he is more worried about intellectuals who stupidly equate British democracy with fascism or despotism: given the current threat from Nazi Germany, he hopes that the common people will have more sense (*CEJL*, 1:409-10).

There are three points to note in this important letter. First, Orwell at this time (January 1940) is not fully pessimistic about the effect of a collectivized state on intellectual freedom. Second, perhaps at Gollancz's prodding, he is exploring in his mind the relationship between freedom of thought and the specific form of *economic* life within a society. We can see his unease with the idea that society might be both "economically totalitarian" and yet intellectually free: it is possible, but somehow not logical. Third, Orwell brings Gollancz back from theory to reality, firmly asserting the value of the freedom currently existing in Britain: capitalist Britain is not a fascist despotism and deserves defending by everyone. This was an idea that set Orwell apart from many leftist intellectuals; it was, in fact, still a relatively new idea for Orwell himself. Deep into 1939 *he* had continued to equate British "democracy" with fascism—the position he now castigated in others.[5] But as is well known, with the coming of war against the Nazis Orwell had experienced a sudden and monumental awakening of patriotism; and this letter to Gollancz shows that one source of it was an appreciation of the freedoms Britain actually provided. Those freedoms formed the reality against which Orwell would henceforth judge socialist theory. Perhaps the effect can already be seen in "Inside the Whale," where we find not merely the vision of a totalitarian future (in Orwell's thoughts since at least 1938), but a true elegy for "liberal-Christian culture."

If in the Gollancz letter Orwell is uncertain about the fate of intellectual freedom in a collectivized economy, nine months later he is definitely and publicly optimistic. In *The Lion and the Unicorn: Socialism and the English Genius* (written in the autumn of 1940, published in February 1941), Orwell proposes a revolutionary program, including nationalization of industry and equalization of incomes via punitive taxation.[6] The capitalist system is doomed in any case, Orwell writes, and socialism is necessary if Britain hopes to win the war. But, he asserts, *his* socialist regime will not degenerate into tyranny, because it will be solidly grounded in the prevailing gentleness of English culture. This last idea seems an amplification of Orwell's remarks to Gollancz about the possibility of a humane—Western—economic collectivism, combined with Orwell's new, patriotic approval of the basic forms of English life (*CEJL*, 2:96-109, especially 101-3 and 107).

And it is probably no accident that, hopeful of an English and democratic socialism, Orwell now is explicitly disdainful of economic liberty per se. In modern England, "the liberty of the individual is still believed in, almost as in the nineteenth century. *But this has nothing to do with economic liberty*, the right to exploit others for profit". (*CEJL*, 2:59; my italics)

Even in *The Lion and the Unicorn*, though, Orwell's direct criticisms of English capitalist society are quite restrained. Basically, it is too economically disorganized to cope with the current military crisis (Orwell believes that centralized coordination and control will be necessary for Britain's survival), and it produces an upper class which is too stupid to win the war (*CEJL*, 2:69-73, 103). But Orwell declares also that capitalism has spread prosperity much farther down the social scale than was previously ever thought possible (*CEJL*, 2:76). And with all its faults, British society is not a fascist dictatorship. Its claim to be democratic is not a complete sham, nor is its claim to respect human rights:

> In England, such concepts as justice, liberty and objective truth are still believed in. They may be illusions, but they are powerful illusions. The belief in them influences conduct, national life is different because of them. In proof of which, look about you. Where are the rubber truncheons, where is the castor oil? (*CEJL*, 2:63)

This passage—and especially the idea that the prevailing belief in legal justice and liberty tends strongly to influence bourgeois social conduct—points directly ahead to "Goldstein's" explanation of relative human freedom in capitalist society before the Ingsoc Revolution.[7] The prevailing English liberty and legality are precisely what Orwell believes his proposed English socialist state—efficient, but gentle—will preserve.

Orwell's confident mood of 1940—the odd euphoria which accompanied the Battle of Britain—did not last long. He soon relapsed into pessimism. Even before "The Lion and the Unicorn" came out in print, his hopes for an immediate, democratic socialist revolution had already faded (see *CEJL*, 2:49-50 [3 January 1941]). Britain was still fighting practically alone against Nazi Germany, and in the spring of 1941 the war news itself turned increasingly bad. England now seemed to Orwell genuinely on the verge of defeat; at the very least, a long, grim struggle was in the offing, with untold negative effects on the character of English society. The result of Orwell's worries in this period were two essays, in April and May 1941, which are significant in the development of his thought but which have never received more than glancing attention from Orwell scholars. Both essays reveal Orwell's increasing concern over the form which socialism (even English socialism) might take, and—concurrently—an appreciation of the virtues offered by the currently existing capitalist society (dreadful though the faults of that society are).[8]

The first essay is the startlingly titled "Will Freedom Die with Capitalism?" published in Victor Gollancz's journal the *Left News* for April 1941.[9] Here, in response to a letter from Douglas Ede, Orwell attempts directly to answer the question: "Can Democracy, as we know it, survive into a collectivist age, or is it simply a reflection of *laissez faire* capitalism?" (WFD, 1682). One must say that the answer Orwell found to this question was complex—and equivocal.

In "Will Freedom Die?" Orwell holds that capitalism is both inherently evil and historically doomed. It is inherently evil because it depends purely on the cash nexus, and has no room in its economic relations for the human (let alone the humane). It is historically doomed because on the one hand, the historical process ineluctably moves from ancient slave states to feudalism to capitalism and then to socialism and communism (the Marxist paradigm), and more specifically because the disorganized nature of capitalism makes it less efficient than a centralized socialist economy. But the example of an efficient centralized socialist economy with which Orwell unfavorably compares capitalism is the economy of Nazi Germany, which Orwell here as elsewhere always insisted was a form of socialism. And this very example of Nazi Germany (the Soviet Union of Stalin also looms in the background) raises for Orwell a disturbing idea:

> As against capitalist democracy nazism must prevail because it is more up to date, therefore more efficiently militarily; but as a way of life it is immeasurably worse. It is a step forward, and a step to the bad. (WFD, 1684)

But how can a step *forward* away from capitalism be, for a socialist, a step to the bad? The reason, according to Orwell, is that it is by no means certain that the change-over to a collectivized economy will make human life immediately happier, easier, or freer. "On the contrary, the transition may make life very nearly unbearable for a long period, perhaps for hundreds of years" (WFD, 1683). The ultimate goal, supported by Orwell, is utopian communism; and socialism is the necessary next step after capitalism toward that goal; but the road "may lead through some dreadful places," and "I think we ought to guard against assuming that as a system to live under, [socialism] will be greatly preferable to democratic capitalism" (ibid.).

This is because, first of all, capitalism itself has been tamed from its original total inhumanity, "and has developed certain virtues of its own" (ibid.). And second, there is the very real possibility, even probability, that socialist states will be horrific dictatorships:

> Just as at the end of the feudal age there appeared a new figure,
> the man of money, so at the end of the capitalist age there appears
> another new figure, the man of power, the Nazi gauleiter or
> Bolshevik commissar. Such men...don't want ease and luxury, they
> merely want the pleasure of tyrannising over other people. And
> since power has not been debunked as money has, they can pro-
> ceed with a self-righteousness...that would be impossible to a
> mere money-grubber. But from the point of view of the underdog
> the rule of power is worse than the rule of money. (WFD, 1684)

It is obvious that important ideas here look forward to the depiction of Ingsoc society in *Nineteen Eighty-Four*. Orwell's 1941 image of
"the man of power," whose ultimate motive is simple joy in the exercise of tyranny, seems to be the root of O'Brien's terrifying disquisi-
tion on power and its ultimate destiny in the torture-chambers of the
Ministry of Love. The concept of a socialism that will "lead through
dreadful places" and "make life very nearly unbearable, perhaps for
hundreds of years," forms the basic structure of the novel itself.

By comparison, Orwell admits in "Will Freedom Die?" that a society of democratic capitalism may well be less repressive—perhaps far
less repressive—than many of the forms of oncoming socialism. That
is one of the virtues of "tamed" capitalism. He even admits, for
instance, that the radical Spanish Republic, for which he himself had
fought and bled, had outraged every principle of democracy far more
grossly than any British government manned by Conservatives would
ever dare to do (WFD,1685). If that turned out to be the case in radical Spain, where Orwell believed innocent idealism had indeed flour-
ished, then the socialist future takes on a very chilling aspect.

Nevertheless, Orwell does see one ray of hope—the same hope that
he suggested to Victor Gollancz in his letter of January 1940, the hope
explicated in more detail in *The Lion and the Unicorn*. Granted that
the transition to a centralized economy must happen, perhaps in
Western Europe the effects will be less destructive to human freedom
than has so far been the case in Nazi Germany and the Soviet Union.
This is because the countries of the West have all developed a strong
tradition of parliamentary democracy and, even more importantly, "a
belief in the *value* of bourgeois Democracy is widespread" (WFD,
1684, Orwell's emphasis). These national habits of thought and behavior are deep-rooted and important: a peaceful socialist revolution
might not disturb them, even if *capitalist* democracy itself disappears.
The prospects for Britain, with its unrepressive upper class, are the
most encouraging of all:

> I think the answer to Mr. Ede's query must be that *if* we can bring
> our revolution about it will be comparatively speaking a bloodless

one, and that many features of capitalist Democracy, whose disappearance he rightly dreads, will be able to survive it. (WFD, 1685, Orwell's emphasis)

But Orwell does not end his essay on this happy note. A socialist revolution in Britain might be "less bloody and disappointing than elsewhere"—but then again, it might not. There is no certainty except that a centralized economy is coming (especially because of pressures induced by the war), and that democratic capitalism cannot be saved. So Orwell grimly urges Douglas Ede to grow up:

> To say that since capitalist Democracy has its points it would be better to retain it in toto, is as though a baby should say that since lying in a cradle is a very pleasant thing, it would be better to remain a baby all your life. No such thing can happen, and to wish for the impossible, even the impossible good, is inherently reactionary. (WFD, 1685)

All this can hardly be called a ringing endorsement of the socialist project, nor does Orwell display here much confidence in the coming of a socialist democracy: it is only a hoped-for possibility. What is also striking for our purposes is Orwell's willing acknowledgment in this depressing essay that capitalist society as currently constituted does provide the genuine virtue of democracy and human rights, and that this is a definite good that ought to be preserved as much as possible. The problem is Orwell's doubt that it can be.

The month after "Will Freedom Die?" appeared (that is, in May 1941), Orwell's mood had become even more somber. The war news was, if anything, growing worse: Britain seemed about to be totally defeated in the crucial Mediterranean theater. And so we find him writing in his diary on 18 May: "Within two years we shall either be conquered or we shall be a socialist republic fighting for its life, with a secret police force and half the population starving" (*CEJL*, 2:401).

Britain defeated (or even occupied), Britain a starving socialist police state: this had not been the vision of 1940 and "The Lion and the Unicorn." Intensifying pessimism about the future now led Orwell to an even sharper appreciation of the virtues of the present, which are specified in the essay "Literature and Totalitarianism."

"Literature and Totalitarianism" originated as a radio talk show for the BBC Overseas Service and was then published in *The Listener*. It appears that Orwell was somewhat self-deprecatory about these BBC radio lectures. But the problem was not their content. Orwell simply felt guilty about beaming discussions of British literary culture to India at a time when India was struggling to gain her independence from

Britain.[10] The lecture "Literature and Totalitarianism" was broadcast on
21 May 1941—that is, just three days after Orwell recorded in his diary
the darkest forebodings about the English future (including the possible nature of English socialism). In fact, this essay is the second full-
scale exposition of Orwell's nightmare vision of worldwide tyranny
(the first being "Inside the Whale").

Orwell begins by warning of "the threat that hangs over the whole
of literature in the coming age" (*CEJL*, 2:134). He explains that European
literature has been the product of the autonomous individual, concerned only to write with honesty. But in "the age of the totalitarian
state," which is likely to be a worldwide phenomenon, the individual
is not going to be allowed any freedom whatsoever (*CEJL*, 2:134-35).
And the origin of the totalitarian state, Orwell now says, is basically economic: it is brought about by the end of "free capitalism" and its
replacement by "a centralised economy" (*CEJL*, 2:135). The result:

> The economic liberty of the individual, *and to a great extent his
> liberty to do what he likes*...comes to an end. Now, till recently the
> implications of this were not foreseen. *It was never fully realized
> that the disappearance of economic liberty would have any effect
> on intellectual liberty.* Socialism was usually thought of as a sort
> of moralised liberalism. The state would take charge of your eco-
> nomic life, and set you free from the fear of poverty...but it would
> have no need to interfere with your private intellectual life.... Now,
> on the existing evidence, one must admit that these ideas have
> been falsified. Totalitarianism has abolished freedom of thought to
> an extent unheard of in any previous age. Can literature survive in
> such an atmosphere?...It cannot. If totalitarianism becomes world-
> wide and permanent, what we have known as literature must come
> to an end. And it will not do—as may appear plausible at first—
> to say that what will come to an end is merely the literature of
> post-Renaissance Europe. (*CEJL*, 2:135-36, my italics)

This is an astonishing passage. The linking of economic liberty with
other liberties represents a complete reversal from Orwell's position
in "The Lion and the Unicorn." The explicit connecting of centralized
control over the economy with centralized control over the private
intellect—this is an analysis worthy of Norman Podhoretz. (In fact, it
is the analysis of Norman Podhoretz, and in an article on Orwell—but
without reference to "Literature and Totalitarianism," so little known
is this essay.[11])

Much of "Literature and Totalitarianism," clearly, is based on ideas
first developed in "Inside the Whale." But there are at least two significant changes. First, the existence of the honest and autonomous
author, and thus of literature as we have known it, is now attributed

not to "liberal-Christian culture" but precisely to the existence of economic liberty itself. Second, a centralized economy, once it becomes totalitarian, will mean the death not just of "bourgeois literature" but of all literature.

Orwell does try to sound a hopeful note at the end, but the attempt only reveals his current despair. Literature's survival, he says, depends on those countries where liberalism has sunk its deepest roots:

> Though a collectivised economy is bound to come, those countries may know how to evolve a form of Socialism which is not totalitarian, in which freedom of thought can survive the disappearance of economic individualism. (*CEJL*, 2:137)

This concept, of course, lay at the heart of *The Lion and the Unicorn*: the "English genius" would lead to a humane socialist regime. In "Will Freedom Die?" such an outcome is suggested as at least a strong possibility (though an oppressive socialist dictatorship is admitted to be a strong possibility too—even in England). But now, in "Literature and Totalitarianism," the idea is canvassed that a "liberal" socialism being founded in certain culturally favorable climates is "no more than a pious hope" (*CEJL*, 2:137). And Orwell ends his exposition with the dry comment, "That, at any rate, is the only hope to which anyone who cares about literature can cling" (*CEJL*, 2:137). He clearly fears that here he is merely whistling past the graveyard, for he knows that even gentle Britain may not be immune to socialist totalitarianism. That, of course, is one of Orwell's main points in *Nineteen Eighty-Four* (and consciously intended to shock)—as he explicitly says in the Henson letter.

After "Literature and Totalitarianism," Orwell never returned to an explicit, full-scale discussion of the connection between economic liberty and intellectual freedom. This is at first sight odd, for Orwell as a writer was capable of repeating ideas *ad nauseam*. The reason for his reticence here seems obvious, however: the implications of this view of the social impact of capitalist economics made Orwell the socialist very uncomfortable, challenging his most cherished ideals about how a "just" society should look. Those ideals he never gave up. Nevertheless, the ideas which evolved in the face of the catastrophe that seemed to loom in spring 1941 had an enduring influence upon his life and work. The simplest evidence comes from the Henson letter and has already been quoted: *Nineteen Eighty-Four* is "a show-up of the perversions to which a centralised conomy is liable." The emphasis on the economic origins of Big Brother points directly back to "Literature and Totalitarianism."

It is also striking that, after 1941, Orwell occasionally wrote passages extolling nineteenth-century capitalism and capitalist society as phenomena characterized, above all, by human freedom. The most famous instance occurs in "Riding Down to Bangor" (1946). In discussing the mood of certain mid-Victorian American novels, Orwell remarks:

> [They have] not only innocence but...a buoyant, carefree feeling, which was the product, presumably, of the unheard-of freedom and security which nineteenth-century America enjoyed.... [It was] a rich, empty country...in which the twin nightmares that beset nearly every modern man, the nightmare of unemployment and the nightmare of State interference, had hardly come into being.... There was not, as there is now, an all-prevailing sense of helplessness. There was room for everybody, and if you worked hard you could be certain of a living—could even be certain of growing rich: this was generally believed, and for the greater part of the population it was even broadly true. In other words, the civilisation of nineteenth-century America was capitalist civilisation at its best. (*CEJL*, 4:246-47)

Such outright praise of anything is rare in Orwell.

Orwell returned more than once to this vision of the nineteenth century as an age of human freedom.[12] And after 1941 we also find occasional brief remarks where he links capitalism directly or indirectly with liberty (especially intellectual liberty) (*CEJL*, 2:335; 3:118, 229-30). He praised unregulated, independent small businessmen, too (*CEJL*, 3:208; 4:25, 176, 465); and, as was already true by 1941, he continued to use the term "capitalist democracy" without irony (unusual in a man of the far Left) (*CEJL*, 2:168; 4:162, 325).

This is not to suggest that Orwell's view of capitalism ever became basically positive. On the contrary, whatever his occasionally idealizing (and even naive) attitude toward a stage of capitalism in the nineteenth-century past, Orwell feared and despised what he saw as the giant "monopoly" capitalism of the present. As powerful and as impersonal as the State, it was just as capable of crushing the individual—through the unemployment line, rather than the interrogation chamber.[13]

But it is also clear that by the early 1940s Orwell had become deeply suspicious of economic collectivism per se, and especially the threat it potentially posed to intellectual freedom. Indeed, he feared the State more than he feared capitalism—perhaps because he felt that the capitalist system was dying, whereas the age of the State was only beginning. It was difficult to reconcile these suspicions with a wholehearted advocacy of socialism. One way of achieving such a reconciliation was to give your socialism a strongly anarchist slant—which is precisely what Orwell always did. Yet it should be emphasized that Orwell himself well knew that in the real world, "centralised control is a necessary pre-condition of Socialism" (*CEJL*, 4:18).

Orwell's difficulty here may help account for the general "paleness" of his pro-socialist writing after 1941. It singularly lacks concrete and convincing detail either about the shape a democratic socialist society might take, or how we are to get there. (This is particularly the case with his proposed Socialist United States of Europe.) Meanwhile, as the Cold War developed, Orwell firmly sided with America (*faute de mieux*, it is true), and castigated those intellectuals who did not do the same (*CEJL*, 4:309, 323, 392, 398). To cite one startling example: a major reason Orwell said he was pleased with the Labour Party's electoral victory of July 1945 was his belief that a Labour government would not be "obliged to adopt an appeaser attitude toward the USSR."

> At some point or another a stand against Russian aggression will have to be made, and when the moment comes a Labour government will be able to unite the country behind it, which a Conservative government for obvious reasons could not.[14]

Indeed, after 1941 Orwell's real focus of social and political concern changed radically: he concentrated his literary energies more and more simply on the defense of civil liberties and intellectual freedom. He had come to see how fragile these things were, and from how many directions they were threatened.[15] Orwell's friend T. R. Fyvel now tells us that when the Labour government began nationalization of industry and punitive taxation of incomes—two of the very measures that Orwell himself had proposed five years before, in *The Lion and the Unicorn*—Orwell "was not against these measures[!]...only he had become profoundly suspicious of any extension of state power."[16] How deeply Orwell had changed since the euphoria of 1940. Fyvel believes that Orwell remained a socialist—but at the last moment introduces a crucial qualification: "He was formally a socialist."[17]

If Orwell was "formally a socialist," what was he really? Obviously, he was a complicated and sometimes self-contradictory human being. Fyvel concludes that more than anything else, Orwell was a pessimist; and this is in line with the final judgment of another of Orwell's friends, Herbert Read.[18] In pointing to the polarity between socialism and pessimism in Orwell's thought, Alex Zwerdling has put the dilemma this way: although Orwell claimed to retain his faith that a democratic socialism could somehow be achieved, his critique of the statist tendencies within the socialist movement was devastating to him, and "a hopeless faith is a contradiction in terms."[19] My point is in a way the reverse of Zwerdling's, but also complements it: Orwell's moods of pessimism made him not only more wary of socialism, but also less hostile to capitalism and capitalist society.

But I would also suggest that besides the polarity of socialism/pessimism, there existed another polarity in Orwell's thought. As a political person he was (or considered himself to be) a socialist, but as a writer he was a liberal. I am not the first to describe Orwell this way; both George Woodcock and Bertrand Russell called him a "nineteenth century liberal."[20] But I mean the term in the specific way Orwell himself used it, the way he felt was vital to a writer: "freedom-loving," especially regarding freedom of thought (see especially *CEJL*, 4:159). Thus, as a writer—as a liberal—Orwell intensely valued the relatively liberal and tolerant surroundings provided by bourgeois Britain, and feared that economic collectivism would lead to their destruction. And this fear eventually came to balance, at least to some extent, the ideals of "social justice" and economic equality which he upheld as a democratic socialist. All this goes a long way toward explaining the special emphasis in *Nineteen Eighty-Four* on the collectivist economic origins of the terrifying Ingsoc society and, conversely, the novel's depiction of pre-revolutionary capitalist society as relatively benign.

Orwell himself was keenly aware of the fundamental ambivalence into which he had fallen. In a 1944 "As I Please" column for *Tribune*, he wrote:

> If one thinks of the artist as...an autonomous individual who owes nothing to society, then the golden age of the artist was the age of capitalism. He had then escaped from the patron and had not yet been captured by the bureaucrat.... Yet it remains true that *capitalism, which in many ways was kind to the artist and the intellectual generally,* is doomed and is not worth saving anyway. So you arrive at these two antithetical facts: (1) Society cannot be arranged for the benefit of artists; (2) without artists civilisation perishes. I have not yet seen this dilemma solved (there must be a solution), and it is not often that it is honestly discussed. (*CEJL*, 3:229-30, my italics)

"There must be a solution." Orwell offers none here, and one may wonder whether he ever found one.

Notes

1. See T. R. Fyvel, *George Orwell: A Personal Memoir* (New York: Macmillan, 1982), 99.
2. See *NEF*, 5, 21 with 118-19, 70, 76, 101, 120, 121-22, 141.
3. See *NEF*, 92 and 164-65, 80; cf. 9-11, 77, 124, 169.

4. The evidence that this is a lie is collected just above. Interviews: *NEF*, 74-78; artifacts: *NEF*, 9, cf. 80 and 81; Goldstein's Book: *NEF*, 152-64.

5. See the wry comment of Crick, *GO*, 258.

6. *The Lion and the Unicorn* appears in *CEJL* 2:56-109.

7. Compare with *NEF*, 168 (cf. above, p. 3). The same holds true with "Goldstein's" claim about the spread of prosperity under capitalism: compare *CEJL*, 2:76 (cited just above) with *NEF*, 168 (and cf. above, pp. 195).

8. Neither of these essays receives more than a bare mention in any scholarly study of Orwell. Sometimes both are simply ignored, as in Crick's monumental biography.

9. "Will Freedom Die?" (*Left News*, April 1941, 1682-85) does not appear in *CEJL* and will hereafter be abbreviated as WFD.

10. See Fyvel, 123-24.

11. See Norman Podhoretz, "If Orwell Were Alive Today," *Harper's*, January 1983, 37.

12. See *CEJL*, 2:325-26; 3:145; 4:7, 17, 444; cf. 2:73.

13. See especially *CEJL*, 3:117-18 (Orwell's bitter remarks at the beginning of his tandem review of F. A. Hayek, *The Road to Serfdom*, and K. Zilliacus, *The Mirror of the Past*); also *CEJL*, 2:282, 429; 3:12; 4:410.

14. George Orwell, "The British General Election," *Commentary* 1 (November 1945): 68. (Not in *CEJL*.)

15. This shift of focus in Orwell's social and political concerns is noted (with disapproval) by Raymond Williams, *George Orwell* (New York: Viking, 1971): 63-68.

16. Fyvel, 114.

17. Orwell as a socialist: Fyvel, 114. The qualification: Fyvel, 208.

18. Fyvel, 208; Herbert Read, in his review of *NEF*, in *George Orwell: The Critical Heritage*, ed. Jeffrey Meyers (London/Boston: Routledge and Kegan Paul, 1975), 285.

19. Alex Zwerdling, *Orwell and the Left* (New Haven/London: Yale University Press, 1974), 109; part of Zwerdling's excellent general discussion of Orwell's pessimism (96-113).

20. George Woodcock, "George Orwell, 19th Century Liberal," in *The Critical Heritage*, ed. Meyers, 246; Bertrand Russell's obituary of Orwell in *ibid.*, 1975), 300.

On the Political Sociology of Intellectuals: George Orwell and the London Left Intelligentsia

John Rodden

I

Contemporary social theorists have written extensively about the modern intellectual's class origins, political allegiances, and social function.[1] Yet, as Charles Kadushin notes, "Despite (or perhaps because of) the many works on intellectuals, there is no adequate sociological theory of intellectuals or intellectual life.... Theory-building in this field has been marred by an abundance of opinion and moralization, a dearth of facts, and a plethora of parochial definitions."[2] Much of the scholarship on the sociology of intellectuals is purely descriptive; and even worse, unlike the case in other subfields of the sociology of occupations, as Robert Brym notes, sociologists have tended to accept the self-descriptions (or "professional ideologies") of intellectuals about their political outlooks at face value.[3] Brym calls for a moratorium on general theories about the correlation between social structure and intellectuals' patterns of mobility, and he instead urges careful study of the relation between partisan affiliation and the intellectual's career trajectory through the changing social structure.[4] Given the observations of Kadushin and Brym about the theoretical imprecision and "intellectual backwardness" of the political sociology of intellectuals,[5] it may prove a modest contribution merely to broach the conceptual issues of the field through the single rich example of a particular intellectual and his intellectual milieu.[6]

George Orwell and the London intelligentsia of the 1930s and 1940s provide an instructive case. The special historical relation of Orwell to the British intellectuals of his day sheds light on the changing situation of the modern Western intellectual. "When the history of intellectuals of the twentieth century is written," William Steinhoff has predicted, "some part of it will be devoted to Orwell's analysis and criticism of his fellow intellectuals."[7] The case of Orwell, however, possesses more than merely historical interest, for it represents not just one man's dispute with his fellow literary intellectuals. Rather, it signals the emergent position of the modern writer-intellectual in Britain, responding to two new, related historical developments in the 1930s: the birth of a radical intelligentsia and the rise in Europe of totalitarianism.

How did English writer-intellectuals react under such conditions? What factors contributed to the rise and decline of widespread intellectual dissidence? What accounts for political rebellion and adaptation occurring variously in political, religious, and aesthetic terms? How do the intellectual's class origins, education, and mature social experience shape his political orientation? Does the writer-intellectual have a special political function to fulfill in society?

These broad historical, conceptual, and normative questions cannot, of course, be addressed adequately in a single example. Moreover, to approach them via the filter of the vivid historical personalities and complicated social conditions of the 1930s and 1940s in Britain runs the risk of generalization from skewed or impoverished data. Yet advantages emerge too. The sociologist's restricted case allows for a combination of observational detail and conceptual delimitation seldom found in cultural history, and the case of Orwell, an unusually rich and suggestive one, is particularly well-suited to a study of the political sociology of intellectuals. His appropriateness arises, perhaps paradoxically, from the adverse stance which he took toward his adopted "class" of fellow intellectuals.

By the very fact of his distinctiveness, Orwell offers insight into the typicality of his intellectual generation. Because he was never directly affiliated with the left-wing writers of the "Auden generation"—"a generation he was in but never part of," in Stuart Samuels' characterization[8]—he could stand at once inside and outside the Left. He thereby could both participate in and give witness to his generation's experience, reflecting its larger dilemma between political detachment and commitment. "To learn what the world then looked like to an English intellectual," wrote his friend and *Tribune* (London) colleague T. R. Fyvel in *Intellectuals Today* (1968), "one can go to George Orwell, who wrote so explicitly and precisely about this, and one can also see how the issues of the time were reflected in his own career." His diverse engagement with poverty, imperialism, fascism, and socialism established Orwell, in Fyvel's view, as "the characteristic literary figure of the thirties," and Fyvel urged readers "to consider Orwell's historical role as an intellectual of his day."[9]

This essay takes this exhortation as a point of departure for addressing the theoretical issues framed by the foregoing questions. Periods of political crisis invariably raise such questions with special directness, whose responses often manifest themselves most clearly in the experience of one centrally involved in the struggle. As his intellectual generation's posthumously proclaimed "conscience" and "voice,"[10] Orwell and his work constitute not only a sociological but also an ethical guide to the contemporary relation of the intellectual and politics.[11]

II

Whereas various continental traditions of intellectuals involved in radical politics stretch as far back as the eighteenth century, Britain alone possessed no dissident left-wing intelligentsia until the 1930s. The "philosophical Radicals" of the 1820s, including James Mill, were parliamentary reformers, and they numbered in any case no more than a coterie of twenty. The nineteenth-century intellectual "Lights of Liberalism"—led by John Stuart Mill, Herbert Spencer, James Bryce, and Henry Sidgwick—were similarly in or close to the corridors of power and fully assimilated into the governing classes by birth and education. Edwardian liberals like L. T. Hobhouse and J. A. Hobson, and Fabian socialists like H. G. Wells and Sidney and Beatrice Webb, likewise invested their progressive hopes in gradualism, social planning, technological advance, and administrative efficiency. With occasional exceptions like Robert Owen, William Morris, and George Bernard Shaw, English intellectuals were traditionally Liberal or Conservative, or frequently apolitical. Historically they have not been models of the "alienated intellectual," Robert Park's "Marginal Man."[12] Indeed, even when an English socialist intelligentsia finally did emerge late in the nineteenth century, its leading members (Shaw, Wells, the Webbs) became Establishment figures, hardly more alienated or distant from the corridors of power than Victorian liberal and conservative intellectuals had been.

The conditions responsible for the traditionally moderate political stance of British intellectuals and their tendency to form part of the ruling consensus rather than a critical opposition or "adversary culture" are numerous and complex. Alan Swingewood cites as significant factors such traditions in English society as

> political stability, historical continuity, a gentrified bourgeois culture, the strength of philosophical currents relying on common

sense, experience, and practicality (utilitarianism, empiricism), combined with the absence of a broadly based revolutionary social-ist movement....[13]

These so-called "peculiarities of the English" have facilitated the inte-gration of the British intelligentsia into society with a smoothness unknown elsewhere in Europe—especially unlike the cases of France and Italy, neither of which possesses an established tradition of coop-erative intellectual participation in government and politics.[14] As Lewis Coser once summed up the distinction, the salons led to the French Revolution and the coffeehouses to the 1832 Reform Bill.[15] British intel-lectuals have typically maintained access to important official channels of communication and power, and have thereby constituted an "intel-lectual aristocracy," in Noel Annan's phrase, closely bound to the rul-ing classes and one another by family, school, and professional ties. As Annan explained:

> The influence of these families [the Stracheys, Darwins, Huxleys, Stephenses, and others] may partly explain a paradox which has puzzled European and American observers of English life: the para-dox of an intelligentsia which appears to conform rather than rebel against the rest of society. The proclivity to criticize, of course, exists; Matthew Arnold flicked Victorian self-confidence with his irony.... But the pro-consular tradition and the English habit of working through established institutions and modifying them to meet social needs only when such needs are proven are traits strongly exhibited by the intelligentsia of this country. Here is an aristocracy, secure, established, and, like the rest of English soci-ety, accustomed to responsible and judicious utterance and skepti-cal and iconoclastic speculation.[16]

The main focus of political sociology is the analysis and explanation of partisan affiliation. In their efforts to explain intellectuals' behavior via correlations between social position and political outlook, political sociologists usually identify "malintegration" within the existing social structure as the chief cause of radical protest. Unemployment and underemployment locate intellectuals on the margins of society. Poorly embedded in Establishment institutions, they feel rootless, estranged, and well-disposed to revolutionary appeals.[17] What the social malinte-gration-political radicalism thesis often ignores, as Brym points out, is whether alienated intellectuals possess "the political resources to change their ire into action"—sufficient numbers, influence on other revolutionary-minded groups, links to communication networks, and high social organization (journals, meeting societies, discussion circles, co-operatives).[18] As we shall see, Britain in the 1930s sustained radical intellectual politics so long as both the social structure failed to absorb intellectuals and their political resources could be maintained. With the arrival of World War II, both conditions for the widespread *political* expression of intellectuals' alienation disappeared.

III

The 1930s witnessed the first society-wide dislocation of British intellectuals. They were cut off from many traditional connections to prestige and power, or their sources of private patronage, following graduation from Oxbridge or London, dried up. As Fyvel recalled it, British intellectuals "searched, some of them desperately indeed, for ways of becoming integrated in their society."[19] The major cause of marginalization was the world depression. Unemployment in Britain hovered above two million for most of the decade. Hard times forced middle-class graduates to make ends meet as journalists, publishers, schoolmasters, and private tutors. W. H. Auden, C. Day-Lewis, Evelyn Waugh, Rex Warner, Orwell, and hundreds of others took poor-paying jobs in private schools. Other graduates traveled to Europe or, like Malcolm Muggeridge, William Empson, and Orwell, observed how the British Empire operated away from home. They saw conditions no better abroad; capitalism seemed to be failing everywhere. At the same time, the new Soviet state and its romantic promise of equality and prosperity—and its celebration, rather than merely toleration, of intellectuals—struck many young intellectuals as a cultural paradise. Pilgrimages to Moscow became routine for socialists, and glowing return reports from the Webbs and others confirmed the happy rumors.[20] Outrage about unemployment at home and admiration for the Soviet Union soon led to the formation, as Samuels puts it, "of a radical intelligentsia in England—a body of creative people who, as a group, openly criticized the existing form of society and who established institutions and intellectual pressure groups to mount a campaign to alter that society."[21]

The criticism actually began in the late 1920s, in the absence of any developed political consciousness, as the college protest of a bourgeois literary elite. The "Left Poets" at Oxford (Auden, Stephen Spender, Day-Lewis) formed the heart of a group (including Warner, Louis MacNeice, Hugh Gaitskell, Isaiah Berlin, Christopher Isherwood, Harold Acton, Edward Upward, and A. J. P. Taylor) known variously as "the gang," "the Happy Few," and "the Lads of the Earth." They resembled an undergraduate Bloomsbury group. They crammed their publications, like *Oxford Poetry*, with insiders' gossip and private allusions. Art was for the happy few, namely themselves, not for what they considered the ill-bred masses. They were quite self-consciously members of Oxford's literary minority (the "arties"), contemptuous of the uncultivated, athletic majority (the "hearties"). They aspired to aesthetic priesthood; their bishop was Auden and their vicar T. S. Eliot. Political commitment, social activism, and "artistic responsibility" were vulgar, alien notions to them.[22]

Around 1930 all this began to change. Auden, Spender, Isherwood, Upward, David Guest, and some others of the Auden "gang" (e.g., John Lehmann from Cambridge) traveled to Berlin. The initial attraction was decadence, for Berlin was to the late Weimar Republic what Paris's Left Bank had been to France a few years earlier. But as Spender put it in 1937: "One began by noticing symptoms of decadence, suffering and unemployment; one looked further and saw, beneath the decay of the liberal state, the virulent reaction of the Nazis and the struggle for a new life of the Communists."[23] Although they themselves were usually quite comfortable because of favorable exchange rates, the young bohemians had brushed up against what they had never encountered before: unemployment, physical suffering, poverty, disease.[24]

Most young intellectuals returned to England shortly before Hitler came to power and near the nadir of the depression in Britain in 1933, when unemployment peaked at 2.75 million. Although the German situation, with six million unemployed, was far worse than Britain's, the social consciences of the Auden group awakened only on their return home, in the face of the hunger marches of 1932 and 1934. As Spender recalled:

> I did not, at first, feel that I could do more than pity [the Germans]. This was partly because, as a foreigner, I felt outside Germany. Only when the crisis spread to Great Britain and other countries did I begin to realize that it was a disease of capitalism throughout the world. Gradually I became convinced that the only cure for unemployment, other than war, was an international society in which the resources of the world were exploited in the interests of all the people of the world.[25]

Thus did the "Happy Few" become aware of the miseries of the unhappy multitude.

The names Auden, Spender, and Day-Lewis first became publicly linked through their joint appearance in a little anthology, fitly entitled *New Signatures* (1932). Although it was primarily a rebellion against esoteric, coterie poetry, it also marked the Left Poets' first halting steps toward political consciousness. In *New Country* (1933) they explicitly repudiated bourgeois values and called for a socialist revolution. They were "concerned no longer with a purely aesthetic approach, with finding a new signature, a new moral code, but with discovering a new country, a new social order."[26] That order was the classless society—but overlaid with a romantic veneer suffused with fellow-feeling, a self-dramatizing "Marxism of the heart." "Prepare the way for an English Lenin," cried Michael Roberts in his introduction to *New Country*. Intellectuals were moving "forward from liberalism," per the title of Spender's 1936 book. They could "no longer remain aloof from politics," declared Roberts. Radical aesthetics had given away to radical politics.[27]

Few young intellectuals did remain aloof from politics. Membership in the Communist Party of Great Britain (CPGB) rose from 1,356 in 1930 to 15,570 in 1938, an increase "due in no small measure to the many middle-class intellectuals who became politically conscious in the 1930s and streamed into the Party ranks."[28] Per Lenin's conception of the Party as revolutionary vanguard, intellectuals began to spearhead left-wing activities, raising workers' consciousness by organizing societies and sponsoring publications. Led by John Strachey, whose *The Coming Struggle for Power* (1932) proved one of the most influential books of the decade, middle-class intellectuals set up in 1934 a section of Writers' International, chaired by Day-Lewis and represented by the journal *Left Review*. A British branch of Artists International was formed that same year. Politically-minded leftist dramatic groups, like Unity Theatre, Left Theatre, and Group Theatre, sprang up. John Grierson's GPO Film Unit also launched a revolutionary movement in documentary film. Founded in May 1936, Victor Gollancz's Left Book Club, boasting 57,000 members by 1938, served as the umbrella group for many of these political and cultural activities. It was as close as Britain got to a popular front.[29]

Still, neither the Left Book Club nor these other activities were really popular. Nor did they ever enjoy strong Labour Party support. "Political radicalism was not popular with the masses," wrote Neal Wood in his history of British Communist intellectuals. "The intellectuals on the Left were somewhat isolated on the whole.... The country tended to be to the right of the intellectuals, as was the government."[30] Nevertheless, participation in socialist programs gave many intellectuals a sense of fellow camaraderie as "radicals," the feeling of being socially useful, of being "in touch" with one another and with "the people."[31] Social malintegration therefore sparked political radicalism, but the partial result was that intellectuals' sense of shared mission integrated the intelligentsia itself. Of course, the interlinked pattern of alienation,malintegration, and radicalization did not cover all intellectuals, nor were those who were alienated and radicalized uniformly and equally so. Yet as Samuels observes:

> By 1935 few young, sensitive English intellectuals could avoid becoming either involved in one of the various intellectual organizations established to mobilize an attack on fascism, economic depression, and war, or convinced of the necessity of making their intellectual products reflect the social crises of the period and serve a genuine social function. Artists became socially aware, poets socially conscious, writers more didactic....[32]

IV

Orwell, however, was one of these uncommitted few, still without what he called "a political orientation." "By the end of 1935," he recalled in "Why I Write" (1946), "I had still failed to reach a firm decision" (*CEJL*, 1:4). That decision was perhaps further complicated by his reported friendship with devout Anglicans, his casual contact with British socialists and Trotskyists, and his serious flirtations with poetry writing and with modernist aestheticism (e.g., his Joycean stylistic experimentation in *A Clergyman's Daughter*, 1935).[33]

Orwell's indecision about his politics in the mid-1930s furnishes a clue to his lifelong "outsider" stance toward the London intelligentsia. Superficially his career does possess a comparable shape and sequence to other 1930s intellectuals: public school, travel abroad, return to teach, occasional journalism, a "new signature," contact with the British unemployed, embrace of socialism, and off to Spain. But that narrative abstract masks and bleaches the very different experience which Orwell actually had from most intellectuals of his generation, at least after public school, and which set him apart from them. Detailed attention to the trajectory of his career suggests both the fallacy of linking mechanically class origins with political affiliation and the necessity of injecting a dynamic, historical dimension into an inquiry on the conditions for intellectuals' political radicalization.

How and why did Orwell differ from the members of the Auden group and the majority of other 1930s intellectuals? Three factors stand out, all of them reinforcing his antagonism toward English "clubbishness" and shaping his evolving "outsider" stance toward the London intelligentsia.

First, although Orwell was from the middle class, his family was poorer than most of those which produced public school boys, from whose ranks the leading intellectuals of his generation emerged. He evidently retained this acute consciousness of his relative poverty throughout his adult years, as the bitterness and anguish of "Such, Such Were the Joys" suggests.[34]

Secondly, Orwell was slightly older than the decade's radicals. Although just a year senior to Day Lewis, he was four years older than Auden and MacNeice and fully six years older than Spender. This age difference may account in part for Orwell's much stronger attachment to pre-World War I England and Edwardian memories. If Cyril Connolly's recollections are accurate, Eric Blair had already read much of Butler, Wells, and Shaw by the time of his entry to Eton (1916), and seems to have possessed an extraordinarily mature (and fatalistic) outlook on the ultimate consequences of World War I for the Empire.[35] It is interesting too that in *Coming Up for Air* (1939) Orwell casts George Bowling, the most autobiographical of Orwell's heroes and a thinly-disguised mouthpiece for many of the author's own views, exactly one decade older than himself. For Eric Blair at 13 evidently had the political sophistication of Bowling at 23. (Orwell, according to Richard Rees, felt guilty throughout his adulthood for being too young to serve in the war—and appropriately enough, Bowling gets wounded in 1916 on a French battlefield.[36]) It may have been that Blair-Orwell was just over the generational divide which permitted a passionate identification with the "eternal summer" of Edwardian England represented by Bowling's long lazy days at the Mill Farm fishing pond.

A third difference was the crucial one: Blair's Burma police service. His Burma years put him on a track which was to divide him permanently and irrevocably from his coevals, even after his return home. Virtually all of the leading intellectuals of the 1930s and 1940s had gone up to Oxford or Cambridge. Very few intellectuals did not go to some university. At the time that Oxford's literary "Lads of the Earth" encircled Auden in 1928, Orwell was already back from five grueling years in Burma—where, as John Wain once remarked, five years would seem like fifteen in a young Etonian's development.[37] Indeed, Blair had missed the relatively prosperous 1920s and the dramatic political events that would give rise to 1930s radicalism: Lloyd George's fall from grace in 1922; the rise to power in 1923 of the first, short-lived Labour government and the May 1926 General Strike, prompted by proposed reductions in the miners' wages. Numerous upper- and middle-class families viewed the strike as a possible syndicalist revolution in the making. With their support—and that of hundreds of undergraduates—Stanley Baldwin's Conservative government put down the strike. The Auden group watched from a distance and treated the whole affair as springtime amusement. Quite probably Orwell met some of these same miners exactly a decade later at Wigan.

Blair had also missed the heyday of the literary revolution. By the early 1920s Eliot's *The Waste Land* (1922) and Joyce's *Ulysses* (1922), and also the doctrines of the publicists of modernism (e.g., Pound, Hulme, Ford Madox Ford) had begun to filter down to the Oxbridge undergraduates. When Blair returned from Paris at Christmas 1929, having spent little more than six months in England during the previous seven years, many of his peers were already well-established in literary London and the new Auden era of committed political art was dawning.[38]

This personal history may suggest that Orwell was always "one step behind" his generation and therefore forever playing intellectual "catch-up" in the 1930s. The political, and even the literary, evidence seems copious. For instance, by choice and circumstance, he never felt completely at home with the modernists and the "committed" thirties' writers: the Victorian and Edwardian avant-garde of his boyhood (Dickens, Charles Reade, Butler, Gissing, Wells) remained his favorite novelists. Thus, he was still reading the advanced writers of two decades earlier, went to Paris to live like a bohemian when the "poet-in-the-garret" vogue about Paris was ending, and saw lower-class life from the gutter up when the university youths were editing manifestoes and publishing books.

Yet this way of explaining Orwell's development—as if he experienced a literary-political "lag" *vis-à-vis* his generation as a result of having gone to Burma rather than university—frames a comparison which, once again, rests on a superficial appearance of mere belatedness to his contemporaries. But it is not just that his experience was *later*; his experience was *different* from theirs, and he learned different things from it. He did, it is true, come to fashions when they were no longer fashionable. For example, like some of his contemporaries, he reached political consciousness abroad, but whereas they arrived *en bloc* as a politicized coterie, he arrived alone, and his stance, unlike theirs, was never simply that of a spectator. Orwell *lived* with the tramps and miners; he *fought* at the Aragon front (significantly, with the POUM dissident Marxist militia rather than the Stalinist-controlled International Brigades), not merely visited it like Auden and Spender (or like the numerous British delegates to the 1937 International Conference of Writers Against War and Fascism in Valencia). Orwell engaged so deeply in the events of the decade that he could digest and reflect on them only somewhat later—approximately when the intellectual spectators, who had observed events at a distance, were no longer caught up in them. But this participant-witness stance, as an outsider able to feelingly describe what he has seen "from the inside,"[39] gave Orwell valuable psychological distance (and subsequently, high credibility and immense authority) which most intellectuals of his generation did not possess.[40] When Orwell made a decision, as he did in 1936-37, to embrace democratic socialism, it was a firm and enduring one.

The fact is, as Samuels remarks in a passage already quoted, Orwell belonged to "a generation he was in but never part of"; he stood outside "a movement he toyed with but never joined."[41] He could stand outside precisely because, in the most literal sense, he was never part of "the Auden generation"—nor of any other. His Burma years had placed him among working-class men slightly older than himself, many of whom had served in World War I; and even after Burma and Paris in the mid-1930s in Hampstead, he associated not with his coevals but mainly with provincial university graduates and other bohemians (e.g., Rayner Heppenstall, Michael Sayers) eight to ten years younger than himself. Some of them looked upon 32-year-old Eric Blair, in Heppenstall's phrase, as "a nice old thing, a kindly eccentric"—"illread," middlebrow, without a university degree, and always going on insufferably about Butler, the *Magnet*, and comic postcards.[42] Thus Orwell found himself always "between" and "outside" generations, not just political groups.[43] That, too, is why his mature experience was so "different" from that of the Auden group, and it is revealing that Hynes opens and closes *The Auden Generation* with quotations from Orwell's *oeuvre*.[44] Orwell possessed neither the generational consciousness of "the Auden generation," which is acquired only by shared participation in psychologically decisive events, nor that of the younger and older generational groups in Hampstead and Burma with which he associated. Yet this separation from his contemporaries, especially in the case of his contact with the provincial graduates, probably helped form Orwell's quixotic, plain-speaking character: he could be less inhibited with such youthful, unthreatening, still-unestablished fellow bohemians, caring less that they disagreed with or mocked him. Generational discontinuity thus nourished Orwell's natural antinomianism, inadvertently furnishing him with a setting in which he could do his own thinking, draw on his own experience, and work out his own positions without the pressure to bend to the institutional and intellectual authority of his already-successful coevals.[45] As Bernard Crick observes:

> His time-out in Burma had made him older than most of the young writers still leading this kind of "floating life"; but it also gave him an emotional detachment from them and immunized him from fashion. (*GO*, 177–78)

Indeed, the singularity of Orwell's early manhood, marked by police work in Burma rather than attendance at Oxbridge, further helps explain the specifics of the distinctive arc of his career in the late 1930s and early 1940s: his exceptional responses to the course of the Spanish Civil War, to the revelations about Stalin's crimes, and to the changing CPGB line. What may have seemed Orwell's non-university "untrained mind," as Crick notes, turned out to be a fiercely independent radical's un*tamed* mind.[46]

Typically, Orwell arrived at the Spanish war late, after the fighting had been on for nearly a half year (December 1936) and just as some leading British Marxist intellectuals (e.g., Ralph Fox, David Guest) were killed in action. The Loyalists' prospects were already dimming by the time Orwell was defending Barcelona in May 1937, and most intellectuals in 1937-38 were quickly growing disillusioned with Stalinism and Left politics. Precisely at this moment, in the face of Franco's looming triumph and the Stalinists' suppression of POUM and other non-Communist militias, Orwell was wholeheartedly committing himself to socialism and penning his eloquent *Homage to Catalonia* (1938). "I have seen wonderful things," he wrote Cyril Connolly from his Barcelona sickbed in June 1937, after having narrowly escaped death from a throat wound, "& at last really believe in Socialism, which I never did before" (*CEJL*, 1:269). Very few other returning leftists felt the same. And for the intellectuals who stayed home, their skin-deep commitment to socialism was waning, largely as a result of an avalanche of evidence no longer deniable about Stalin's betrayal of the Revolution during the 1930s: the Kirov murder, the brutal extermination of the *kulaks*, the deliberate scheme of mass famine in the Ukraine, the labor camps, the wholesale purges of rival Party members, the mock show trials of fellow Old Bolsheviks, the ferocious repression of all dissent. Just at the time when most Left intellectuals were beginning to doubt the Marxist pieties, Orwell had met his Italian militiaman in Catalonia and found his communitarian vision.

For Orwell had never been attached to Marxism, Stalin, or Russia, unlike most 1930s radicals, and so he (unlike the Auden group, the Webbs, Kingsley Martin and the *New Statesman*, and thousands of other CPGB members and fellow-travellers) had nothing to lose by branding "the Soviet myth"—"the belief that Russia is a Socialist country"—for what it was. The USSR, he declared, embodied "the corruption of the original idea of Socialism..." (*CEJL*, 3:404-5). While many British leftists became defensive about the transformation of Bolshevism into "oligarchical collectivism," Orwell only became more confirmed in his negative judgment of Stalinism, which he claimed to have arrived at as early as 1931—long before the purges and show trials, the Spanish war, and the 1939 Ribbentrop-Molotov pact. To CPGB members like Day Lewis and Spender, Russia was "the god that failed." Not for Orwell. For he had already experienced his period of disillusion, much earlier in Burma. He had seen "the dirty work of Empire at close quarters"—and he had hated and finally rejected it (*CEJL*, 1:236). His attempts to expunge his guilt and his search for social reintegration followed in Paris, London, and Spain. By the time his fellow intellectuals were touting the organized efficiency of the Soviet state, Orwell's Burma years had confirmed and deepened "my natural hatred of authority" (*CEJL*, 1:4). This early experience—his ordeal in Burma and his subsequent vocational and political crises in the 1920s and early 1930s—was probably no less traumatic than his contemporaries' agonized reappraisal of Stalin and communism a decade later. It did, however, act as an ideological vaccine: he became no Stalinist dupe. Thus, what Orwell once described as a waste of five years in a tropical swamp may have actually inoculated him against leader-worship and literary cliques, and thereby saved him from the more serious political errors of his generation, particularly "the stupid cult of Russia" (*RWP*, 216). He had "chucked" Burma; many of his con- temporaries would not do the same with Stalin and the CPGB until years later. In this respect Orwell was not only "behind" but also"ahead" of his generation, as well as "between" and "outside" it.

When his intellectual contemporaries finally did repudiate commu- nism, as Orwell pointed out in "Inside the Whale," the "something to believe in" which they embraced was not a political party line but rather a religious orthodoxy or aesthetic doctrine (*CEJL*, 1:515). Many intellectuals in the 1930s and 1940s discovered the Anglican or Catholic churches; others opted out of politics and rededicated them- selves to Art. Cyril Connolly's editorial policy in the inaugural issue of *Horizon* (March 1940) ushered in the latter aspect of the new mood of the 1940s: "Our standards are aesthetic, and our politics are in abeyance." Or, as Connolly put it two years later in *The Unquiet Grave*: "The true function of a writer is to produce a masterpiece...no other task is of any importance."[47]

The turn toward Art in 1940 was, however, sharply different from the case of the 1920s: whereas the undergraduates of the 1920s rebelled via Art, young and maturing intellectuals of the 1940s escaped into it. Whereas political detachment was the posture of the 1920s and commitment of the 1930s, disenchantment was the attitude of the 1940s. One notes here that radicalism and conservatism can take many forms. Religious or aesthetic radicalism may not only accommodate but also often entails political quietism. What determined the outbreak of radicalism in a specifically political form in the 1930s was in part British intellectuals' recent rejection of other possible manifestations: God was already dead and Art had failed as Hulmean "spilt religion."

In the middle of a depression and with a revolution eastward already succeeding, Marxism and Russia offered intellectuals of the day a model and a plan of action.

By the decade's close, however, many leading London Left intellectuals were politically deradicalized. The advent of World War II catalyzed the process by giving them something productive to do *as intellectuals*—in the BBC, the Ministry of Information, the War Office selection boards, military intelligence—and thereby *re*integrating them into society.[48] "Probably in no belligerent country had the intelligentsia volunteered so wholeheartedly as in England to serve the State at war," Fyvel later observed. "The meaningful social integration which had been talked about in the Thirties was suddenly easier."[49] The English tradition of intellectuals' cooperative participation in government and official politics—or what one critic has termed the venerable British practice of "massive cooptation of intellectuals by the State"[50]—had reasserted itself. It would continue largely undisturbed—through the war years, the Labour government under Attlee, and the consensus politics of "Butskellism"—until the Suez crisis and the birth of the New Left in 1956-57.[51]

However, because Orwell was so alienated from and malintegrated within the London Left intelligentsia, he was never quite so well socially reintegrated as a BBC broadcaster in the early 1940s, either. The ideological moderation characteristic of most other wartime Left intellectuals began at a time when Orwell was at his most revolutionary and optimistic about the possibilities for an English socialist revolution (1939-1941). In *The Lion and the Unicorn* (1941), he argued that the war would transform Britain into a democratic socialist nation. It was not his hope alone, but few others held such a rosy view, and his own faith soon dimmed.[52] Although he enjoyed much of the social contact of his BBC work, he formally reassumed his stance as intellectual "outsider" and radical iconoclast in 1943, eagerly accepting the literary editorship of *Tribune*, Aneurin Bevin's still-struggling dissident Left paper (*GO*, 318-24).

V

This brief sketch of the interrelations among the Left intelligentsia, British politics in the 1930s, and Orwell's development highlights important theoretical issues and inadequacies in the accepted sociology of intellectuals. For the intellectual is that difficult creature, neither worker nor owner. He is, as it were, ideologically ambidextrous according to the literature of the sociology of occupations, which argues variously that the intellectual invariably serves the elite, allies with the workers, constitutes a separate class, and is essentially "class-less."[53]

Thus, functionalists (S. N. Eisenstadt, Daniel Bell) have portrayed intellectuals as gradually becoming coopted into the service of the presiding bureaucracy and becoming what C. Wright Mills in *White Collar* (1951) termed "Brains, INC." They experience *embourgeoisement*. Classical Marxist sociology has also cast the intellectual with the middle class, as a *petit bourgeois*, a tag once much applied by Stalinist critics to Orwell and generating more heat than light. Conversely, neo-Marxists (Bettina Aptheker, Alain Touraine), influenced by New Left social theory, have taken the opposing view that the intellectual's institutional incorporation effectively "proletarianizes" him, making him a wage earner. The necessity for "teams" to pursue sophisticated scientific projects, the modern corporation's demand for the "expertise" of a wide range of specialist consultants, and the existence of large bureaucratic research staffs alienate intellectuals from the fruits of their labor. They become radicalized "Brain Workers." Classical and recent elite theorists (Robert Michel, Alvin Gouldner) have held that intellectuals constitute a class in their own right, a "New Class." In developing countries they often form the political elite; under advanced capitalism intellectuals become a credentialed professional class deriving income and status from their "cultural capital" (technical and language skills). Finally, in his *Ideology and Utopia* (1929), the first influential discussion of intellectuals via the sociology of knowledge, Karl Mannheim characterized them famously as "a relatively classless stratum which is not too firmly situated in the social order." Mannheim held that intellectuals constitute a unique, socially "rootless" class of their own whose spiritual preoccupations enable them to transcend ordinary, material class interests. Intellectuals emerge from various classes, and their education, rather than their class origin, decisively shapes their development and unites them in political outlook. Their education makes it possible for them to place "ideals before interests," in Martin Malia's phrase, to see political issues sensitively and with an open mind. Intellectuals thus *choose* their partisan affiliations; their class background is a secondary influence.[54]

It requires no attempt to apply these categories mechanically to the case of Orwell and his contemporaries in order to glimpse how and where these theories fall short as heuristic tools for understanding the relationship between interwar politics and the British intellectual. The old Marxist notion of class origins as the lifelong determinant of political allegiance is obviously insufficient. Although Orwell had a similar middle-class birth and rearing to most thirties' intellectuals, his course in the educational system and his subsequent occupational experience led him to adopt an "outsider" stance toward the intelligentsia at large—for example, his early anti-Stalinism and brief active member-ship in the anti-war Independent Labour Party (1938-39) (*GO*, 245–57).

Nor are intellectuals necessarily "embourgeoisified"—or radicalized—by government or official institutional employment. For many intellectuals in the 1930s who were formerly dislocated from English society, wartime service brought reintegration and a renewed feeling of usefulness, identity, and power. For Orwell, however, the war years first brightened and then clouded his socialist hopes, and he sought by 1943 to escape "integration" and London for indepen-dent work and greater privacy (e.g., his purchase in 1944-45 of a home on Jura in the Scottish Hebrides (*GO*, 353-70). The divergence of Orwell from the patterned responses of his generation makes it imper-ative to approach the multivalent relationships among class, educa-tion, occupation, and partisan affiliation in dynamic, concrete, and interpersonal terms, rather than simply according to theoretical paradigms: the conditions of political allegiances are not reducible to a single factor or invariable structural pattern.

Yet this does not mean that the intellectual constitutes a separate class or is socially unanchored, as the elite theorists and Mannheim have argued, respectively. Rather, as Brym notes, and as the case of Orwell's distinctive career exemplifies, it is to intellectuals' *shifting* patterns of *rootedness* that attention must be paid, to the dynamics of political affiliation and disaffiliation.[55] The case of Orwell points up, in the first place, the significance of how *evolving* intellectual attach-ments to *other* mass agents (the British worker, the British war machine) and how "generational consciousness" condition partisan affiliation. The intellectual is not "relatively classless" and "rootless" but rather variously and complexly rooted in the spongy, ever-malleable soil of social and historical relations. His political behavior can therefore only be understood by appreciating the institutional web and stages of his complicated mobility pattern within and among dif-ferent classes and groups, that is, by scrutinizing the course of his class origins, education, and employment and career experience. As Brym, following Gramsci, notes, partisan allegiance is not noncausal but radically contingent:

> ...intellectuals' partisan loyalties [are not] mere mechanical and static responses to their current class and other group locations.... In order to explain intellectuals' partisan affiliations one must trace their paths of social mobility, from their origins to their social des-tinations, as these are shaped by the capacity of classes and other groups to expand the institutional milieu through which they pass in the course of their careers.... [T]he determination of intellectuals'

ideological outlooks is really a problem of multivariate causation. That is to say, social origins, school, and economic and political opportunities are independent causes of political allegiance, and one variable may reinforce or, at the other extreme, cancel out the effects of another.[56]

Thus, unlike Orwell, British intellectuals in the 1930s were radicalized during or after their university years; their disenchantment with communism late in the decade and absorption into the literary Establishment and the war bureaucracy produced political moderates. On the other hand, Orwell's Burma service, his "belated" bohemianism, and the Wigan Pier and Spain trips radicalized him and effectively "canceled out" the integrative potential of his BBC work. The political orientations and actions of intellectuals evolve according to their career mobility paths. No single general factor conditions or freezes their partisan affiliations.

Moreover, contrary to what Gouldner and Mannheim imply, the example of Orwell makes clear that "*the* intelligentsia" is not monolithic, nor does education lead to uniform intellectual-political outlooks, as the postwar decline of the Left's dominance of intellectual life and the rise of strong conservative and neoconservative intellectual movements throughout the West in the 1970s and 1980s demonstrates. Despite our casual use of the word "intelligentsia" in the singular, intellectuals constitute a multiform, heterogeneous stratum whose members' diverse ideologies are linked to various mass institutional groups and classes (business, labor, working-class movements, etc.). Intellectuals do not constitute an ideological bloc, and even in the British Thirties the degree and intensity of their radicalism was by no means uniform.

Third and finally, what this case study suggests about the frenzied embrace of communism by European intellectuals throughout the West in the 1930s also problematizes Mannheim's thesis that intellectuals grandly "choose" their political allegiances, dispassionately and with reasoned calculation, as if immune to the historical pressures acting upon lesser men. Intellectuals do *in part* choose their loyalties, as do other historical actors, but their choices are enabled and constrained by their historical situation. The personal and group histories of intellectuals are bound up in social history, just the same as that of other individuals and groups. Hence the need to enrich the political sociology of intellectuals with the empirical concreteness of intellectual history: one must approach the study of their political allegiances in historical and social context, for intellectuals' ideas are developed in an engagement with events and thus can only be understood via an attempt to recover that engagement.[57]

VI

Orwell's independent stance toward the Left intelligentsia of his generation furnishes one man's answer by word and deed to a normative issue in the sociology of intellectuals with an even longer history of controversy than the previous historical and conceptual ones, that is, Does the intellectual have a "proper" social function? What should be his special role, if any, in the modern age of ubiquitous ideology and totalitarian politics? The adversaries alternately define these questions in terms of personal integrity (Julien Benda, Ortega y Gasset, Allen Tate) and social responsibility (Trotsky, Sartre).[58]

The *locus classicus* of the traditionalist position advocating intellectual disengagement from politics is Benda's *La Trahison des Clercs* (1927). Writing in the aftermath of World War I, Benda saw the danger of the intellectual's Hegelian tendency to spiritualize history and political leaders, to "deny God and then shift Him to man and his political work."[59] Instead, Benda argued that the intellectual, the rightful heir of the medieval clerk, betrayed his vocation and legacy if he abandoned the universal and attached himself to the particular and practical. Again Benda's view has been the Marxist-existentialist "responsible artist" position. Radicals and existentialists have argued that the rise of totalitarianism has ushered in a new age of pervasive ideology, in which all cultural activity is politicized and therefore precludes the luxury of detachment. The intellectual "objectively" supports injustice and tyranny by political disengagement. He must be willing to "change" the world, not just "interpret" it, to risk getting "dirty hands," per the title of one of Sartre's plays.

Orwell stands firmly in the latter tradition, but in a characteristically unorthodox way. His pragmatic stance signals a reluctant commitment that is spiritual in its defiant insistence on a higher, objective, thisworldly truth. In "Writers and Leviathan" (1948) he gave his ambivalent answer to the intellectual's "proper" social function. Acknowledging the "invasion of literature by politics," Orwell insisted on "the need to take sides politically" in "an age of State control."[60] The totalitarian leviathan had to be confronted and resisted. "Keeping out of politics" was not possible, Orwell said. One possibility presented itself: the split self. Orwell urged *engagement*, but only on the condition that the writer-citizen divide himself in two—and that the "literary" self remained untainted:

> ...we should draw a sharper distinction than we do at present between our political and literary loyalties, and should recognize that a willingness to do certain distasteful but necessary things does

not carry with it any obligation to swallow the beliefs that usually go with them. When a writer engages in politics, he should do so as a citizen, as a human being, but not as a writer. I do not think that he has the right, merely on the score of his sensibilities, to shirk the ordinary dirty work of politics. Just as much as anyone else, he should be prepared to deliver lectures in draughty halls, to chalk pavements, to canvass voters, to distribute leaflets, even to fight in civil wars if it seems necessary. But whatever else he does in the service of his party, he should never write for it. He should make it clear that his writing is a thing apart. (*CEJL*, 4:412)

To get one's hands dirty yet keep one's spirit clean: this was Orwell's pained compromise. He recognized that his stance amounted to an "orthodoxy" like any other, insofar as it entailed "unresolved contradictions" (*CEJL*, 4:411). He was not blind to the tensions in his position:

To suggest that a creative writer, in a time of conflict, must split himself into two compartments, may seem defeatist or frivolous: yet in practice I do not see what else he can do. To lock yourself up in an ivory tower is impossible and undesirable. To yield subjectively, not merely to a party machine, but even to a group ideology, is to destroy yourself as a writer. (*CEJL*, 4:413)

Caught between the ivory tower and the party machine, "between the priest and the commissar," as Orwell put in a 1936 poem, one had to reject both (*CEJL*, 1:5). Politics was merely another aspect of the supreme dilemma which he had first identified at St. Cyprian's: "The good and the possible never seemed to coincide" (*CEJL*, 4:360). Politics was always a choice of lesser evils, "and there are some situations from which one can only escape by acting like a devil or a lunatic" (*CEJL*, 4:413). These escape routes, which he associated with the aestheticism of a Dali and the derangement of a Pound, respectively, Orwell himself would never take. The quandary of commitment versus detachment was *the* torturous predicament of the modern intellectual as citizen-artist, and it could be neither evaded nor reconciled. Orwell rightly saw that the writer faced the general problem in a particularly acute way:

If you have to take part...and I think you do...then you also have to keep a part of yourself inviolate. For most people the problem does not arise in the same form, because their lives are split already. They are truly alive only in their leisure hours, and there is no emotional connection between their work and their political activities. Nor are they generally asked, in the name of political loyalty, to debase themselves as workers. The artist, and especially the writer, is asked just that—in fact, it is the only thing that politicians ever ask of him. (*CEJL*, 4:413-14)

Orwell finally, in effect, argued that the writer's spiritual self, the noble Don Quixote inside him, could and must act independently of the fat little Sancho Panza within:

> If [the intellectual] refuses [to compromise himself], that does not mean that he is condemned to inactivity. One half of him, which in a sense is the whole of him, can act as resolutely, even as violently if need be, as anyone else. But his writings, in so far as they have any value, will always be the product of the saner self that stands aside, records the things that are done and admits their necessity, but refuses to be deceived as to their true nature.[61]

To love truth more than power: that was Orwell's injunction to his fellow intellectuals. The special function of the intellectual in a totalitarian age was to bear witness to historical and political Truth—the "record" as objective reality and social fact. Orwell's allegiance to "truth" was the screeching brake on his political commitment: beyond or outside it he would not go.

However satisfactory Orwell's attempt to negotiate between the Scylla and Charybdis of commitment and detachment, contemporary advocates of both traditional positions—the intellectual as activist and as *clerc*—have hailed Orwell for his *praxis*, if not his theory. To Noam Chomsky, Orwell is no dispassionate critic but the model of "the responsible intellectual," whose documentary "honesty, decency, and concern with the facts" in *Homage to Catalonia* signified his exemplary commitment to democratic socialism.[62] To John Wain, Orwell the truth-teller was the intelligentsia's relentless critic, whose role was to "keep their consciences alive": "As for his relevance, who can feel that the situation that faces free men has changed much from what it was in the '30s and '40s. The thing to be feared is still a *trahison des clercs*: freedom still needs to be defended against those whom Nature most favours, whom she showers with advantages."[63]

As Wain notes, to argue, as some New Left critics have done, that Orwell, given his pragmatic ethos and distaste for theory, was no intellectual whatsoever, is to misconceive the nature of his intellectuality and of his dispute with his fellow radical intellectuals. For Orwell indicted precisely their cowardly flight into Abstraction, their "pea-and-thimble trick with those mysterious entities, thesis, antithesis, and synthesis..." (*RWP*, 177). He was indeed their harshest critic; he held them to the same ruthlessly severe standards that he set for himself.[64] As the intelligentsia's scourge, particularly toward his own side, he may thereby seem "the supreme example of the intellectual who hated intellectuals."[65] But this elides the point; in fact, he hated not intellectuals but rather their readiness to do dirt on the intellect and betray their spiritual vocation: the defense of truth, liberty, *and* social justice. Orwell was no intellectual-baiter. He mercilessly criticized the intelligentsia's literary cliques "just because I do take the function of the intelligentsia seriously." To keep Civilization's conscience alive, thought Orwell, was the intelligentsia's function, and his own self-appointed task did indeed become to keep the consciences of the intellectuals themselves alive. He castigated their equivocations about Stalinist Russia and their prolix jargon "not because they are intellectuals but because they [are] not...true intellectuals..." True intellectuals thought and spoke clearly, independently, courageously. Clique members took their ideas and language prefabricated.[66]

By this standard, Orwell was indeed a "true" intellectual. Furthermore, his criticism was almost always directed at social*ists*, not social*ism*: he railed at socialists because he wanted socialist intellectuals to be worthy of socialism. A "conscience of the Left" *does* criticize from within; and though Orwell may sometimes have been the guilty or excessively scrupulous "wintry conscience of his generation," he flayed the Left intelligentsia in order to fortify it, not to weaken or abandon it.[67] In this respect his distinctive career not only illumines the complex conditions underlying the formation and fluctuations of intellectual rebellion, adaptation, and radicalization. It also serves, as so many admirers of George Orwell have testified, as a radiant example of how to live the intellectual life.

Notes

1. See, e.g., Bennett Berger, "Sociology and the Intellectuals: An Analysis of a Stereotype," *Antioch Review* 17 (September 1957): 12-17; Lewis Coser, *Men of Ideas: A Sociologist's View* (New York: The Free Press, 1965); A. Gella, ed., "An Introduction to the Sociology of the Intelligentsia," in *The Intelligentsia and the Intellectuals: Theory, Method and Case Study* (Beverly Hills, Calif.: Sage, 1976), 9-34.
2. Charles Kadushin, *The American Intellectual Elite*, quoted in Robert J. Brym, "The Political Sociology of Intellectuals: A Critique and a Proposal," in *Intellectuals in Liberal Democracies: Political Influence and Social Involvement*, ed. Alain G. Gagnon (New York: Praeger, 1987), 208. I am much indebted to this article and Brym's *oeuvre* throughout this essay.
3. Brym, "Political Sociology of Intellectuals," 199.
4. Ibid., 206-8. See also Robert J. Brym, *Intellectuals and Politics* (London: George Allen & Unwin, 1980), 70-73.
5. Brym, "Political Sociology of Intellectuals," 208.
6. No attempt is made here to define the term "intellectual" precisely. The word first entered the French lexicon in the 1890s as a description of a

group of prominent defenders of Alfred Dreyfus. It should be taken in this essay as a general characterization of those who are producers, rather than merely consumers, of ideas, especially through the medium of writing. On the problem of defining the term "intellectual," see Alain G. Gagnon, ed., "The Role of Intellectuals in Liberal Democracies," in *Intellectuals in Liberal Democracies: Political Influence and Social Involvement* (New York: Praeger, 1987), 4-6.

 7. William Steinhoff, *George Orwell and the Origins of 1984* (Ann Arbor: University of Michigan Press, 1976), 57.
 8. Stuart Samuels, "English Intellectuals and Politics in the 1930s," in *On Intellectuals*, ed. Philip Rieff (New York: Doubleday, 1969), 247.
 9. T. R. Fyvel, *Intellectuals Today* (London: Faber, 1968), 44.
10. See, e.g., V. S. Pritchett, "George Orwell," *New Statesman and Nation* 39 (28 January 1950): 96; and George Woodcock, "Orwell's Conscience," *World Review* 14 (April 1950): 28-33.
11. On this relation, see G. E. Hanson, "Intellect and Power: Some Notes on the Intellectual as a Political Type," *Journal of Politics* 31 (1969): 28-31; and Martin Malia, "The Intellectuals: Adversaries or Clerisy?" in *Intellectuals and Tradition*, ed. S. N. Eisenstadt and S. Graubard (New York: Humanities Press, 1973), 206-16.
12. Robert Ezra Park, *Race and Culture* (Glencoe, Ill.: Free Press, 1950), 373. See also Coser, *Men of Ideas*, 37-82, 171-80.
13. Alan Swingewood, "Intellectuals and the Construction of Consensus in Postwar England," in *Intellectuals in Liberal Democracies: Political Influence and Social Involvement*, ed. Alain G. Gagnon (New York: Praeger, 1987), 87.

    Among the other reasons for "British exceptionalism" is the fact that workers have traditionally dominated the British socialist movement, a trend which the CPGB has also reflected since its founding in 1920. Possibly British Protestantism has also played a role. Intellectuals have enjoyed high authority in Catholic France and Italy, where communism has also proven popular, arguably because it has served as a substitute religion.
14. Cf. E. P. Thompson, "The Peculiarities of the English," *Socialist Register* 2 (1965), reprinted in his *The Poverty of Theory and Other Essays* (London: Secker and Warburg, 1978), 35-91. Thompson was replying to Perry Anderson's critical history of the English intelligentsia, "Origins of the Present Crisis," *New Left Review* 23 (1964): 26-53.
15. Coser, *Men of Ideas*, 11-26. On the differences between the French and British intelligentsias, see Keith A. Reader, "The Intellectuals: Notes toward a Comparative Study of Their Position in the Social Formations of France and Britain," *Media, Culture and Society* 4 (1982): 263-73.
16. Noel Annan, "The Intellectual Aristocracy," in *Studies in Social History*, ed. J. H. Plumb (London: Longmans, Green, 1955), 241-87.
17. See Brym's chapter, "Radicals and Moderates," in his *Intellectuals and Politics*, 14-34.
18. Ibid., 25.
19. Fyvel, *Intellectuals Today*, 39.
20. Cf. Paul Hollander, *Political Pilgrims: Travels of Western Intellectuals to the Soviet Union, China and Cuba* (New York: Oxford University Press, 1981), especially chaps. 3 and 4.

21. Samuels, "English Intellectuals," 196.
22. See Samuels, "English Intellectuals," 198-211. As Spender put it decades later: "[A]t Oxford it was possible to forget human injustices or at least to think that they were not the business of 'the poet.'" See his contribution to *The God That Failed*, ed. Richard Crossman (New York: Bantam [1950] 1965), 211.
23. Stephen Spender, "Oxford to Communism," *New Verse* 26-27 (November 1937): 10. Quoted in Samuels, "English Intellectuals," 202. See also Spender's *The Destructive Element* (London: Faber and Faber, 1935).
24. See Samuels, "English Intellectuals," 201-4. Also Humphrey Carpenter, *W. H. Auden: A Biography* (Boston: Houghton Mifflin, 1981), 96-110.
25. Spender, *The God that Failed*, 212.
26. Samuels, "English Intellectuals," 206.
27. Michael Roberts, ed., *New Country* (London: Hogarth Press, 1933), 12. See also Samuel Hynes, *The Auden Generation: Literature and Politics in England in the 1930s* (London: Bodley Head, 1976), especially ch. 3, "1933"; and Edward Mendelson, *Early Auden* (New York: Viking, 1981), 137-51.
28. Samuels, "English Intellectuals," 238. On CPGB membership figures, see Neal Wood, *Communism and British Intellectuals* (New York: Columbia, 1959), 23-24.
29. Hynes, *The Auden Generation*, 125-293; Wood, *Communism and British Intellectuals*, 60-63; Stuart Samuels, "The Left Book Club," *Journal of Contemporary History* 1 (1966): 65-86.
30. Wood, *Communism and British Intellectuals*, 69.
31. Fyvel, *Intellectuals Today*, 46.
32. Samuels, "English Intellectuals," 228. Orwell considered the attitude, "We're all socialists nowadays," hypocritical and dangerous to the socialist movement. In *Keep the Aspidistra Flying* (1936) the *beau monde* girlfriend of wealthy Ravelston remarks that she finds workers "absolutely disgusting," and then says to him a moment later:
    > Of course I know you're a Socialist. So am I. I mean we're all Socialists nowadays. But I don't see why you have to give all your money away and make friends with the lower classes. You can be a Socialist *and* have a good time, that's what I say (*KAF*, 98).
33. On Orwell's life during this period, see Bernard Crick, *George Orwell* (Boston: Little, Brown, & Co., 1980), 104-80.
34. Cf. "Such, Such Were the Joys," *CEJL*, 4:330-69. On Orwell's compulsion to place himself, with anatomical precision, in the "lower-upper-middle class," see *RWP*, 121-53. One old colleague of Orwell's at the BBC, Henry Swanzy, has also recalled a conversation around 1942 with Orwell about being "the poorest boy in the school" at Eton (*GO*, 281).
35. Cyril Connolly, *Enemies of Promise* (New York: Macmillan, 1948), 164.
36. Richard Rees, *George Orwell: Fugitive from the Camp of Victory* (Carbondale: Southern Illinois University Press, 1961), 123-24. See also *RWP*, 138.
37. John Wain, "Here Lies Lower Binfield," *Encounter* 17 (October 1961): 75.
38. On the influence of Eliot and Joyce on Auden and his circle, see Hynes, *The Auden Generation*, 27-37. On Orwell during the period 1922-1929, see *GO*, 76-104.

39. This "outsider" stance of a man who had once been "inside" was first identified by Q. D. Leavis in her influential *Scrutiny* essay-review on Orwell
in September 1940. She noted that Orwell belonged, "by birth and education," to "'the right Left people," a leftist "nucleus of the literary world
who christian-name each other and are in honour bound to advance each
other's literary career." But she noted that Orwell was "in" yet not "of" his
generation: "He differs from them in having grown up. He sees them
accordingly from outside, having emancipated himself, at any rate in part,
by the force of a remarkable character." Quoted in Jeffrey Meyers, ed.,
George Orwell: The Critical Heritage (London: Routledge & Kegan Paul,
1975, 187.

Note also John Wain's shrewd observation that Orwell was "able to
observe the intelligentsia both from the inside and the outside," because
he was an intellectual yet with much of the common-sense temper of a
non-intellectual. Wain, "Orwell and the Intelligentsia," *Encounter* 21
(December 1968): 75.

40. Francis Hope's analysis of Orwell's reputation as a "witness" is acute:

> He always overgeneralized from his own experience: just because he
> went to Lancashire or to Catalonia, exposed himself to something he did
> not enjoy, and then wrote it up very well, he was taken as The Authority
> on a much wider problem—the communists and the Spanish Civil War
> as a whole, or British working class life in general. But at least he went
> there, and if his first-hand reports were then made to bear more general
> application than they should have, it is largely because so few other
> reporters put themselves forward.... It is remarkable how few people go
> even as far as Orwell did. ("My Country Right or Left," *New Statesman*
> 78 [19 December 1969]: 893)

41. Samuels, "English Intellectuals," 247.

42. Rayner Heppenstall, *Four Absentees* (London: Barrie and Rockliff, 1960),
59. Heppenstall adds that, at 32, Orwell seemed to him and Sayers "a great
age," and they thought it "a little odd in itself that he should have wanted
to share premises with us rather than with men more precisely of his own
generation...."

43. On Orwell's "outsider" stance toward all political groups, see my "The
Separate Worlds of George Orwell," *Four Quarters*, Summer 1988.

44. On the generational consciousness of "the Auden generation," see Hynes,
The Auden Generation, 17-37. Hynes does note that other 1930s writers
possessed Orwell's guilt for having been too young and having "missed"
World War I. The key generational "break" between them, as we have
seen, was Orwell's five years in Burma.

45. Cf. S. N. Eisenstadt, "Generational Conflict and Intellectual
Antinomianism," *Annals of the American Academy*, 68-79.

46. *GO*, xx. Angus Wilson is among those who argues that Orwell, "by leaving
Eton not for Oxford or Cambridge, but for 'experience of the world,'...lost
more than he gained." As a result, says Wilson, Orwell looked down on
education and never understood well the English middle class and professional tradition. Wilson, "Orwell and the Intellectuals," *Observer*, 24
January 1954, 8.

47. "Comment," *Horizon* 1 (1940): 5; Cyril Connolly, *The Unquiet Grave*
(London: Gollancz, 1942), 1.

48. Already by 1937-38, however, as "Macspaunday" became disillusioned with communism, they were "reintegrating" themselves within British society, partly for careerist reasons. By 1938 Auden had accepted the King's Gold Medal for poetry, Day-Lewis had joined the Book Society selection committee, and Spender had begun writing for Geoffrey Grigson's highbrow *New Verse*. On the tensions within the Auden group over these decisions, see C. Day Lewis, *An English Literary Life* (London: Weidenfeld & Nicolson, 1980), 115-17.

49. Fyvel, *Intellectuals Today*, 49. Fyvel also quotes a BBC acquaintance of Orwell's, Lawrence Gilliam, head of the BBC Home Service during the war, on the socially integrative effect of the intellectuals' war contributions *as intellectuals*:

    ...above all I remember no separation between people. What was happening here was a closing of the gap between intellectual and community. The intellectual found himself not out on a limb, not on a small magazine, writing his poems or articles or critical essays for a tiny audience, but temporarily reunited with the community as a whole and able to service it with his special talents, without losing his poetic identity or his independence.

50. Swingewood, "Consensus in Postwar England," 94.

51. Indeed, as late as April 1955, Edward Shils could ask in his report on the British intelligentsia: "Who criticizes Britain now in any fundamental sense, except for a few Communists and a few Bevanite irreconcilables?" Shils went on:

    [I]n the main...scarcely anyone in Great Britain seems any longer to feel that there is anything fundamentally wrong.... To the British intellectual of the mid-1950s [Britain is] fundamentally all right and even much more than that.... Never has an intellectual class found its society and its culture so much to its satisfaction. ("The Intellectuals in Great Britain," *Encounter* 4 [April 1955]: 8).

52. On the optimistic "revolutionary socialism" briefly espoused by Orwell, Fyvel, Fred Warburg, and a few others associated with the Searchlight Books group, see Fyvel, *George Orwell: A Personal Memoir* (London: Macmillan, 1982), 125-35.

53. For an overview of these positions, see Gagnon, *Intellectuals in Liberal Democracies*, 6-10.

54. Karl Mannheim, *Ideology and Utopia* (New York: Harcourt Brace, 1936), 137-38. For this summary I have relied chiefly on Gagnon's overview and Brym's analysis in *Intellectuals and Politics* and "The Political Sociology of Intellectuals." Malia is quoted in the latter (200).

55. Brym, *Intellectuals and Politics*, 13.

56. Brym, "The Political Sociology of Intellectuals," 206, 208.

57. Neglecting the historical dimension of political sociology not only blurs the process whereby radical movements form and fragment. It can also impose a false set of polarized categories on the past, which, if they persist, skew analyses of subsequent political configurations. And, as George Watson argues, the dissident politics of the 1930s has bred precisely such distortions. That single, aberrant decade of British radicalism has drawn a false line of demarcation between supporters of the "Left" and "Right"

which stretches into the 1990s. The very language of "spectrum" politics, imported from the continental (especially French) tradition of ideological politics, is historically inappropriate to the liberal, British political heritage. Indeed, the entry of the terminology of "Left" and "Right" into the English political lexicon around 1930 invited the "reclassification" of figures from the Victorian age—who had not thought in terms of the sharply dichotomous, near-monolithic, party-line ideological taxonomies of Left and Right. Thus Dickens, Cobbett, and others soon became "writer[s] well worth stealing" by Marxists and Tories alike. The irony is that Orwell's reputation, subject to repeated grave-robbing by intellectuals of all political stripes, has fallen victim since his death in 1950 to the very same oversimplifications from the 1930s which he so clearly saw through. See George Watson, *Politics and Literature in Modern Britain* (Totowa, N.J.: Rowman and Littlefield, 1977), 85-97.

58. For an overview of these two traditions and their exponents, see G. de Huszar, ed., *The Intellectuals: A Controversial Portrait* (Glencoe, Ill.: Free Press, 1960).

59 Julian Benda, *The Betrayal of the Intellectuals* (Boston: Beacon Press, 1955), 32.

60. *CEJL*, 4:410-11, 407-8. I have inverted the order of the last quotation.

61. Ibid., 413-14. One is struck by the similarity of Camus's formulation of the problem in his interviews of the 1950s (e.g., "The Artist and His Time [1953]," in *The Myth of Sisyphus and Other Essays* [New York: Vintage, 1982], 147, 149-50):

> Artists of the past could at least keep silent in the face of tyranny. The tyrannies of today are improved; they no longer admit of silence or neutrality. One has to take a stand, be either for or against....
>   Considered as artists, we perhaps have no need to interfere in the affairs of the world. But considered as men, yes....

Camus admired Orwell's work, which may have influenced Camus's thinking on the artist's responsibilities. Cf. Herbert Lottman, *Albert Camus* (Garden City: Doubleday, 1979), 413.

62. Noam Chomsky, *American Power and the New Mandarins* (New York: Pantheon, 1967), 95-102, 144-48. The second quotation is from Chomsky's interview on Melvyn Bragg's BBC-TV program on Orwell, "The Road to the Left", broadcast 10 March 1971. See also Chomsky's distinction between "responsible" and "combative" intellectuals in *Intellectuals and the State* (Amsterdam: Het Wereldvenster Baarn, 1978), 12-13.

63. Wain, "Orwell and the Intelligentsia," 76-77.

64. On Orwell's excruciating integrity, see Arthur Koestler, "A Rebel's Progress to George Orwell's Death," in *The Trail of the Dinosaur* (New York: Harcourt Brace, 1955), 102-5.

65. Watson, *Politics and Literature*, 45.

66. *CEJL*, 2:229. Orwell's key example of the intellectuals' collective self-betrayal of their trust was, of course, the issue of Stalinism: "The sin of nearly all left-wingers since 1933 is that they have wanted to be anti-fascist without being anti-totalitarian" (*CEJL*, 3:125).

His harsh criticism of Stalinism derived from his concern with truth-telling, freedom, and justice, not any reflex anti-communism. In 1944 Orwell told his friend John Middleton Murry, a wartime pacifist:

> I consider that willingness to criticise Russia and Stalin is *the* test of intel-
> lectual honesty. It is the only thing that from a literary intellectual's point
> of view that is really dangerous.... The thing that needs courage is to
> attack Russia, the only thing that the greater part of the British intelli-
> gentsia now believe in.... But to be anti-Russian makes enemies, whereas
> the other [criticism of British imperialism] doesn't—i.e. not such enemies
> as people like us would care about. (*CEJL*, 3:203-4)

Indeed, Orwell made it clear in a 1946 exchange with communist Randall
Swingler that he considered calculated appeals to emerging anti-commu-
nist intellectual orthodoxy just as corrupt as a reflexive pro-communism.
His reply to Swingler seems almost prescient in light of the rise of
McCarthyism in 1950:

> In five years it may be as dangerous to praise Stalin as it was to attack
> him two years ago. But I should not regard this as an advance. Nothing
> is gained by teaching a parrot a new word. What is needed is the right
> to print what one believes to be true, without having to fear bullying or
> blackmail from any side. ("Annotations to Swingler's 'The Right to Free
> Expression,'" *Polemic* 5 [1946]: 53)

67. *GO*, 237; Pritchett, "George Orwell," 96.

"The Rope That Connects Me Directly With You": John Wain and the Movement Writers' Orwell

John Rodden

I

No British writer has had a greater impact on the Anglo-American generation which came of age in the decade following World War II than has George Orwell. His influence has been, and continues to be, deeply felt by intellectuals of all political stripes, including the Marxist Left (Raymond Williams, E. P. Thompson), the anarchist Left (George Woodcock, Nicolas Walter), the American liberal-Left (Irving Howe), American neoconservatives (Norman Podhoretz), and the Anglo-American Catholic Right (Christopher Hollis, Russell Kirk).[1]

Perhaps Orwell's broadest imprint, however, was stamped on the only *literary* group which has ever regarded him as a model: the Movement writers of the 1950s. Unlike the above-mentioned groups, which have consisted almost entirely of political intellectuals rather than writers—and whose members have, understandably, responded to him as a political critic first and a writer second—some of the Movement writers saw Orwell not just as a political intellectual but also as the man of letters and/or literary stylist whom they aspired to be. As we shall see, as their aspirations evolved, they revised and remolded their model into the political and literary model they needed. Eventually they projected an outsized, translucent image of him, bending him into a figure who could help resolve problems within the Movement of personal and group identity.

The Movement writers were primarily an alliance of poet-critics. The "official" members numbered nine poets and novelists; a few writers and critics loomed on the periphery. Their acknowledged genius, if not leading publicist, was Philip Larkin, who later became one of Britain's leading poets and an oft-mentioned candidate for poet laureate. Orwell's plain voice influenced the tone and attitude of Larkin's poetry and that of several other Movement poets, especially Robert Conquest and D. J. Enright.[2] But Orwell shone as an even brighter presence among the poet-novelists, particularly John Wain and Kingsley Amis, whose early fictional anti-heroes were direct descendants of Gordon Comstock in *Keep the Aspidistra Flying* (1936) and George Bowling in *Coming Up for Air* (1939).

For Wain, above all, Orwell has been a literary-intellectual model, "a moral hero."[3] Wain's admiration for Orwell—unlike Amis's—has never wavered; he cherishes, and muses on, the unfulfilled tributes to him in the 1950s as "Orwell's natural successor." Into the 1980s he continues to hold fast to "the rope that...connect[s] me directly with you," however frayed his Orwell connection sometimes seems to unsympathetic observers and however rough-and-tumble his tug-of-war with other political intellectuals for Orwell's mantle sometimes becomes.[4] Across four decades, Orwell has remained a constant presence in Wain's life, though his history of impassioned responses has modulated with changes in his personal life and on the contemporary literary-political scene.

Wain's and the Movement writers' image of Orwell has developed against a wide panorama of cultural history, evolving in four stages. This reception history alters focus through the Movement's ascendency in the mid-1950s, through its breakup in the late 1950s and its members' growing fear of totalitarianism in the early 1960s, through the years of the New Left and Vietnam War, and through the Reagan-Thatcher era of renewed East-West hostility. Like Amis and most other Movement writers, Wain in the 1960s and 1970s adopted Toryism ("Experience is a Tory," Amis once quipped)[5] and a fierce anti-Communism—and, in turn, projected a sharply ideological, conservative image of Orwell. Thus, in searching for the Orwell in himself, Wain came to spotlight the John Wain which he perceived in George Orwell. In 1983, during the political showdown that would lead to the longest miners' strike in British history, he went so far as to try to "explain" to "Dear George Orwell" why the sympathetic view of the miners in *The Road to Wigan Pier* was obsolete and why Wain's harder line toward trade unionism was necessary.[6] Wain's reception history of Orwell thus constitutes not only a barometer of the fluctuations in the postwar British cultural climate and a glimpse into the ideology and aspirations of an important group in British literary history. It also furnishes insight into the mentality of a postwar generation who have agonized over their status as "successors" to the 1930s radicals, as latecomers deprived of "good brave causes"—and who have not infrequently justified their rightward turns by pointing to the example of the author of the quietist "Inside the Whale" and the antitotalitarian *Nineteen Eighty-Four*. Ultimately Wain's response also raises larger conceptual questions—pursued herein only suggestively—about the dynamics of literary response, the nature of author-reader relationships, the formation of readers' identities, the construction of intellectual genealogies, and the sociology of artistic reputation.

II

The Movement belongs both to the history of publicity and the history of poetry. The group's rise to prominence owed partly to the BBC Third Programme broadcasts made by 28-year-old Wain in 1953 ("First Reading"), in which he aired published Movement poems and work-in-progress, and also to favorable promotions by sympathetic literary journalists at the *Spectator* (e.g., Anthony Hartley, a fringe member of the group). Charter documents include Wain's *Hurry On Down* (1953), Amis's *Lucky Jim* (1954), and the Movement anthologies *Poets on the 1950s* (1955, edited by D. J. Enright) and *New Lines* (1956, edited by Robert Conquest). Officially launched in March 1954 when the literary editor of the *Spectator*, J. D. Scott, first tagged several of the writers with the label, "the Movement" was a tight alliance of old Oxford friends (Phillip Larkin, Amis, Wain) and of postgraduate acquaintances of similar age from London literary circles in the early 1950s.[7]

The Movement fit with and formed the temper of postwar reconstruction. In the aftermath of a global war and in the shadow of the bomb, Wain has recalled, the Movement writers felt "the impulse to *build*...." Writing "regular and disciplined verse forms" seemed to them a stay against postwar exhaustion and ennui; it was a small effort to "make something amid the ruins."[8] Orwell's limpid style and pragmatic ethos served as blueprint and cornerstone; his empirical, workaday sensibility undergirded the Movement's call to reassert order, tradition, and restraint.[9] His example and the Movement's priorities seemed to match the decade's, an Arnoldian epoch of concentration, or more exactly "consolidation,"[10] rather than expansion. In revolt against the obscurantism of Eliot's followers, the agitprop verse of the 1930s, the apocalyptic mysticism of some wartime pacifists, and the neo-Romanticism of Dylan Thomas, the Movement poets exalted (in Wain's words) "the return to a more level tone, the disappearance of panache and 'prophetic' pomp,...the submission to a new discipline of form, the refusal to make large gestures...."[11] Formal strictness, clear expression, concrete imagery, and a controlled voice summed up the Movement credo. The Movement writers maintained that poetry was a form of public communication, not an occasion for display of personality or ideological solidarity. Given their emphasis on reason, ordinary language, familiar allusions, everyday feelings, accessibility, and the wider audience, it is hardly surprising that they came to admire Orwell's straightforward prose and demonstrable appeal to the general reading public.

During this opening phase of his reception (c. 1950-56), then, Orwell stood before the Movement writers explicitly as a literary-intellectual figure. Most highly valued were Orwell's realistic novels and essays; three new collections of the latter appeared during this period (1950, 1953, 1956). Orwell was not a great novelist or artist, the Movement writers agreed. But he was practically the only twentieth-century Englishman to whom the Movement novelists could turn to for examples of "the compromising hero," as Blake Morrison has observed.[12] The picaresque anti-heroes in Wain's *Hurry on Down* and Amis's *Lucky Jim* and *That Uncertain Feeling* (1956)—so ambivalent toward issues of class and inequality, social "compromise" and "adjustment," bourgeois "conventionality" and political involvement—closely echo the confused, self-alienated Gordon Comstock of *Keep the Aspidistra Flying*. Moreover, Wain insisted in 1954, as a critic Orwell was "as good as any in English literature."[13] Wain argued that the permanent value of Orwell's work lay in his criticism, indeed, that a piece like "Lear, Tolstoy and the Fool" would ultimately gain more readers than *Animal Farm*.[14]

The Movement's particular attraction to Orwell, however, was not merely to his prose technique but to his literary persona. "Literary integrity" and "moral uprightness" go "hand in hand," Wain argued, casually accepting that *le style c'est l'homme*:

> It was Orwell's aim to forge a style in which it would be *impossible* to tell lies.... That bareness, that clarity, that directness, that fertility in images drawn from everyday life could only be achieved by two means: first, constant vigilance and imitation of the best models; second, by being that kind of person. In reading a page of Orwell one knows instinctively, even without knowing anything about his personal story, that here was a man who would be prepared to give his life for what he believed in. There is no short cut; a pusillanimous man cannot write a forthright prose; if he tries, he will sink into heartiness and that is all.[15]

That closing verdict could apply as self-criticism; even in the 1950s, and more so in later years, Wain's prose sometimes degenerated into "Jolly Jack" bluffness or mannered bluntness.[16]

But no Movement writer contested Wain's high assessment of Orwell's character. In 1954, J. D. Scott noted that "admiration for...Orwell above all" represented a "sign by which you may recognize the Movement."[17] Conquest's memorial poem "George Orwell" was a hymn to a "moral genius":

> Moral and mental glaciers melting slightly
> Betray the influence of his warm intent.
> Because he taught us what the actual meant
> The vicious winter grips its prey less tightly....
>
> We die of words. For touchstone he restored
> The real person, real event or thing;
> —And thus we see not war but suffering
> As the conjunction to be most abhorred.
>
> He shared with a great world, for greater ends,
> That honesty, a curious cunning virtue
> You share with just the few who won't desert you,
> A dozen writers, half-a-dozen friends.[18]

In his introduction to *New Lines*, Conquest added:

> One might, without stretching matters too far, say that George Orwell with his principle of real rather than ideological integrity, exerted, even though indirectly, one of the major influences on modern poetry.[19]

The Movement writers therefore embraced not only Orwell's "pure" prose style but also his "authentic" style of life. They strongly identified with their image of "the man within the writings," with the "decent," "trustworthy" "voice" of the essays and documentaries. Wain's recollections possess group significance:

> ...I had no political opinions, except a vague general sympathy with the social revolution that started in England in 1945.... As I gradually came to have some notion of politics, both domestic and international, it was two books of yours, *The Road to Wigan Pier* and *Homage to Catalonia*, that opened my eyes most. What I had in you was an instinctive trust: I knew I was hearing the voice of a decent, unselfish man, ready to make sacrifices for others, while at the same time enjoying his own life and getting on with it; and also the voice of a writer, which I hoped to be.
> I was twenty-five when you died, and I shall never forget the shock, the sense of a profound *personal* disappointment, with

which I heard the news. There were to be no more books and
articles by George Orwell! I felt robbed....[20]

It had been absolutely uncanny. They were like a series of
books that had been written expressly for me.[21]

The other Movement writers were in "vague general sympathy" with
the Labour Party too. Yet all of them were "neutralists" who scoffed at
politics. This stance certainly owed something to Orwell's disillusion-
ment with left-wing utopianism, particularly his caustic deprecation of
political "idealism" in "Inside the Whale." Blake Morrison has aptly
termed him a "maturing influence" on the Movement writers.[22] Their
nonpolitical attitudes, however, were also part of the larger current of
"end of ideology" and "consensus" politics ("Butskellism") prevalent in
the mid-1950s among a generation of Cold War liberals proud of the
recent successes of welfare-state capitalism. Kingsley Amis probably
exaggerated the direct effect of Orwell's anti-ideology stance on British
intellectuals, insofar as he suggested it was a primary, exclusive influence. His observations leave no doubt, however, as to Orwell's privileged place in the Movement canon by August 1956:

Any intellectuals who may submit to have a list of their heroes
wrung from them are likely to put him in the first two or three
whatever their age (within reason), whatever their other preferences, and—more oddly at first—whatever their political affiliations. And if they have none, incidentally, this is as much Orwell's
doing as anyone else's.[23]

Anti-wet, anti-phoney, undeceived, uncommitted: the Movement's
politics was an anti-politics, and Orwell served as a sort of *negative*
political model. "It is for us to keep Orwell's example constantly
before us," urged Wain in 1954.[24] The focus on Orwell's intellectual
and moral purity allowed the Movement writers to indulge their own
tendencies to equate acumen and virtue with political inactivity, so
that to follow "Orwell's example" entailed detachment, even cynicism,
toward politics. Overlooking the historical conditions which generated
Orwell's pessimism in the dark days of World War II in 1940 when
"Inside the Whale" was written, Movement writers identified his politics with the "sophisticated" withdrawal of the figure whom he criticized, Henry Miller, for whom all political affiliations were foolish.[25]

III

The Suez crisis and the ruthless Soviet suppression of the Hungarian
uprising in October-November 1956 transformed the meaning of
"Orwell's example" to the Movement writers overnight. British

intellectual opinion now regarded political indifference as passive, not sophisticated. As public debate over British foreign policy heated up, the Movement writers were widely criticized for their detachment. And some of them, in turn, blamed Orwell. The shift in attitude is most apparent in Amis's Fabian pamphlet, *Socialism and the Intellectuals*, written in November 1956. Amis had paid homage to Orwell's quietist influence just three months earlier, but this time its baneful consequences are noted:

> Of all the writers who appeal to the post-war intelligentsia, he is far and away the most potent.... No modern writer has his air of passionately believing what he has to say and of being passionately determined to say it as forcefully and simply as possible. Most passionately he believed that left-wing politics are a trap for what I have called the political romantic; so passionately, indeed, that the trap becomes a trap and nothing else. Orwell's insistence that the political *can* be dirty and dishonest and treacherous, that it *often* is, betrays him into implying that it *must* be and *always* is....
>
> He was the man above all others who was qualified to become the candid friend the Labour party needed so much in the years after 1945. But what he did was to become a right-wing propagandist by negation, or at any rate a supremely powerful—though unconscious—advocate of political quietism....[He] completed his long-impending development into a hysterical neurotic with a monomania about the depravity of British intellectuals.[26]

The man whom Amis saw as an "intellectual's hero" in the summer had become a "hysterical" intellectual-basher by autumn; the man of toughminded common sense had turned into a political romantic.[27]

The deflation reflected not only Amis's turmoil over the events of 1956. It also betokened a change of heart toward Orwell among his intellectual generation. Many postwar admirers soon began focusing on Orwell as the author of *Wigan Pier* and *Homage to Catalonia*—rather than "Inside the Whale"—and so began valuing him precisely for his stirring activism.

No longer were the Movement writers being depicted in the literary press as generational spokesmen after Suez. Young Britons were now described as "angry," and though Wain and Amis were portrayed in the press as Angry Young Men (a catch phrase belonging almost entirely to the history of publicity), fictional heroes like Charles Lumley in *Hurry on Down* and Jim Dixon in *Lucky Jim* actually exhibited no more than irritation and frustration, not outrage.[28] The critical success of *New Lines* in 1956 had marked the "arrival" of the Movement; already by 1957, Wain was speaking in the past tense, announcing that "there was a 'movement' and it did cohere. Then, as always, each moved away on his own path...."[29] Suez and Hungary hastened the dispersal, as the consensus shared by the Movement unravelled, with most members (unlike the rest of their generation) remaining neutralist about British neo-imperialism in Suez but some speaking out against the Soviet invasion.[30] Eden's disastrous, widely-condemned decision to send troops to Egypt had undermined Britain's moral authority and exposed its loss of power in the postwar world, developments on which the Movement writers looked with mixed feelings; and Hungary had made clear the price of "peaceful co-existence." October 1956 thus rendered the Movement's quizzical anti-political stance widely suspect as irresponsible attitudinizing. The age of noncommitment had ended. Anger replaced langour as the de rigeur emotion of the hour.

The 1957 manifesto *Declaration*, to which Wain (along with several other "Angries") contributed, captured the new mood in a word. British intellectuals moved, in E. P. Thompson's phrase, "outside the whale."[31] Some New Left spokesmen, including Thompson and later Raymond Williams, echoed Amis in "blaming" Orwell. "We can write Berlin, Algiers, Aden, Watts, Prague in the margins of Orwell's passivity," wrote Williams. "What in Orwell was a last, desperate throw became for many others, absurdly, a way of life."[32] This negative assessment of Orwell was one of the few topics on which Amis and his New Left coevals agreed.

In no way did it signify, however, the consensus of their generation. Rather, many young intellectuals, caught between the inclination to adapt and the impulse to rebel, felt both an anxiety of influence and the inspiration of the heroic toward Orwell. Indeed, some young writers began calling attention precisely to Orwell's "generously angry" side, giving rise to a more feisty and political, less noble and "pure," public image. This new emphasis is broadly discernible in the work of Wain and certain Movement-affiliated writers (Hartley) and a few of the Angry Young Men (John Osborne, John Braine, Alan Sillitoe), and it represents an equally strong current within the second stage of Orwell's reception (c. 1957-1963) by postwar British writers. "Personally, I always think of him as he thought of Dickens:...the face of a man who is *generously angry*...," wrote Hartley. Taking issue with Amis's and Thompson's harsh judgments, Hartley insisted that the author of *Wigan Pier* was "far and away the most powerful advocate of a fair deal for the British working classes" and that the apathy of postwar intellectuals arose not from reading Orwell but "because of what they read in the newspapers." Events, not Orwell, caused their political disillusion. "If, as is fashionable to say, he was not a Socialist," concluded Hartley, "so much the worse for Socialism." And yet, even while noting gratefully that "the no-nonsense air of a generation came from

Orwell," Hartley admitted that the limitations in vision and aspiration implied by that attitude had entailed "jettisoning some valuable cargo": "Something, I feel, was lost by my generation. Perhaps we played too safe, were too concerned not to be criticized for romantic or sentimental nostalgia. Perhaps the something was youth...."[33] A flexible, down-to-earth habitude has ossified into the earthbound doctrine of a generation.

Post-Suez fiction and drama indirectly promoted both the "angry" and "quietist" (or "neurotic") images of Orwell. Joe Lampton in Braine's *Room at the Top* (1957) and Arthur Seaton in Sillitoe's *Saturday Night and Sunday Morning* (1958) were widely recognized anti-phoney cousins to the choleric Gordon Comstock—who is usually taken as a thinly autobiographical Orwell—all of them provincial boys alternately defiant and craven toward "the money god" and "bourgeois" family values. ("This Angry Young Man of the Thirties...," blazoned the cover of the 1962 Signet edition of *Keep the Aspidistra Flying*.) Orwell is clearly the Angry Young Man of the Thirties towering behind Osborne's *Look Back in Anger*, key scenes of which echo "Inside the Whale," "Reflections on Gandhi," and *The Lion and the Unicorn*.[34] Indeed, the play reflected and reinforced the split in Orwell's post-Suez reputation: Was he an erstwhile Jimmy Porter? Or did the heroic father whom young Jimmy watched die on his return home from the Spanish Civil War evoke Orwell (who had almost died of a throat wound in Catalonia)?

Wain remained Orwell's biggest champion—and Orwell remained, of Wain's and the Movement's onetime master from the older generation, Wain's single abiding enthusiasm.[35] Implicitly challenging the reassessments by Amis and other contemporaries (e.g., Anthony West's psychoanalytic reading of "Such, Such Were the Joys")[36] who began devaluing Orwell after 1956, Wain declared in a 1957 essay ("Orwell in Perspective") that his hero was being "grotesquely misjudged." Preoccupied with his life rather than his work, critics were devoting excessive attention to his "idiosyncrasies," charged Wain.[37] Ironically, of course, the keen critical interest in "the man" was partly due to Wain's own preoccupation with Orwell persona just a few years earlier.

Rather than discuss Orwell's impact on his generation, Wain sought to "update" Orwell in the new activist climate and to furnish a critical approach to his work which would properly value his achievement. Wain's previous characterization of Orwell as "critic" was inadequate, he now realized. Nor would "novelist" or "essayist" do. An entirely new "perspective" was needed, a category which would foreground the *engagé* Orwell and do justice to his literary strengths. If one stepped back and considered Orwell's work collectively and from a wide historical angle, Wain argued, his *oeuvre* fell within the tradition of the polemic:

> He was a novelist who never wrote a satisfactory novel, a literary critic who never bothered to learn his trade properly, a social historian whose history was full of gaps. Yet he matters. For as polemic his work is never anything less than magnificent; and the virtues which the polemic demands—urgency, incisiveness, clarity and humour—he possessed in exactly the right combination.[38]

Partly in reaction to the rise of the British New Left in the late 1950s and a harrowing one-month visit to the Soviet Union in 1960 (both satirized in *The Young Visitors*, 1965),[39] Wain himself was becoming more politically active. Wain's catalogue of "virtues which the polemic demands" constituted a personal inventory: a polemical Orwell was precisely the new model whom he needed. And so Wain again remolded Orwell as he assimilated him, bending him into the shape he now required—less a lonely figure of intellectual integrity and more a committed pamphleteer, though one of anti-radical convictions. (That both Osborne and Wain could admire and use the "rebel" Orwell from opposite ends of the ideological spectrum suggests how politically ambidextrous and culturally fashionable "rebellion" had become in the 1950s—and it shows that Orwell's reputation had become remarkably protean.)

Russia was Wain's Catalonia. "In retrospect these four weeks have expanded steadily until they now seem the equivalent of four years," Wain wrote on his return home. Having "fallen for a lot of the stuff I'd read about the thaw" during the de-Stalinization period under Khrushchev, Wain was "shocked" to encounter "a real, fully fledged totalitarian system." The experience contrasted sharply with an enjoyable visit to America in 1959: it was almost as if the drama of the Cold War were being enacted in his life. His Soviet trip "depressed me almost suicidally" and "taught me to revalue all my political experience.... It taught me what totalitarianism, even with its mild face,...is like.... Quite simply, it altered my entire view of the world."[40]

Putting Orwell "in perspective" thus soon became not just a critical stratagem but a personal necessity. As he gradually developed into a romantic Conservative in the mold of Samuel Johnson, Wain came in turn to see Orwell not merely as a dissident socialist but as an anti-revolutionary altogether. Pointed reference to Orwell's contempt for "progressives"—the word usually enclosed within arch quotation marks—soon became standard practice in Wain's criticism. By 1961 Wain was profiling what Conor Cruise O'Brien later called Orwell's "Tory growl."[41] Highlighting Orwell's romanticism, patriotism, and nostalgia, Wain stressed "the hatred felt for him by 'progressives' with their money on the future and their heads full of Revolution."[42]

Ignoring his 1957 plea that critics avoid psychologizing Orwell, Wain returned in 1961 ("Here Lies Lower Binfield") to the subject of his enduring fascination: his model's character, now approached in light of Wain's own newly-felt romanticism, patriotism, and nostalgia, attributes which he projected as the whole of Orwell's personality and work. *Coming Up for Air*, Wain argued, was Orwell's "central book," and "his most important character creation" was George Bowling. "If all his books disappeared without a trace," said Wain, "we should be able to tell, from this one, what kind of writer he was, what his major themes were, and how he treated them."[43] *Coming Up* represented the clearest instance of Orwell's unconscious literary strategy for expressing fully his love of nature, his "Englishness," and his sentimental faith in the common man, said Wain. There was indeed a "thin man" inside George Bowling, struggling to get out: his name was George Orwell. *Coming Up* disclosed the dynamics of Orwell's imaginative life as a series of substitutions: Blair needed Orwell to speak in his own voice about politics; Orwell needed Bowling to speak about personal matters.[44] Bowling thus growled the Tory truths, Wain implied, which Blair-Orwell could seldom speak.

IV

By the mid-1960s a new "Movement" had arisen. The radicalization of the British New Left after 1962 gave birth to the student movement and counterculture. Several former Movement writers turned further right in response (Wain, Amis, Larkin, Conquest, Donald Davie), and they suddenly found themselves united in ideological solidarity much as they had been joined on literary grounds a decade before. By 1970 they had become defenders rather than critics of the status quo, unabashedly conservative domestically, pro-American internationally. The avant-garde had become a rearguard.

Orwell's Tory growl thundered in this third phase of the Movement writers' reception history of him (c. 1964-1974). The rumbles sounded loudest in the works of Amis and Wain. Their attention shifted away from Orwell's essays and early fiction and toward *Homage to Catalonia* and *Nineteen Eighty-Four*, with the image of Orwell the anti-"progressive" skeptic giving way to an explicitly anti-Communist figure.

In 1956 Amis had called Orwell "one of those writers you can never get away from because no view of him can ever be final."[45] Amis's use of the second person probably indicated his own urge to evade Orwell's influence; but by the early 1960s his politics and his fluctuating view of Orwell were stabilizing and converging. "Hungary turned me into a violent anti-Communist," he admitted;[46] indeed, Hungary was Amis's Catalonia. A "callow Marxist" during 1940-1942 in his early twenties, an undergraduate editor of Oxford's *University Labour Club Bulletin*, and an ambivalent supporter of the Labour Party throughout the 1950s, Amis confessed that by 1960 his tempestuous relationship with Labour and socialism "had got to the name-calling and walking-out stage."[47] By the mid-1960s Amis had effectively broken with the Left and embraced Wain's anti-totalitarian "perspective" on Orwell. The mark of the late Orwell is clear in *The Anti-Death League* (1966), a militaristic, apocalyptic, nightmarish world much like Oceania. Amis's own political maturation, he later recalled, gave him more sympathy for the trajectory of Orwell's development in the 1940s:

> I had once thought Orwell a man of utter integrity—the one intellectual from the older generation who had not compromised himself. Later I came to modify that view, but also to realize that part of growing up is that you can still have a hero whom you know to be impure, whom you can value for what he got right and not condemn for what he got wrong.[48]

Amis became aware of the odd doubleness of Orwell's public persona, which allowed different generations—both angry young men and their chastened elders—to identify with distinctive aspects of him. Orwell as a model was not a "trap," as Amis had once thought, but a mirror of his past and a lamp for his future. The figure of Orwell as "young man's hero" possessed the appeal of an idealist; one could identify with his romantic dreaming, his passionate defiance, and his apparent purity. Conversely, the figure of Orwell as "mature man's hero" spoke to the worldly-wise; one could admire his skepticism toward, even his cynicism about, utopian high-mindedness.[49] Orwell had once been Amis's youth hero; now the mature Amis recognized the value of his hero's realistic side and even of his flaws, no longer feeling any need to "get away from" Orwell.

Indeed, just the reverse. In the late 1960s Amis's skepticism led him to adopt a combative traditionalism hostile to all innovation, and his self-image developed into that of an intellectual rebel not unlike Orwell—though with the major difference that Amis became a curmudgeonly Establishment defender possessed of none of Orwell's attachment to the Left-liberal fold. Martin Green, noting the perverse pleasure which Amis seemed to derive from his numerous unpopular positions, acutely observed that "it seemed as if he could have no orthodoxy except an unrespectable one like Toryism"[50]—almost as if

Amis were trying to outdo Orwell as a fashion-hating rebel. Or adopting another model along with Orwell: in his crotchety defense of the Establishment, Amis seemed to be modeling himself even more after Evelyn Waugh than after Orwell.

Thus, as Amis finally "broke off my lingering love affair with the Left" and voted Conservative for the first time in 1966, he became almost reactionary in his cultural politics.[51] In his fiction and criticism he attacked new idioms "corrupting" the English language, deprecated rock and modern jazz in preference to early jazz, dismissed free verse and "pop" poetry in favor of metrical laws and regular forms, inveighed against "totalitarian" ideas (promoted by "trendy Lefties") threatening "humane" (conservative) values, opposed university expansion ("MORE WILL MEAN WORSE" went his much-quoted slogan) in defense of educational "standards" and elitism,[52] and castigated communitarian schemes in support of individualism and free enterprise.[53] Occasionally he implied, indulging in the "If Orwell Were Alive Today" speculations of the period, that Orwell might have done the same.

One sign of Orwell's importance for Amis at this time came in his opening salvo as regular columnist for London's *Daily Express* (19 March 1969). Promising to "sound off" against "left-wing idiocy," Amis portrayed Orwell as his predecessor, gratefully characterizing him as "a thorn in the side of the Left." By this time Amis had also become an outspoken supporter of the American presence in Vietnam—together with Wain, practically the only leading British intellectuals to do so[54]—a position for which Amis was pilloried on both sides of the Atlantic. Inevitably he mused on where Orwell would have stood on Vietnam, though he recalls that he was no more certain than many of his radical critics—most notably, Mary McCarthy[55]—as to the answer. Would Orwell, always the iconoclastic enemy of Left faddism, have had the grit to stand alone—outside the Left—as Kingsley Amis did?

> Which way would he have gone? He would have had a horrible time. Certainly I think that he would have wanted to have supported the American side, which meant supporting the fight against Communist aggression. Whether he would have done so or not—I don't know. I don't know whether he would have had the courage.[56]

Wain, though less vocal about the war, similarly "thank[ed] my stars" that "the Americans refuse to retreat before Communist bluster" and instead "stand firm against Soviet and Chinese threats."[57] Significantly, Wain also revised his judgment about Orwell's "most important book" for "understand[ing] [his] mind": the clear-sighted anti-Communist *Homage to Catalonia*, not *Coming Up for Air*, now received Wain's vote.[58] To Wain, the 1960s were a replay of the 1930s. The age of the hypocritical "right Left people" had returned—but fortunately accompanied by Orwell's pointed, conscience-pricking jibes:

> ...[I]t is once more the fashion to decry Orwell, as it was in the Thirties. Now as then, his truth-telling is dismissed as perverse, and his warnings are shrugged off by what he called "the huge tribe known as 'the right left people.'" Now as then, the most vicious digs at Orwell come from men whose basic intellectual position is totalitarian, the sort of people who are always ready to point out the flaws in an untidy democracy, but see nothing disturbing in the dreadful tidiness of, say, a classroom of North Vietnamese children squawking in unison: "No one loves Uncle Ho more than the children." We are plagued with these people now, as we were in the Thirties, and for much the same reasons.
>
> It is a testimony to the continuing vitality of Orwell's work that totalitarian-minded critics hate him so much. They hate him because he is a thorn in their sides. May he stay there forever.[59]

Wain's new image of Orwell was that of a salty political "conscience," a figure fusing Wain's previous portraits of the intellectual paragon and brilliant polemicist. Orwell's Johnsonian service to his fellow intellectuals, said Wain, had been to clear their slogan-sogged minds of radical cant, to "keep their consciences alive."[60] Writing in December 1968, just one month after the biggest anti-war demonstration in London, Wain nominated himself for a similar task to his own generation to intellectuals—for the long-vacant office of Orwell's "successor":

> ...I know that when I hear the pronouncements made by various influential people in the England of the '60s, I long for Orwell back again. But, since we can't have him, it is good to be able to use his work for its purpose: as an example, an incitement, and a justification....
>
> [W]ho can feel that the situation that faces us has changed much from what it was in the '30s and '40s...? The thing to be feared is still a *trahison des clercs*: freedom still needs to be defended against those whom she most favours, whom she showers with advantages. At whatever point we are engaged in the never-ending battle against cant, whether we are trying to reckon up the myriad ways in which Western writers can get a good price for their integrity behind the Iron Curtain, or sorting out the multiple confusions in the latest pronouncement from someone like Cohn-Bendit,...it is Orwell who provides us with the best model of how to do it, and the most generous and communicable vision of why it should be done.[61]

V

The decade-long "countdown on 1984" raised the "If Orwell Were Alive Today" speculations to a fever pitch. The Soviet occupation of Afghanistan, the Iranian hostage crisis, the politicized 1980 and 1984 Olympics, the imposition of martial law in Poland and the Philippines, the Soviet shooting of KAL 007, the American military involvements in Lebanon and El Salvador and Nicaragua and Grenada, the Falkland Islands invasion, the birth of the Social Democratic Party: so enveloping was Orwell's ever-lengthening shadow that hardly a single major event of the late 1970s and early 1980s did not tempt some intellectual or journalist to wonder aloud about *Orwell Redivivus* all over again.[62]

Neither Amis or Wain hesitated to weigh in with their own predictions. Amis believed that Orwell would have spoken out against *Sandinismo* just as he had attacked communism in Republican Spain. Likewise, he suggested, the liberal-minded, patriotic Orwell would have supported the Thatcher government's Falkland Islands mission as a just defense against Argentinian aggression and of the islanders' right to self-determination.[63]

Having already moved in the late 1960s to take Orwell's place as a rebel not just against but *outside* the Left, Amis came in the 1970s and 1980s to assume, though now as a self-declared "man of the Right," another role often ascribed to Orwell: the dire anti-totalitarian prophet.[64] Amis's *The Alteration* (1977) depicted a horrific, theocratic, quasi-Nazi state; and *Russian Hide-and-Seek* (1980) portrayed Britain under Soviet occupation. Thus Amis and Wain—among the leading men of letters of their generation and two of the major voices within the British intellectual Right—have wound up filling, as it were, distinct places in English cultural life once occupied by the socialist Orwell, adjusting them to fit their conservative politics. The more truculent, insouciant Amis has chosen to become a wide-ranging cultural commentator, an aggressively provocative opponent of radical chic, and an almost gleeful sounder of apocalyptic alarms. The more earnest, sometimes moralistic Wain has settled into his narrower, self-ordained role as the clerisy's "conscience."

The elder Wain seems to accept that along with the office comes the charge, as his younger self had put it, "to keep Orwell's example constantly before us." But as he follows that radiant model, he freely jerks rightward "the rope that connects me directly with you," often dragging Orwell along rather than dutifully trailing behind. In the *American Scholar*, edited by neoconservative Joseph Epstein, Wain discussed the 1983 British domestic scene in a letter to an absent correspondent—"Dear George Orwell." He boxed rival claimants for

"St. George's" halo, arguing that Orwell would have opposed anti-Zionism, Scottish and Welsh nationalists, noisy pubs, the "Peace Movement" ("Personally I would not use the word 'peace' if what I really meant was 'surrender'"), and especially the "anti-democratic Left."[65] The Communists "hated you because you saw through them and said so" and "they still hate you," Wain told Orwell, but some current radicals employ devious tactics "to undermine your influence from within, claiming to admire you but actually working to destroy your credibility."[66] Less blatantly than *Commentary* editor Norman Podhoretz, but no less certainly, Wain suggested that, if Orwell were alive today, he would be standing with the Anglo-American neoconservatives and against the Left.[67] Reemphasizing the significance of *Homage to Catalonia*, Wain denied that Orwell's radical "admirers and inheritors" (e.g., Raymond Williams, Bernard Crick) belonged in any tradition that included him—thereby making no distinction between the Marxist and democratic Left:

> The[ir] technique is to represent you as a founding father of the present-day Left—so that it is perfectly fitting to keep your grave tended and even to lay flowers on it—but as someone who has been left behind by the developing situation and can't any longer be taken seriously. When done skillfully, this is a highly effective technique, and some of your most untiring enemies have managed to muddy the waters so successfully that they are habitually named as your admirers and inheritors. I can only offer one piece of practical advice to people who might wonder whether they are being conned or not. The mark of all such anti-Orwell smear jobs is that they underplay *Homage to Catalonia*.[68]

No issue, however, exercised Wain more than the 1984-85 miners' strike, led by the self-declared Communist Arthur Scargill and already on the horizon when Wain's letter appeared. Wain, who had grown up among miners in Stoke-on-Trent, reserved his hottest fire for Scargill and appealed to the author of *The Road to Wigan Pier* to bless his hard-line position.

> The new breed of trade union leader is not like the ones you saw in action and heard speak at meetings.... As I write, the National Union of Mineworkers has got itself under the leadership of a man [Scargill] who spouts Marxist cliches as copiously as Fidel Castro; he has already announced [that]...the strike weapon will be used not as a means for getting the miner a fair day's work...but as a political battering ram in the service of the anti-democratic Left. Now, what would you, George Orwell, make of this? Would you say, "The miners forever—the common man right

or wrong?" But then, who, nowadays, is the common man? Isn't it the case that highly organized key workers, in a position to bring the economy to a standstill and wreck everybody's hopes, form an aristocracy, in the sense of power handed on from generation to generation and unanswerable to the moral authority of a democratic state?[69]

Wain's use of direct address bares his feeling of closeness to Orwell. However fair or correct Wain's stand, Orwell's place as a guiding star in his life impels him to explain his positions to his model less by arguing them in their own terms than by framing them so that they fit Orwell's pronouncements on related, and sometimes anachronistic, subjects. As he settles into middle age, readily "disclaim[ing]" the title "Orwell's natural successor" as "too big for me,"[70] Wain wonders aloud in this fourth stage of his reception history (c. 1975–) about his relationship with Orwell, more conscious than earlier of its tensions and yet unequivocal in his allegiance. In an interview he mused on "Wain's Orwell" then and now:

> In my youth I was a great propagandist for Orwell. I was always pushing him on people, quoting him at people—I was always saying, "As George Orwell remarked...." I wanted to bang the drum for Orwell—which no doubt led some people to think that I was trying to be the next Orwell....
> He's always somebody I've enjoyed keeping company with. I'm very fond of the man in the writings, and I think I would have been fond of the man himself—though I don't feel any confidence that Orwell would have liked me. Still, to me he's an endearing, funny figure. You can't really love someone you can't laugh at, and sometimes I have a good laugh about him. But I think that, in his political opinions, he was absolutely right. He rings absolutely right....[71]

"Love" is not too strong a word for the fealty which John Wain has shown since his twenties toward George Orwell. If Wain's admiration "early and late" has sometimes been uncritical and self-serving, it nevertheless seems genuine. Indeed, Wain's reception history of Orwell represents an unusually deep and open instance of reader identification with an author, suggesting how readers turn writers into luminous heroic "presences" to whom they can look for direction in their lives.[72] As Ernest Becker explains it, the fascination of the perceiver for the admired is an attempt to "address our performance of heroics" to another single human being. We "beatify" an Other so that we can know whether our performance is adequate. When it proves inadequate, we can look to him or her alone and change. Contra Freud, Becker sees this as natural, healthy projection, a reaching out for plenitude, and he terms this localized, intense charge of affect "transference heroics." Most of the time we construct composite models, with a mixture of different (and sometimes conflicting) features of persons constituting our image of the heroic, of our ideal selves. And typically we choose living models. But between a willing admirer like Wain and a strong literary personality and autobiographical writer like Orwell the identification can be sweeping, passionate, and enduring. It may also be that the great dead author, particularly for those readers who are themselves writers, is most amenable to idealization as a secure model, since he is incapable of compromising himself by further action and possesses a living "voice" which "re-presents" him before his readers at their will and always at his best. The man is dead, but the magnificent work—and the man within the work—cannot die.[73]

Wain is not the only reader, of course, to have exalted Orwell into a radiant figure in his life. Nor is Orwell the only writer who has engaged Wain's emotions as an inspirational model. As he moved rightward, Wain began comparing Orwell with the Tory Samuel Johnson— another cherished "moral hero" of Wain's and in some ways a more comfortable political model—thereby recasting Orwell in his own image through Johnson's.[74] In such ways do readers struggle to resolve problems of identity and authors acquire reputations. "The rope that connects me directly with you" has many intricately woven strands, inevitably yanked and twisted and reeled in as readers' needs and aspirations compel and as authors' personas and writings invite. A reader's history of response to an author is not merely a literary critique but also a complex autobiographical and cultural act. As John Wain's and the Movement writers' variegated reception history of George Orwell attests, the fabric of reputations is dyed the color of our lives.

Notes

1. On Orwell's reception by some of these groups, see my "Ideology, Revisionism and the British Left: Orwell's Marx and the Marxists' Orwell," *Papers in Comparative Studies* 5 (1984): 45-60; and "Orwell on Religion: The Catholic and Jewish Questions," *College Literature* 11 (1984): 44-58.
2. Blake Morrison has discussed Orwell's influence on Larkin in *The Movement* (London: Oxford University Press, 1980), esp. 178, 234.
3. John Wain, Introduction to *A House for the Truth* (London: Macmillan, 1972), 1.
4. John Wain, "Dear George Orwell: A Personal Letter," *American Scholar*, February 1983, 22.
5. See Kingsley Amis, "Why Lucky Jim Turned Right," *What Became of Jane Austen and Other Questions* (New York: Harcourt Brace Jovanovich, 1971), 202.

6. Wain, "Dear George Orwell," 31-32.

7. See Morrison, *Movement*, 10-54. Wain and Amis also reviewed regularly for the *Spectator* during the key years of the emergence of the Movement, 1954-55.

8. Quoted in Morrison, *Movement*, 89.

9. Indeed, the Movement's character owes something to the rise of logical positivism and the postwar vogue in the British academy for the ordinary language philosophy of the late Wittgenstein and Gilbert Ryle. To some degree, the Movement writers received this influence through Orwell; Hartley calls the author of "Politics and the English Language" and "Notes on Nationalism" the "great popularizer of logical positivism" in the 1950s. See Anthony Hartley, *A State of England* (New York: Harcourt Brace, 1963), 50. It has also been argued, however, that the "collective solipsism" of *Nineteen Eighty-Four* is a satire of logical positivism.

10. The role of "consolidation" served as a key concept in the Movement's vocabulary. See Morrison, *Movement*, 89-91.

11. John Wain, "English Poetry: The Immediate Situation," *Sewanee Review* 65 (1957): 359.

12. Morrison, *Movement*, 73.

13. John Wain, "The Last of George Orwell," *Twentieth Century*, January 1954, 71.

14. Ibid.

15. John Wain, "Orwell," *Spectator*, 19 November 1954, 632.

16. On the "Orwell-derived manner" of much Movement prose, see John Lucas, "Aspidistra Flyers," *New Statesman* 99 (23 May 1980): 286-87.

17. [J. D. Scott], "In the Movement," *Spectator*, 1 October 1954. This article was anonymous. Scott discusses it and its role in the publicity campaign launched by the *Spectator* to promote the Movement in "A Chip of Literary History," *Spectator*, 16 April 1977.

18. Robert Conquest, "George Orwell," in *George Orwell: Collected Writings*, ed. George Bott (London: Secker & Warburg, 1958), 1.

19. Robert Conquest, ed., Introduction to *New Lines* (London: Macmillan, 1956), 4.

20. Wain, "Dear George Orwell," 22.

21. John Wain, interview with the author, 14 March 1985.

22. Morrison, *Movement*, 92.

23. Kingsley Amis, "The Road to Airstrip One," *Spectator*, 31 August 1956, 292.

24. Wain, "The Last of George Orwell," 78.

25. On Miller's view of Orwell as a foolish idealist for going to fight Spanish fascism, see Henry Miller, "The Art of Fiction," *Paris Review* 7 (1962): 146-47.

26. Kingsley Amis, *Socialism and the Intellectuals* (London: Fabian Society, 1957), 8.

27. On Williams' similar volte face between 1955 and 1956, see his essay-review "George Orwell," *Essays in Criticism* 5 (1955): 44-52; and his chapter "George Orwell," in *Culture and Society*, ed. Raymond Williams (New York: Columbia University Press, 1958), 331-47, which was written during 1956.

28. On the relation between the Movement and the Angry Young Man phenomenon, see Morrison, *Movement*, 246-48.

29. Wain, "English Poetry," 359.

30. Cf. Morrison's *Movement* for a discussion of the impact of the events of 1956 on some of the Movement writers, 249-51.
31. See Thompson's influential, hostile essay on Orwell of that title in his *Out of Apathy* (London: New Left Books, 1960), 158-65, 171-73.
33. Raymond Williams, *George Orwell* (London: Fontana, 1971), 96.
33. Hartley, *A State of England*, 53-55.
34. Cf. Daniel Rogers, "'Look Back in Anger'—To George Orwell," *Notes and Queries*, August 1962, 310-311; and Geoffrey Carnall, "Saints and Human Beings: Orwell, Osborne and Gandhi," in *Essays Presented to Amy G. Stock*, ed. R. K. Raul (Jaipur: Rajasthan University Press, 1965), 168-77.
35. Already by 1957 Wain, as he was defending Orwell, was distancing himself from William Empson and F. R. Leavis. Empson's ambiguity and anti-Romanticism and Leavis's methods of textual "scrutiny" had exerted decisive influence on Movement poetry and criticism. But Wain and other Movement writers came to see "Empsonianism" as arid intellectualism and "Leavisism" as pretentious academicism. The aesthetic-political contradictions in the Movement's credo and the inherent instability of the Movement's program, given the family tree formed by its three models thus finally revealed themselves. Though the trio shared an emphasis on "Englishness" and pragmatism, Empson's scientific formalism and Leavis's aggressive elitism were fundamentally at odds with Orwell's sociological literary criticism, democratic socialism, and commitment to the common reader. Professional reasons probably also weighed in Wain's and Amis's preference for Orwell. Wain and Amis rejected the route which Empson and "Dr." Leavis had taken: the academic career. Wain left Reading University in 1955 to pursue free-lance writing full-time; Amis stopped teaching in 1963. No doubt it was also easier to embrace Orwell because, unlike Empson and Leavis, he was a nonthreatening (or already slain) father figure, no longer a judge or rival. (Amis in particular was attacked by Leavis for his "pornographic" fiction.)
36. Anthony West, "Hidden Wounds," *New Yorker* (28 January 1956): 71-79.
37. John Wain, "Orwell in Perspective," *New World Writing*, reprinted in *George Orwell: A Collection of Essays*, ed. Raymond Williams (Englewood Cliffs, N.J.: Prentice-Hall, 1974), 89.
38. Ibid., 90.
39. Some of Wain's other poetry and fiction of the period also bore the marks of his Soviet experience. *Wildtrack* (1965) included several couplets entitled "Attitude of Humanity Toward the Irreducible I." His novel *A Winter in the Hills* (1970) told the story of individualistic Welsh nationalists resisting creeping totalitarianism. (By 1983, as we have seen [p. 250], Wain had turned against Welsh nationalists.)
40. John Wain, *Sprightly Running: Part of An Autobiography* (New York: St. Martin's Press, 1962), 233-34; "John Wain," interview in *The Writer's Place*, ed. Peter Firchow (Minneapolis: University of Minnesota Press, 1974), 327.
41. Conor Cruise O'Brien, "Orwell Looks at the World," in *George Orwell: A Collection of Essays*, ed. Raymond Williams (Englewood Cliffs, N.J.: Prentice-Hall, 1974), 158.
42. John Wain, "Here Comes Lower Binfield," *Encounter* 17 (October 1961): 71.

43. Ibid. 74, 79.
44. Ibid., 76.
45. Amis, "The Road to Airstrip One," 292.
46. "Kingsley Amis," interviewed by Clive James, *New Review* 1 (July 1974): 24.
47. "Callow Marxist": Amis, *Socialism and the Intellectuals*, 5; "Name-calling and walking-our stage": quoted in Morrison, *Movement*, 252.
48. Kingsley Amis, interview with the author, 12 March 1985.
49. I discuss the duality of Orwell's appeal in *The Politics of Literary Reputation: The Making and Claiming of "St. George" Orwell* (New York: Oxford University Press, 1989).
50. Martin Green, interview with the author, 8 November 1984. Green, a long-time English expatriate, first became friendly with Amis when they were colleagues at Cambridge University in 1961-62. For Green's views of Orwell's influence on Amis, see his *A Mirror for Anglo-Saxons* (London: Longmans, 1961), and *Children of the Sun* (New York: Basic Books, 1972).
51. Amis, "Why Lucky Jim Turned Right," 202.
52. Amis, "Lone Voices," in *What Became of Jane Austen and Other Essays*, 161.
53. See Morrison, *Movement*, for a discussion of Amis's outspoken cultural conservatism, 252-55. See also Philip Gardner, *Kingsley Amis* (Boston: Twayne, 1981), 13-22, 144-52.
54. Cecil Woolf and John Bagguley, eds., *Authors Take Sides on Vietnam* (London: Gollancz, 1967), 48-49.
55. Mary McCarthy, "The Writing on the Wall," *New York Review of Books*, 6 (January 1969): 3-6.
56. Amis, interview with the author, 12 March 1985.
57. John Wain, "Our Situation," *Encounter* 11 (May 1963): 8.
58. John Wain, "In the Thirties," in *The World of George Orwell*, ed. Miriam Gross (London: Weidenfeld and Nicolson, 1971), 79. Interestingly, whereas New Left radicals sympathetic to Orwell seized on his revolutionary zeal in *Homage to Catalonia*, comparing American imperialism to Spanish fascism and seeing Orwell as an erstwhile Che Guevara, Wain and anti-radical critics emphasized Orwell's anti-Communism in *Catalonia*. One comparison of Orwell and Guevara is in a letter to the *New Statesman*, 13 December 1968. See also Noam Chomsky, *American Power and the New Mandarins* (New York: Pantheon Books, 1969), 95-102, 144-48.
59. Wain, "In the Thirties," 90.
60. John Wain, "Orwell and the Intelligentsia," *Encounter* 21 (December 1968): 74.
61. Ibid., 80.
62. See, for example, Norman Podhoretz, "If Orwell Were Alive Today," *Harper's*, January 1983, 30-37.
63. Amis, interview with the author, 12 March 1985.
64. Amis's politics have been strongly influenced by the anti-Communism of Conquest, a self-made Soviet scholar of the Stalin period (best known as author of *The Great Terror*, 1968). Amis's view is sardonically referred to in the interview as "Conquest's Law." This "law" holds that one's radicalism extends only to those issues irrelevant to one's interests or sphere of

competence; one is invariably "conservative" about issues one has a stake in or is knowledgeable about. Transforming various institutions (family, education, law, etc.) sounds appealing to a radical outside those institutions, Amis says, but he or she tends to emphasize the need to "understand" the "difficulty" and "complexity" of such schemes when radical proposals involve overturning arrangements benefiting him or her.

65. Wain's proprietary attitude toward Orwell is nothing new for him. See his heated exchange with Tom Hopkinson, author of the first book on Orwell (*George Orwell*, 1953), in *Twentieth Century*, March 1954, 235-36. Wain charged that George Woodcock, one of Orwell's anarchist friends, was "out to steal [Orwell], to kidnap him and keep him in the 'anarchist and libertarian' menagerie." See also John Wain, "On George Orwell," *Commentary*, June 1969, 28-29. Wain also castigated the "Left Establishment" and Raymond Williams' *George Orwell* in the *Observer*, 10 January 1971, 9. By the late 1960s, Wain was among the most prominent of the so-called "Encounter Orwellians," who themselves have been accused by the Left (e.g., Conor Cruise O'Brien and Bernard Crick) of "stealing" Orwell.

66. Wain, "Dear George Orwell," 26-27.

67. Podhoretz, "If Orwell Were Alive Today," 30.

68. Wain, "Dear George Orwell," 26.

69. Ibid., 30-31.

70. Ibid., 22.

71. Wain, interview with the author, 14 March 1985.

72. One easily overlooked source of Wain's impassioned identification with Orwell is surely the striking resemblances of their schooldays and adolescence. In his *Sprightly Running* Wain recalls, in language that echoes Orwell's "Such, Such Were the Joys," his miserable schooldays and how they shaped his outlook. Even the character and themes of some of Wain's novels, not to mention his prose style, bear a direct relation to Orwell's work. For example, one cannot help but wonder whether Wain's already-discussed psychological reading of *Coming Up for Air* reflected his own struggles with his novel *The Contenders*, written near the same time (1958) as his critical essay and also about a fat man (Joe Shaw) who is really a thin man ("Clarence") inside.

73. Ernest Becker, *The Denial of Death* (Detroit: Free Press, 1973), 127-58.

74. Cf. Wain, "Orwell and the Intelligentsia," 76-77; and Wain's award-winning biography, *Samuel Johnson* (New York: Viking Press, 1975).

NOTES ON CONTRIBUTORS

VICTORIA CHALIKOVA was Professor of Philosophy and a doctoral candidate at the Institute for Scientific Information on the Humanities, Academy of Sciences, Moscow. She worked with Yelena Bonner to organize the pro-democracy movement in the USSR. In 1988 and 1989 she published commentaries on Orwell in several Soviet journals, including *Novy Mir, Znamya, Filosofskie Nauki,* and *Rodnik.* She died in Germany in May 1991.

ARTHUR M. ECKSTEIN is Associate Professor of History at the University of Maryland, College Park. He has written extensively on both ancient and modern history (including George Orwell). His latest book is *Senate and General: Individual Decision-Making and Roman Foreign Relations* (1987). His most recent article is "Is There a 'Hobson-Lenin Thesis' on Late Nineteenth Century Colonial Expansion?", *Economic History Review* 44 (1991).

W. RUSSEL GRAY is Professor of Liberal Arts at Delaware County Community College in Media, Pennsylvania. He writes about aspects of popular culture, including the mass media, futuristic films and novels, detective fiction, Victorian prize-fighting, and *Nineteen Eighty-Four.*

DANIEL KIES is Associate Professor of English and Linguistics at the College of DuPage in Glen Ellyn, Illinois. He writes about linguistics, modern English grammar, and stylistics. He is currently working on a functional linguistic analysis of the prose of college composition students.

WILLIAM E. LASKOWSKI, JR. is Assistant Professor of English at Jamestown College. He has written about Leon Edel, science fiction and Richard Wagner, and is currently working on a study of Rupert Brooke.

SUE LONOFF is Associate Director of the Derek Bok Center at Harvard University. She is the author of *Wilkie Collins and His Victorian Readers* (1982), as well as numerous articles on Victorian literature. She is currently preparing an edition of Charlotte and Emily Bronte's essays.

LAURENCE M. PORTER is Professor of Romance Languages at Michigan State University. He is the author of *The Literary Dream in French Romanticism: A Psychoanalytic Interpretation* (1979), *"The Interpretation of Dreams": Freud's Theories Revisited* (1987), two other books, and numerous articles on French and comparative literature.

JOHN RODDEN teaches rhetoric at the University of Texas at Austin. He is the author of *The Politics of Literary Reputation: The Making and Claiming of "St. George" Orwell* (1989).

JONATHAN ROSE is Associate Professor of History at Drew University and President of the Northeast Victorian Studies Association. He is the author of *The Edwardian Temperament 1895–1919* (1986) and co-editor of the historical dictionary *British Literary Publishing Houses, 1820–1965* (1991). Currently he is writing an intellectual history of the British working class and he is organizing the Society for the History of Authorship, Reading and Publishing.

ALEX ZWERDLING is Professor of English at the University of California, Berkeley. He is the author of *Yeats and the Heroic Ideal* (1965), *Orwell and the Left* (1974), and *Virginia Woolf and the Real World* (1986).

Index

The Revised Orwell

Production Editor: Julie L. Loehr
Design: Michael J. Brooks
Copy Editor: Ellen Link

Text composed by Desktop Productions in 10pt. Garamond.

Printed by Bookcrafters on 55# Booktext Natural, bound in 80# Enamel and smyth sewn in Roxite B with gold foil stamp.